Caring for children who have experienced domestic abuse

A guide to supporting foster carers, adopters and kinship carers

Hedy Cleaver and Wendy Rose

Published by
CoramBAAF Adoption and Fostering Academy
41 Brunswick Square
London WC1N 1AZ
www.corambaaf.org.uk

Coram Academy Limited, registered as a company limited by guarantee in England and Wales number 9697712, part of the Coram group, charity number 312278

© Hedy Cleaver and Wendy Rose, 2022

British Library Cataloguing in Publication Data
A catalogue record for this book is available from the British Library

ISBN 978 1 913384 13 5

Project management by Jo Francis, Publications, CoramBAAF
Designed and typeset by Helen Joubert Design
Printed in Great Britain by The Lavenham Press

All rights reserved. Apart from any fair dealing for the purposes of research or private study, or criticism or review, as permitted under the Copyright, Designs and Patents Act 1988, this publication may not be reproduced, stored in a retrieval system, or transmitted in any form or by any means, without the prior written permission of the publishers.

The moral right of the authors has been asserted in accordance with the Copyright, Designs and Patents Act 1988.

For the latest news on CoramBAAF titles and special offers, sign up to our free publications bulletin at https://corambaaf.org.uk/subscribe.

Contents

Introduction		**1**
	Aims of the guide	1
	Limitations of the research drawn on in this publication	2
	A note about language	2
	Structure of the guide	3
1	**Protecting women and children through the law**	**4**
	Protecting women	5
	Protecting children and young people	7
	To sum up	10
2	**Who is affected?**	**11**
	Prevalence of domestic violence and abuse	11
	Perpetrators and victims	12
	Impact of the pandemic on domestic abuse	13
	Types of domestic violence and abuse	14
	Physical assault	14
	Sexual abuse	15
	Controlling or coercive behaviour	16
	Economic abuse	18
	Psychological and emotional abuse	19
	Domestic abuse is rarely a single issue	20
	The impact on parenting	21
	Children as innocent bystanders?	22
	Domestic abuse and child protection	23
	Children most at risk of significant harm	25
	The impact on children of different ages and stages of development	27
	To sum up	28
3	**Impact of domestic abuse on children under five years**	**30**
	The unborn child	30
	Infant development (under five years)	32
	Health	32
	Expected developmental progression	32
	Possible impact of domestic abuse	33
	Education: cognitive and language development	35
	Expected developmental progression	35
	Possible impact of domestic abuse	36
	Emotional and behavioural development	37

Expected developmental progression	37
Possible impact of domestic abuse	37
Identity and social presentation	39
Expected developmental progression	39
Possible impact of domestic abuse	40
Family and social relationships	40
Expected developmental progression	40
Possible impact of domestic abuse	41
To sum up	42
Key problems for the unborn child	42
Key problems for children aged under five years	43

4 Impact of domestic abuse on middle childhood — 45

Health	45
Expected developmental progression	45
Possible impact of domestic abuse	46
Education and cognitive development	48
Expected developmental progression	48
Possible impact of domestic abuse	48
Emotional and behavioural development	50
Expected developmental progression	50
Possible impact of domestic abuse	50
Identity	53
Expected developmental progression	53
Possible impact of domestic abuse	53
Family and social relationships	55
Expected developmental progression	55
Possible impact of domestic abuse	56
Social presentation and self-care skills	58
Expected developmental progression	58
Possible impact of domestic abuse	59
To sum up	59
Key problems for children aged 5 to 11 years	59

5 Impact of domestic abuse on adolescence — 61

Health	61
Expected developmental progression	61
Possible impact of domestic abuse	63
Education and cognitive ability	65
Expected developmental progression	65
Possible impact of domestic abuse	67
Emotional and behavioural development	69
Expected developmental progression	69
Possible impact of domestic abuse	70
Identity	71
Expected developmental progression	71
Possible impact of domestic abuse	73

Family and social relationships	74
Expected developmental progression	74
Possible impact of domestic abuse	75
Social presentation and self-care skills	79
Expected developmental progression	79
Possible impact of domestic abuse	79
To sum up	80
Key problems for adolescents	80

6 The right family for the right child — 83

The long-term consequences of domestic abuse	83
Planning for children	84
Planning for permanence	85
Assessing the child's needs	87
Placing siblings together?	88
Finding families for children	91
Assessing potential families	91
Preparing families	92
Making a good match	94
Making the move to a permanent family	95
Support available for carers	97
To sum up	99

7 Looking after infants who have experienced domestic abuse — 101

Preparing and supporting families	101
Effects of exposure to domestic abuse	102
Effects on attachment patterns	103
Contact with birth family	103
Contact with previous carers	104
Promoting attachment	106
Preparing and supporting the child	109
Explaining the family culture	109
Developing self-esteem	110
Supporting cognitive development	110
To sum up	111

8 Looking after middle years children who have experienced domestic abuse — 113

Preparing and supporting families	113
Joining a new family	115
Maintaining relationships with significant people	116
Building a relationship	119
School and education	123
Identity	125
To sum up	126

9 Looking after adolescents who have experienced domestic abuse	**129**
Preparing and supporting families	130
Welcoming teenagers into the family	130
Supporting young people	132
Staying in touch with birth family	132
Contact with previous carers	132
Emerging issues	133
School and education	135
Identity development	136
Forming relationships	138
Indications of risk-taking behaviour	138
Going missing	139
Drug and alcohol misuse	139
Gangs – mixing with the "wrong crowd"	140
Drugs and county lines	143
Risks of child sexual exploitation	144
To sum up	146
10 Support for carers and their children	**149**
Local authority support	149
Therapeutic services	150
Educational services	152
Independent visitors and mentors	153
To sum up	155
11 Epilogue: The carer's tale	**157**
Inviting in the storm	157
Appendix: Resources for practitioners, carers and children	**171**
Making the move to a new family	171
Support for carers and children of carers	172
Attachment programmes	174
Preparation courses	174
Placing siblings – together or apart	175
Life story work	175
Mentoring	176
Behavioural change – therapeutic services	177
Traumatised children	178
Self-harm	179
Drugs and alcohol	179
Gang involvement	180
Criminal exploitation of children	180
Sexual exploitation of children	180
CoramBAAF publications	181
References	**183**

Notes about the authors

Dr Hedy Cleaver is an Emeritus Professor at Royal Holloway College, University of London. Her experience as a social worker and child psychologist informs her research on vulnerable children and their families and the impact of professional interventions. She has written extensively on domestic abuse and how children are affected. Relevant publications include *Child Protection, Domestic Violence and Substance Misuse: Family experiences and effective practice* (2007); and *Children's Needs – Parenting Capacity: child abuse, parental mental illness, learning disability, substance misuse and domestic violence* (2011). Most recently, she was part of the research team responsible for the last triennial review of serious case reviews (Brandon *et al*, 2020). The guiding principle underpinning her work is a desire to improve the quality of life for children living in circumstances that place them at risk of abuse and neglect. The findings from her research have had an identifiable impact on policy and practice in the UK in respect of children and families throughout the last 30 years.

Wendy Rose OBE held children's policy responsibilities at the Department of Health as Assistant Chief Inspector, following social work and senior management experience in the NHS and local authority. As a Senior Research Fellow at the Open University, she worked on research and development projects. During this time, she acted as a professional adviser to the Scottish Government on developing its children's policy, *Getting it Right for Every Child*. Latterly, she worked with the Welsh Government on its safeguarding reforms and was an Honorary Research Fellow at Cardiff University. Her research and development work has focused primarily on improving outcomes for children and families and evaluating the effectiveness of service provision. She has published widely.

Hedy Cleaver has previously written *Parenting a Child Affected by Domestic Violence*, for CoramBAAF (2015) and with Wendy Rose the following two books, *Safeguarding Children living with Foster Carers, Adopters and Special Guardians: Learning from case reviews 2007–2019*, and *Safeguarding Children living with Foster Carers, Adopters and Special Guardians: A guide to reflective practice* (both 2020).

Acknowledgements

The prominence of domestic abuse issues has escalated since we were commissioned by CoramBAAF to produce this practice guide. This can be partly attributed to the well-reported airing of issues during the passage of the Domestic Abuse Bill through Parliament, which gained Royal Assent in 2021. The support for the new legislation was against a backdrop of positive public response to the broadening definition of domestic abuse to include coercion and control and acknowledgement of the plight of victims of abuse. More significant was the worrying increase in domestic abuse reported during the Covid-19 lockdowns in 2020–21. Concerns were widely expressed about the impact this was having on the children who were living in abusive families.

Our focus in this guide has been on those children who have experienced or witnessed domestic abuse and are now unable to live with their birth families, either temporarily or permanently. These are children growing up in alternative family care with foster carers, adopters or kinship carers. Research suggests that the prevalence of such prior experience is high for children in care, but no specific data are collected on a regular basis, nationally or locally, that record domestic abuse as a feature of their young lives.

Hedy Cleaver has brought her findings and extensive experience of researching domestic abuse and its impact on children and families to developing this practice guide.

We have been grateful for the encouragement given to us throughout by Jo Francis, CoramBAAF's Publications Team Manager. We are also indebted to Shaila Shah for her invaluable support and editorial skills. We appreciated the help given by the professionals and academics, who peer reviewed the final draft, for their valuable comments and suggestions, as well as their interest and encouragement. Adrian Thompson gave excellent assistance at the final editing and proof reading stages. Finally, our gratitude goes to Melinda Rigopoulo for allowing us to conclude this guide with her account of adopting Luca.

We would want to acknowledge the debt owed to families who are looking after children who may have been deeply hurt and damaged by what they have witnessed and absorbed, sometimes from a very early age. The need for skilled and committed professionals to be available and to work alongside the carers and children comes across very strongly. We still have a way to go. As one adoptive parent put it, 'Although our society wants "hurt" children to have a chance of healing, there appears to be a wish to hide the problems away behind the doors of families who open them to welcome the child in, but who then struggle to be understood or to get their child's needs recognised' (Hirst, 2005).

Introduction

This Good Practice Guide is the first to focus primarily on supporting children who have witnessed and/or experienced domestic abuse prior to living with foster carers, adopters, special guardians or family and friends carers (also known as kinship carers or connected persons).

These children are potentially vulnerable because exposure to domestic abuse can have long-term consequences for children's health and their emotional, psychological and behavioural development. How children are affected may pose considerable challenges for the families who wish to provide them with love, stability and support.

Most previous work has looked at how domestic abuse has affected children and birth families, with the overall aim of keeping families together and preventing children from becoming looked after. Not all children can remain or return to living at home safely. There is strong evidence to show that domestic abuse is linked to child abuse and neglect (CAADA, 2014; Department for Education (DfE), 2018a). Research suggests that up to 50 per cent of children living with alternative families have been exposed to domestic abuse while living with their birth parents. There is limited information available on how these children fare in their new families and how best to support carers in looking after them.

Local authorities have a duty to provide a child with an alternative family life where this cannot be achieved by the birth parents, secured by an appropriate legal order. The priority is 'a placement with an individual who is a relative, friend or other person connected with the child and who is also a local authority foster parent' (Public Law Working Group, 2020, p.17).

AIMS OF THE GUIDE

This guide has been written for social workers placing and supporting children exposed to domestic abuse and those managing, providing and developing services for them. It offers information on how domestic abuse affects children at different ages and stages in their development, and the skills that alternative families will need to care for them and promote their welfare. The guide will assist managers and practitioners in understanding how they can best support the alternative families in order to improve outcomes for children.

The guide also aims to provide carers with an understanding of how domestic abuse may have affected the children for whom they are now caring. It is hoped that, with greater insight into these issues, carers will be better able to give the quality of day-to-day care and develop the caring relationships that are key to successfully turning around children's lives. With the support of practitioners, it is hoped that carers will more easily find the services and resources they require.

LIMITATIONS OF THE RESEARCH DRAWN ON IN THIS PUBLICATION

The cohorts used in much of the research we accessed have been drawn from specific groups, such as women and children living in refuges or those attending general practitioners' clinics. Consequently, knowledge of how domestic abuse affects children tends to be biased towards its impact on women as carers. Although there are a few surveys of abused men, there is little knowledge on how it affects their parenting capacity.

It is often not possible to measure the extent of the domestic abuse because there are numerous factors that prevent the abused parent and their children from revealing what is happening. This reluctance may be driven by fear, shame, or failure to understand that the relationship is abusive.

Far less is known about families in the general population which do not seek help or do not come to the attention of statutory agencies. Caution, therefore, must be taken in any extrapolation from the research findings.

Despite these limitations, there is a great deal of consistency in the research with regard to how domestic abuse directly affects children and impacts on parents' capacity to meet their children's developmental needs.

A NOTE ABOUT LANGUAGE

As we worked on this practice guide, it became clear that changes were taking place in the official language about domestic abuse over the last decade. In England and Wales as well as in Scotland, the most recent legislation is titled the Domestic Abuse Act 2021. This was not the case in March 2013, when the Home Office produced *Information for Local Areas on the Change to the Definition of Domestic Violence and Abuse*. That document announced that the Government definition of domestic violence was being widened to 'include those aged 16–17', and that the wording was being changed to reflect coercive control as 'a core part of domestic violence'. With the broadening of the definition, *domestic abuse* now appears to be the accepted umbrella term. We have taken the decision in this guide to use both domestic abuse and domestic violence as appropriate to the circumstances being discussed.

In addition, we found reference in some Government reports, and in the wider literature, to Intimate Partner Violence (IPV) (Office for National Statistics (ONS), 2016; Office on Women's Health, 2018) as well as Intimate Personal Abuse (IPA), Adolescent Family Violence (AFV), Intimate Partner Filicide, and Femicide (IPF). These terms appear in the text when a particular author has used them.

Finally, there is currently some fluidity about what, in the past, has been called "kinship care" and, more recently, "family and friends care" or "friends and family care" or care by "connected persons". We have used *kinship care* as an umbrella term to describe one of the options for alternative family care, but note that it also relates to a number of different kinds of arrangements, such as family approved foster carers and special guardianship.

STRUCTURE OF THE GUIDE

The first chapter in this guide, *Protecting women and children through the law,* outlines the changes in law pertaining to domestic abuse and violence. Chapter 2, *Who is affected?*, explores in detail the prevalence and types of violence and abuse perpetrated, the impact on parenting, and the link to child abuse and neglect. The following three chapters focus on children of different ages and stages of development: *Children under five years, Middle childhood,* and *Adolescents*. Each chapter discusses children's expected developmental progression before exploring the possible impact of domestic violence and abuse. Chapter 6, *The right family for the right child*, focuses on matching children with the most appropriate carers and supporting their transition to new families. Chapters 7, 8 and 9 return to the three different age groups of children and explore the challenges facing carers and the professional support they may need to address them successfully. The chapters take into account that some carers may be looking after children who have been exposed to domestic abuse early in their lives while for others the experience of abuse may have been more recent. Chapter 10, *Support for carers and their children*, identifies the support and services available to help carers and the children who have been affected by domestic abuse. Chapter 11, the *Epilogue*, tells the story of a carer and her family's lived experience of adopting a young boy exposed to domestic abuse. Finally, the *Appendix* lists organisations, networks, resources and further reading for professionals, carers and children.

Chapter 1
Protecting women and children through the law

This chapter explores the legal and societal changes introduced to protect women and children since the mid-19th century. In order to understand the present legal framework, it is important to know how it developed. Domestic abuse and violence are not recent phenomena. The subjugation of women has a long history, although the concept of domestic abuse did not exist until recently. In Victorian times and before, when a woman married, her independent legal existence was forfeited: she and any subsequent children became the property of her husband. Her wealth passed to him and, if she worked after marriage, her earnings also belonged to her husband. A husband's rights included: to correct and chastise his wife, provided the stick or rod was no thicker than his thumb, and to have sexual intercourse with her.

Physical chastisement could be taken to extremes, and it was not uncommon for men to appear before the magistrate in the 1800s on charges of aggravated assault on their wives:

> *Of the cases that were heard, the commonest methods of inflicting violence included dragging a wife out of bed by her hair; grasping a fistful of her hair and slamming her head repeatedly against the floor; knocking out her teeth; breaking her jaw, nose or ribs; throwing her out of a window; beating her, most commonly over the head, with whatever came to hand (poker, broomstick, hobnailed boot, hammer); throwing her to the floor and administering kicks all over the body or jumping on her belly; strangulation; punches to the face; stabbing with a domestic knife; throwing a woman onto the fire or burning her with a hot iron poker.*
>
> (Magistrate from the 1800s, quoted in Wojtczak, 2009, para: Types of Assault)

Physical violence was not the only form of domestic abuse acknowledged during this period. Coercive control and degradation were also recognised by some, and the impact that this had on children. Anne Bronte vividly conveyed this in her novel, *The Tenant of Wildfell Hall* (1848).

PROTECTING WOMEN

Women and children had little protection from domestic abuse and violence until the passing of the Matrimonial Causes Act 1878. The Act gave magistrates in the UK the power to grant a separation order with maintenance to a wife whose husband had been convicted of aggravated assault. In 1882, the Women's Property Act allowed women to obtain full control over their own money and property.

Subsequent Acts, such as the Matrimonial Causes Acts 1937 and 1973, and the Divorce Reform Act 1969, steadily broadened the scope for women exposed to domestic abuse to gain a divorce. The Domestic Violence and Matrimonial Proceedings Act, passed in 1976, allowed women to access court orders to prevent further violence and to have the right to stay in the matrimonial home without the abuser. The Act also provided police with powers of arrest for breach of an injunction. The objective was to protect women suffering domestic abuse; however, the ways in which the orders were enforced meant that abused women continued to be inadequately protected (Summers and Hoffman, 2002).

Further legislative change took place in the 1990s. In 1991, the House of Lords made a landmark ruling stating: 'Nowadays it cannot seriously be maintained that by marriage a wife submits herself irrevocably to sexual intercourse in all circumstances' (The Law Commission, 1992, p.2). The illegality of rape within marriage was laid out explicitly under the Sexual Offences Act 2003.

The Family Law Act 1996 provided increased protection to women and children with the creation of two specific types of civil court order: non-molestation orders and occupation orders. A non-molestation order seeks to prevent the victim of domestic abuse and any relevant children from being pestered, harassed or molested, but does not deal with the issue of who can occupy the family home. The occupation order offers that protection, and will be granted by the court if it believes that the applicant will suffer significant harm if the order is not made.

Women were provided with greater protection by legislation that came into force between 1981 and 2018. For example, the Domestic Violence, Crime and Victims Act 2004 introduced major changes to the law in England and Wales by making the breach of non-molestation orders, obtained under the Family Law Act 1996, a criminal offence. In addition, it made all members of a household liable for the offence of causing or allowing the death of, or serious physical harm to, a child or vulnerable adult. The Family Law Act 1996 is a:

> ..."gender-neutral" document which recognises that domestic abuse occurs across society regardless of age, gender, race, sexuality,

> *disability, wealth and geography, while also acknowledging that it is predominantly women who suffer as a result of it.*
>
> (BMA Board of Science, 2014, p.3)

Progress has continued; in March 2018, the Westminster Government launched a nationwide consultation, *Transforming the Response to Domestic Abuse*, which in turn led to the Domestic Abuse Bill being laid before Parliament and vigorously debated during 2019–2021. A campaign calling for it to include a free-standing offence of non-fatal strangulation, often a precursor to domestic homicide, was launched. Underpinned by research (Bichard *et al*, 2020) and supported by Dame Vera Baird, Victims' Commissioner, and Nicole Jacobs, Domestic Abuse Commissioner, they argued for such an amendment because:

> *Non-fatal strangulation or asphyxiation is an utterly terrifying experience and can cause significant long-term mental and physical trauma to victims and survivors. It can also be a matter of life and death. Over a quarter of all female homicides are by strangulation and non-fatal strangulation is widely recognised as a risk indicator – victims are seven times more likely to be killed at the hands of their partner if they have previously been non-fatally strangled.*
>
> (Victims' Commissioner, 2021)

The Domestic Abuse Act 2021 received Royal Assent on 29 April. Non-fatal strangulation and suffocation of another person is now a new offence under the Domestic Abuse Act 2021, s.70. The majority of provisions in the Act apply to England and Wales, or England only.

The Act defines domestic abuse in the following way:

> *Behaviour of a person ("A") towards another person ("B") is "domestic abuse" if–*
>
> *(a) A and B are each aged 16 or over and are personally connected to each other, and*
> *(b) the behaviour is abusive.*
>
> *Behaviour is "abusive" if it consists of any of the following–*
> *(a) physical or sexual abuse;*
> *(b) violent or threatening behaviour;*
> *(c) controlling or coercive behaviour;*
> *(d) economic abuse;*
> *(e) psychological, emotional or other abuse;*
>
> *and it does not matter whether the behaviour consists of a single incident or a course of conduct.*
>
> *For the purposes of this Act A's behaviour may be behaviour "towards" B despite the fact that it consists of conduct directed at another person (for example, B's child).*

There have subsequently been concerns raised by the Local Government Association calling for more funding for social housing on the basis that the recent legislation focuses on accommodation-based support and has not taken into consideration the need for wider community-based support services.

Legislative changes in Scotland also afford increased protection to victims of domestic abuse. The Domestic Abuse (Scotland) Act 2018 recognises domestic abuse as a crime and the multiple ways in which people are affected. The Act expands the definition of what domestic abuse is in criminal law in Scotland and how the police and courts investigate and prosecute this crime.

The Domestic Abuse (Protection) (Scotland) Act 2021 gives more powers to police and courts to protect people at risk of domestic abuse. The Act enables police and courts to ban suspected abusers from re-entering the home, and from approaching or contacting the person at risk for a period of time, enabling them to consider longer-term options around safety and housing. The Act permits social landlords to end the tenancy of a perpetrator and/or transfer it to the victim. Together, these measures should reduce the risk that victims of domestic abuse end up becoming homeless in order to escape their abuser.

In Northern Ireland, a specific offence of domestic abuse was introduced in March 2021 under section 1 of the Domestic Abuse and Civil Proceedings Act (Northern Ireland) 2021. The new legislation also has the effect of criminalising coercive and controlling behaviour, therefore bringing Northern Ireland into line with the other jurisdictions within the UK and Ireland, and with relevant human rights standards.

PROTECTING CHILDREN AND YOUNG PEOPLE

Parallel with the growing acknowledgment of the need to establish legal protection from domestic abuse for women in the late 1880s, there was increasing concern about the numbers of children in poor health and living in extreme conditions of poverty, neglect and cruelty.

The Prevention of Cruelty to, and Protection of, Children Act 1889 was the first Act of Parliament to address these issues. Significantly, it enabled the state to intervene in relations between parents and children. Police could arrest anyone found ill-treating a child, and they could enter a home if a child was thought to be in danger and remove them to a place of safety. These were important steps even though it was made clear that the Act did not take away the right of any parent, teacher or others having control or charge of a child, to administer punishment to such a child.

Subsequent Children Acts of 1908, 1948 and 1989, together with other legislation in 1932/33 and 1968, dealt with the major issues of:

- the establishment of juvenile courts and the orders available to the judiciary;
- the care of children unable to live at home;
- the registration of foster carers; and
- the establishment of local authority children's services.

The right of children to have their welfare promoted and safeguarded, and to have protection from abuse and exploitation, was made explicit under the Children Act 1989 in England and Wales. The Children (Scotland) Act 1995 offered similar protection to children in Scotland. The Acts were underpinned by the United Nations Convention on the Rights of the Child (1989). The UK signed the Convention on 19 April 1990, ratified it on 16 December 1991 and it came into force on 15 January 1992.

Knowledge about what constituted child abuse and neglect was broadening. However, it was not until 2002 that it was acknowledged that children could be at risk of suffering harm as the result of witnessing domestic abuse. In s.120 of the Adoption and Children Act 2002, an amendment was made to the meaning of "harm" as defined in s.31 of the 1989 Act, with the insertion: 'including, for example, impairment suffered from seeing or hearing the ill treatment of another'.

Nearly 20 years after recognition in law of the potential harm to a child of witnessing a parent being abused, violated or intimidated, it has received surprisingly little specific policy and practice attention other than being listed as a form of emotional abuse (*Working Together to Safeguard Children*, HM Government, 2018a, p.107). This may change with the implementation of the Domestic Abuse Act 2021.

During debates at the Bill stage, questions were raised by charities working with victims and survivors of domestic abuse. On 3 March 2020, SafeLives, although welcoming the Bill, called for funding for frontline community specialist services to provide support for adults, teens, child victims and survivors of domestic abuse. The NSPCC expressed concerns that the Bill failed 'to recognise the needs of children affected by domestic abuse despite repeated calls from multiple experts, including the Domestic Abuse, Children's and Victims' Commissioners, and the Home Affairs Select Committee' (NSPCC, 2020a, para 3).

In June 2020, following the Covid-19 lockdown in March 2020, contacts to the NSPCC helpline about the impact of domestic abuse on children increased by 32 per cent. The NSPCC's Senior Policy and Public Affairs Officer reported that: 'This crisis has shone a spotlight on children living with the daily nightmare of domestic abuse.' They called for the

Government to 'grasp the landmark opportunity offered by the Domestic Abuse Bill and ensure children get the protection and opportunity they need' (NSPCC, 2020a).

The following amendments were made to the Bill on 30 June 2020 and welcomed by the Victims' Commissioner:

- *Provide that a child who sees or hears, or experiences the effects of, domestic abuse and is related to the person being abused or the perpetrator is also to be regarded as a victim of domestic abuse;*
- *Prohibition of domestic abuse perpetrators cross examining their victims in person in family proceedings in England and Wales; and*
- *Automatic provision of special measures in civil and family proceedings.*

The Commissioner went on to stress that:

> *It is essential that children are recognised as not mere bystanders when it could not be clearer that they are victims in their own right, who can be profoundly affected by domestic abuse in their childhood.*
> (Victims' Commissioner, 2020, para 7)

The Act incorporated this concern in the legislation and considers children to be victims of domestic abuse:

> *Any references in this Act to a victim of domestic abuse includes a reference to a child who –*
- *sees or hears, or experiences the effects of, the abuse, and*
- *is related to A or B*

> *A child is related to a person for the purposes of subsection (2) if –*
- *the person is a parent of, or has parental responsibility for, the child, or*
- *the child and the person are relatives*

The Domestic Abuse Act 2021 sets out to provide greater protection for children through the role of the Domestic Abuse Commissioner, one of whose duties is to identify children affected by domestic abuse. The Act will also ensure that the state issues guidance about domestic abuse that includes its effect on children.

In Scotland, legislation includes domestic abuse in the definition of child abuse (Section 24, Family Law (Scotland) Act 2006). The Domestic Abuse (Scotland) Act 2018 also makes it a statutory aggravation for domestic abuse to involve or affect a child (this includes a child hearing, seeing or being present during an abusive incident).

TO SUM UP

- Domestic violence and abuse are not recent phenomena. In the Victorian era, a wife belonged to her husband, who had the legal right to chastise her, which could involve beatings, and have sexual intercourse with or without her consent.

- Towards the end of the 19th century, the Matrimonial Causes Act 1878 and the Women's Property Act 1882 gave women some limited protection. Nonetheless, women still had no legal rights to separation unless their husband had been convicted of aggravated assault.

- Further legal changes in the first half of the 20th century enabled women exposed to domestic violence to gain a divorce and have the right to remain in the marital home.

- It was not until the Sexual Offences Act 2013 that women had legal protection from marital rape.

- The Domestic Abuse Act 2021 provides greater safety to women by defining what constitutes abusive behaviour, including coercive control, and makes non-fatal strangulation a new offence.

- Similar progressive changes to the law have been introduced in Scotland and Northern Ireland.

- Historically, children have been very vulnerable to parental abuse and neglect and until the late 19th century had no legal protection. The Prevention of Cruelty to, and Protection of, Children Act 1889 made child maltreatment a crime.

- A series of Children Acts in the 20th century provided increased protection for children, for example, the Children Acts of 1989 and 1995 (in England and Wales, and Scotland respectively) gave children the right to have their welfare promoted and safeguarded. More recently, the Adoption and Children Act 2002 acknowledges the harm to children of being exposed to domestic abuse.

- Children have also been acknowledged in the Domestic Abuse Act 2021, which considers them to be victims if they see or hear, or experience the effects of the abuse. The Domestic Abuse (Scotland) Act 2018 similarly acknowledges the effect of domestic abuse on children.

Chapter 2
Who is affected?

Abi's mum warned her one day that she would end up in a body bag. Five days later her words almost came true, when Swamy kicked and stamped on Abi's body with such force that he damaged her spinal cord, punctured a lung and broke her ribs. As she lay injured, he shouted that he had had enough of her and she needed to shut up.

(The story of Abi, almost killed by her abusive husband Swamy, reported by BBC News, 2020)

PREVALENCE OF DOMESTIC VIOLENCE AND ABUSE

Identifying the prevalence of domestic abuse is hampered by its being mainly a hidden crime occurring primarily within the home. It is a crime that victims frequently do not report or disclose to the police, and may be under-reported in surveys and interviews (ONS, 2019). Men are particularly reluctant to report, when victims of domestic abuse. A study by Mark Brooks (2020) found that men were practically three times less likely than women to talk to anyone about their abuse (49% of men failed to tell anyone compared with 19% of women). A comprehensive understanding of domestic abuse is hampered because prevalence estimates do not take account of whether the abuse caused fear, whether the victim had been subject to multiple incidents, and what type of violence or abuse had been perpetrated.

A variety of agencies collect information on domestic abuse, and police statistics are also a valuable source of data. The Crime Survey for England and Wales estimated that 5.5 per cent of adults (8.1% of women and 4.0% of men) experienced domestic abuse during the year ending March 2020. Offences that were flagged as domestic abuse increased by seven per cent in the period March to June 2020, compared with the same period in 2019 (ONS, 2020a). The Covid-19 pandemic may have contributed to the rise, although there has been a gradual increase in these offences over recent years. Emma Williamson and colleagues point out:

While this increase may be linked to "triggers" – isolation, pressure, boredom, frustrations, anger and so on – coronavirus should not be positioned as a cause of DVA.

(Williamson *et al*, 2020, p.290)

PERPETRATORS AND VICTIMS

Domestic abuse is not confined to any particular group in society. It crosses class boundaries, disregards ethnicity, and has no respect for religion. Neither is it restricted to heterosexual couples, but also occurs within lesbian, gay, bisexual and transgender relationships, and can involve other family members, including children (Elliot, 1996; Donovan *et al*, 2006; Rolle *et al*, 2018).

Most domestic abuse is perpetrated by men against women. In three-quarters of domestic abuse-related crime, women are the victims. This proportion is similar for all types of abuse, except for sexual offences, where women account for 96 per cent of victims. The degree of violence women experience places them at much greater danger than men. The data on domestic homicides in England and Wales, for the two-year period March 2016 to the year ending March 2018, show that 260 women were killed by their male partner/ex-partner, compared with 46 men killed by their female partner/ex-partner (ONS, 2019). The lockdown resulting from the Covid-19 pandemic exacerbated the situation. In June 2020, Amanda Taub reported that in the UK:

During the first month after lockdown in late March, 16 women and girls were killed in suspected domestic homicides – more than triple the number from the same period in 2019. At least 10 more have died in the two months since.

(Taub, 2020)

In cases where men are the victims of domestic abuse, they are more likely to be abused or killed by a male partner than by a female partner. Data collected by the Office for National Statistics (ONS) found that half the suspected perpetrators of domestic homicides involving a male victim were men (ONS, 2018a). Brooks' (2020) study supports this, showing that the percentage of gay men (3.2%) and bisexual men (3.3%) who suffered partner abuse in 2018/19 was greater than for heterosexual men (2.8%).

Although domestic abuse can affect anyone, some people are more at risk. The ONS data (2019) showed that women aged between 21 and 40 years with young children are very vulnerable. Rates amongst the black and minority ethnic groups were proportionally higher than for their white counterparts and highest amongst those of mixed ethnicity. Women in some communities are particularly vulnerable. For example, a key problem cited by the Sikh Women's Action Network (SWAN), based in the West Midlands, is forced marriage, 'with women often becoming totally isolated and losing their friends and family when they move to live with their husband'. Calls during the Covid-19 lockdown to SWAN 'were up by 244 per cent, with almost 60 families helped over the past year' (Kaur, reporting for the BBC, 12 March 2021). Research has shown that this disparity is due to long standing structural inequalities (Platt, 2007).

In addition, men and women with a disability were twice as likely to experience domestic abuse as those without. Pregnancy can also trigger the onset of abuse: a UK study of 500 pregnant women booking at an antenatal clinic found that 17 per cent reported having experienced domestic abuse during their current pregnancy (Johnson *et al*, 2003).

The likelihood of experiencing such abuse also increases for those who are unemployed, in single-parent households, and those living in urban areas (ONS, 2019). Poverty is also an important risk factor. The 2001 British Crime Survey found that women in the poorest households were more likely to be subjected to domestic abuse than those in more affluent households (Walby and Allen, 2004). Work by Hind Khalifeh and colleagues (2013) also highlighted the link between poverty and domestic abuse, identifying social deprivation to be associated with an increased lifetime prevalence of intimate partner violence. There is now considerable research that shows that vulnerability to domestic abuse is associated with low income, economic stress and benefit receipt (Fahmy *et al*, 2015). A recent Scottish-based study (Skafida *et al*, 2021) reinforces these findings and identifies the importance of understanding how dimensions of disadvantage overlap and interlock with each other:

> *The highest predicted prevalence of experiencing any domestic abuse was for mothers who were both in the youngest and the poorest groups. Among this group it is predicted that 1 in 3 of all mothers of young children experience some form of abuse. By contrast, 1 in 10 mothers who were neither in the youngest nor poorest categories are predicted to experience some form of abuse.*
>
> (Skafida *et al*, 2021, p.3)

IMPACT OF THE PANDEMIC ON DOMESTIC ABUSE

Domestic violence and abuse are fundamentally about one person's need to have total control of every aspect of their partner's behaviour. The opportunities for perpetrators to abuse their partner increased with the lockdown on 23 March 2020, imposed to prevent the spread of Covid-19. Once this was in place, victims of abuse and their children were, to quote the Home Secretary, 'trapped in the horrific cycle of abuse' (*The Observer*, 2020). Practically two-thirds (61.3%) of women included in a Women's Aid (2020) survey, who were living with their abuser, reported a worsening of the abuse during the pandemic. Women had more difficulty seeking support and reported that their abuser used the lockdown restrictions to exert control:

> *Hard to get any privacy or time to make calls to anyone who can help. Can't physically leave the house…he doesn't have any routine.*
> (Women's Aid, 2020, p.16)

Women also reported that during the lockdown their fear increased; they felt that they had no one they could turn to for help. As one survivor explained, 'I'm lonely, feel isolated, like a sitting duck' (Women's Aid, 2020, p.10).

Women's experiences during the pandemic were reflected in an increased demand for refuge services, a service already under stress due to local government financial cuts. The Covid-19 lockdown resulted in a further reduction in refuge spaces. This was caused by a number of issues, including staff shortages, restrictions on the numbers of women and families that could be received as per Government guidance, and a lack of personal protective equipment (Women's Aid, 2020). The pandemic also showed an increase in visits to victim service websites: there was a 700 per cent increase in the number of visits to the National Abuse helpline between April to June 2020 compared with the same period in 2019 (ONS, 2020a).

TYPES OF DOMESTIC VIOLENCE AND ABUSE

Domestic abuse may include actual physical violence as well as the many other subtle ways in which control over an individual can be exerted. The following sections describe the types and consequences of different forms that such abuse may take, bearing in mind that these are not mutually exclusive and often co-exist. For example, the dataset of 2,500 victim cases, used by Co-ordinated Action against Domestic Abuse (CAADA), found that:

> *Three-quarters of victims experience multiple types of abuse and 70 per cent experience at least one form of severe abuse such as strangulation, rape or threats to kill.*
> (CAADA, 2012, p.7)

Physical assault

The British Crime Survey suggests that over one-quarter of all victims of domestic abuse suffered a physical injury that required some sort of medical attention (ONS, 2018a):

Minor injuries included bruising or a black eye and scratches, while severe injuries included internal injuries and broken bones or teeth. Death is the most severe consequence of domestic abuse.
(BMA Board of Science, 2014, p.16, para 3.1.1)

As previously noted, partner abuse is not gender-specific, although research suggests that the reasons behind the abuse are different for men and women (see for example, Moffitt and Caspi, 1998; Corry *et al*, 2001). In general, it has been reported that women's use of violence against their male partner is motivated by self-defence and fear, and for some in response to "being pestered". In contrast, men's physical abuse is more likely than women's to be driven by the wish to control and dominate (Swan *et al*, 2008).

The consequences of domestic conflicts, however, are very different. Men's physical strength generally means that women are at greater risk of sustaining injuries that require medical attention. Caroline McGee's (2000) qualitative study of domestic abuse found that 83 per cent of the 48 mothers included in her sample had experienced physical violence:

He threw that brass ashtray at me. I had seven stitches in my head – that was the start of it, and once they've done it once, it goes on and on and on, you know.
(Kim, quoted in McGee, 2000, p.40)

This disparity between the sexes was illustrated in the results of the 2018 British Crime Survey. Practically three-quarters (73.6%) of women needed medical attention compared with just over one-quarter (26.4%) of men, following an incident of domestic abuse (ONS, 2018a).

There has been much less research directed at exploring the patterns of physical abuse perpetrated by women against men. A small UK-based survey of 100 male victims of domestic abuse found that two-thirds said their female partner had used a weapon against them, with just fewer than one-quarter (22%) having been stabbed (Brown, 1998). A larger Portuguese study of 535 male victims of intimate partner violence (all perpetrators were women) showed that injuries were usually mild; the women had perpetrated psychological abuse and minor acts of physical violence (Carmo *et al*, 2011).

Sexual abuse

Women in an abusive relationship were found to be four times more likely than men to have experienced a sexual assault (ONS, 2018b). Research by Andrea Parrot and Nina Cummings (2006) showed that marital rape often coexists with other forms of abuse such as beatings, torture and psychological control. Once again, a woman in McGee's study (2000) provides a moving example of being sexually abused and psychologically controlled, as she spoke of her fears that her abuser would rape her daughter:

> *He raped me once, and it frightened me that he would actually do it to Marilyn. And I think he must have known what was frightening me because he said, 'When you've outgrown your usefulness there's another female in the house', and that is what frightened me.*
> (Camilla, quoted in McGee, 2000, p.40)

The rate of sexual assault within a relationship may be underreported and underestimated because women and men find it a particularly difficult issue to talk about. For others, religion and culture may influence their actions and decisions not to speak out. Marital rape is a concept largely unknown in traditional Islamic law (Saleem Khan, 2020). As a result, Muslim women may be reluctant to report marital rape fearing they would risk losing everything, including their home and family. This reluctance is not exclusive to Muslim women but is shared more widely – patriarchal cultures demand that a woman submits to her husband and many women will be silenced by this and other factors, including economic dependence, having young children, the lack of a supportive network, and their legal status in the UK.

Controlling or coercive behaviour

Chapter 1 explained how controlling or coercive behaviour, including financial, psychological and emotional abuse in an intimate or familial relationship, became a criminal offence in England and Wales in 2015 under s.76 of the Serious Crime Act (Home Office, 2015). In 2018, the Domestic Abuse Law in Scotland also made coercive control illegal.

Controlling or coercive behaviour is defined in the following way:

> *Controlling behaviour is: a range of acts designed to make a person subordinate and/or dependent by isolating them from sources of support, exploiting their resources and capacities for personal gain, depriving them of the means needed for independence, resistance and escape and regulating their everyday behaviour.*

> *Coercive behaviour is: an act or a pattern of acts of assault, threats, humiliation and intimidation or other abuse that is used to harm, punish, or frighten their victim.*
> (Home Office, 2015, p.3, Section 2: para 12)

> *Controlling or coercive behaviour is primarily a form of violence against women and girls and is underpinned by wider societal gender inequality.*
> (Home Office, 2015, p.7, para 22)

Jane Monckton Smith's study (2021) of dangerous relationships and the risk of homicide provides insight into the identification and recognition of coercive control. Her work broadens the focus to include both the motivation and the abuse, with the aim of transforming the way professionals think about risk and homicide:

> *The motivation is in the controlling person – it is that need to have control and power over their partner's life, enforcing compliance. The abuse is the limits this places on the partner and their ability to do what they want, but also the fear they live with, of the consequences of upsetting the controlling person.*
>
> (Monckton Smith, 2021, p.95)

Early research findings from a study working in conjunction with Merseyside Police suggested that, of 156 crimes of coercive control, 95 per cent involved a female victim and a male perpetrator (Johnson and Barlow, 2018). The following experience of one mother provides a vivid illustration of coercive control:

> *We were kept like prisoners, not allowed out – sometimes all weekend. We weren't allowed to see friends or have friends back...he used to physically drag the children back in the house. They were upset that they were not allowed to visit their grandfather who was ill in hospital.*
>
> (NCH Action for Children, 1994, p.27)

The lockdown and quarantine rules imposed by the Covid-19 pandemic resulted in abusers and victims spending more time together. During this time, a range of factors may have increased perpetrators' stress levels, including loss of financial resources, increased use of alcohol and drugs, increased isolation, and presence of vulnerable others such as children or pets, leading to greater controlling or coercive behaviour (Lyons and Brewer, 2021).

This can take an extremely intrusive form, as the experience of the following mother illustrates:

> *It was terrifying when we cut open a teddy bear my husband had given our daughter. It had a hidden camera. He could see everything we were up to.*
>
> (Jenny, quoted in Hestia, 2016, p.10)

Such behaviour is aimed at making a person dependent through one or more acts of assault, threats, humiliation and intimidation or other abuse. It is used to harm, punish or frighten the victim. Disabled victims may be particularly vulnerable because they have to overcome greater hurdles when seeking help. 'They may be dependent upon their abuser also to be their carer' (Humphreys and Mullender, 1999).

In some circumstances, threats and acts of violence towards a pet are used to coerce, control and intimidate. An overview of research by Sherry Ramsey and colleagues (2010) found that 'as many as 71 per cent of battered women reported that their pets had been threatened, harmed, and/or killed by their partners' (p.17). Threats of violence directed at pets are generally used to manipulate the victim to remain with their abuser or to ensure that children do not reveal their home circumstances (Newberry, 2017):

> *He said 'I've told you you're not going, and if you do I will drown that cat, and don't think I'm joking' – so I didn't go.*
>
> (Newberry, 2017, p.14)

Victims of domestic abuse, both adults and children, often form very close bonds with their pets. They are grateful for the animal's affection and emotional support and in some cases for the protection they offer from violent partners. Refuges have no facilities for pets, so, in deciding to leave an abusive partner, some victims are faced with an unresolvable dilemma. Do they leave their abuser but abandon a much-loved animal, or stay to try and protect their pet? There are limited options for victims in such situations, although some charities organised through the Links Group do offer pet fostering services specifically to those fleeing domestic abuse.

When women and children decide to flee to a refuge and must leave a much-loved animal with their abuser, the perpetrator may use threats and violence towards their pets to ensure their return. Newberry (2017) provides another example:

> *He sent me a video of him putting his hand over the dog's mouth and nose to suffocate it and then threw it against the cupboard. He told me if I didn't return for good the dog would die next time, so of course I went back.*
>
> (Newberry, 2017, p.15)

Economic abuse

Economic abuse occurs when an individual deprives their partner of financial resources or the ability to make any money: the power to make choices is curtailed and their dependency is ensured. It is yet another way of controlling their partner and ensuring that they do not leave the relationship. Reports of domestic abuse suggest that women are more likely than men to experience being financially controlled.

> *Female victims of partner abuse were more likely than male victims to report experiencing non-physical abuse (emotional, financial) (72.6% for women and 57.0% for men)...*
>
> (ONS, 2018b, p.3)

The key findings in a report commissioned by Women's Aid included the following:

- *Nearly one-third of respondents said that their access to money was controlled by their partner* (p.5).

- *Over two-fifths described their partner as refusing to pay his share or taking money from her* (p.5).

- *A quarter said that their partner would not let them have money for essentials during the relationship (p.5).*

- *A third of respondents had to give up their home as a result of the abuse or on leaving the relationship, and nine found themselves homeless as a result of leaving (p.8).*

- *43.1% of respondents told us they were in debt as a result of the abuse (p.7).*

- *56.1% of our sample who had left a relationship with an abuser felt that the abuse had impacted on their ability to work (p.8).*

(Women's Aid, 2019)

The story of one woman's experience provides a vivid picture of economic abuse:

> Mary married an older, high-income man. She had a job but he pressurised her to give up work. He then deposited money into her account for household bills. This account was almost empty at the end of the month and she had to keep asking for extra cash. He said the allowance was enough, so she was bad at managing money. On several occasions the allowance was withheld. 'I realised that I was trapped and controlled. His income was high and we had savings, but I never felt I was his partner, I was more like his slave.'
> (Mary, reported by Women's Aid and TUC, 2015)

Government policies to help those on low or no income can have unexpected consequences for women living with domestic abuse. For example, the UK income support system may trap women in abusive relationships. Joint payments of the benefit, paid out to one claimant, allows perpetrators to control all family finances, and further restricts women's ability to leave an abusive partner (Skafida *et al*, 2021).

Psychological and emotional abuse

Psychological and emotional abuse is aimed at reducing a partner's confidence and self-esteem in order to make them reliant and dependent. This is achieved through tactics such as intimidation, bullying, constant criticism, and ignoring or using silence against the victim. Ann Pietrangelo (2018) provides an overview of the obvious signs of psychological and emotional abuse in intimate partner relationships. Included are examples of humiliation, negating and criticising; control and shame; accusing, blaming and denial; and emotional neglect and isolation.

A review of 62 empirical studies examining the prevalence of female perpetrated intimate partner violence found that the highest rates were for emotional abuse (Williams *et al*, 2008). Nonetheless, women are at greater risk of being victimised by their male partners in this way (Karakurt and Silver, 2013):

> ...they grind you down mentally, they make you feel totally useless and inept and unable and incapable, and then it's easy for them to just intimidate you without...just the threat of physical violence is enough...
> (Lucy, quoted in McGee, 2000, p.35)

DOMESTIC ABUSE IS RARELY A SINGLE ISSUE

There are strong links between the consumption of alcohol and domestic violence and abuse. Research by the Institute of Alcohol Studies (2014) suggests that between one-quarter and one-half of those who perpetrate domestic abuse had been drinking at the time of the assault. Where the physical violence is severe, it is twice as likely that alcohol was used when compared with cases of less severe physical violence. Whether there is a causal link between alcohol misuse and domestic abuse is open to debate. The impact is complicated and there is considerable evidence that alcohol is not the root cause of domestic abuse but a compounding factor. People who are violent and aggressive will behave in these ways whether or not they drink alcohol. Alcohol consumption makes it more likely to predict aggression and violence but is no excuse for such behaviour (Galvani, 2004).

The perpetration of domestic abuse is also linked with mental health issues and substance misuse. Gail Gilchrist and colleagues' (2019) meta-ethnography found an interplay between poor mental health (depression, post-traumatic stress disorder and anxiety), substance misuse (intoxication, withdrawal and addiction) and the perpetration of interpersonal violence. Both survivors and perpetrators blamed intoxication as disinhibiting existing violent traits:

> *Alcohol, it brings out the worst in me, you know. You know, when you're not drunk, you're calm and you can just ignore someone or walk out. But when you're drunk, something flicks a switch and you become violent.*
> (Wayne, in treatment for heroin and hazardous drinking, quoted in Radcliffe *et al*, 2017, p.68)

The dependency, withdrawal and addiction to substances means that these issues can take priority over relationships and make survivors vulnerable to domestic abuse, as illustrated by the following:

> *My son's father used to beat me when he didn't have money to get straight. He used to hit me when he was going through withdrawal [from heroin] when I didn't ... give him money.*
> (Domestic abuse survivor, quoted in Gilbert *et al*, 2001, p.525)

There is also considerable evidence to demonstrate a link between being a victim of domestic abuse and poor mental health. For example, two-thirds of women with depression were found to have experienced domestic abuse (Bradley *et al*, 2002):

> *Domestic violence causes several kinds of mental disorder, the most important of which are depression and anxiety and that of post-traumatic stress disorder (PTSD).*
>
> (Walby, 2004, p.54)

Exposure to domestic abuse is associated with alcohol and drug misuse. Victims may use alcohol or substances to manage the symptoms of post-traumatic stress disorder, such as sleep disorder and hyper-vigilance, which have resulted from their experience of abuse and violence (Kaysen *et al*, 2006; Overup *et al*, 2015).

For those who see no way out of the abuse, suicide may become the only option. It is estimated that one in eight of all suicides and suicide attempts by women in the UK are due to domestic abuse (SafeLives, 2016). Further information is provided by a study involving 3,500 women attending the charity Refuge, which found that one-quarter (24%) had felt suicidal at one time or another and 18 per cent had plans to end their life (Aitken and Munro, 2018).

THE IMPACT ON PARENTING

> *Parenting can be defined as those activities and behaviours of caregiving adults that are needed by children to enable them to function successfully as adults within their culture.*
>
> (Jones, 2001, p.283)

There are many aspects to parenting, ranging from physical care to sensitive, timely responsiveness, where the child's needs should be centre stage. Domestic violence and abuse will affect the capacity of parents to look after and care for their children and meet their basic needs (Department of Health *et al*, 2000).

In the majority of families, mothers assume the main responsibility for parenting the children. As a consequence, the prevalence of mothers being the target of domestic abuse, coupled with their increased risk of severe injury, impacts on children to a greater extent than when fathers are the victims.

A mother's capacity to look after her children will be significantly affected by the degree of violence inflicted on her. Assaults can take the form of being kicked, punched, slapped, choked and bitten, scalded and poisoned, the use or threat of weapons, objects thrown and, in the most extreme cases, being killed (Cleaver *et al*, 2007). Meeting the physical needs of children is perhaps most affected when mothers have been disabled by the violence or hospitalised.

As has already been discussed, domestic abuse is rarely confined to physical assaults. Emotional and psychological abuse often consists of a constant barrage of criticism, undermining and humiliation – behaviours that can have a profoundly negative impact on a woman's mental health. This can result in women losing confidence, becoming fearful, and feeling denigrated. It can lead to the over-use of medication, illicit drugs and/or alcohol, all behaviours that may impact negatively on their ability to look after children and which are associated with child neglect (Cleaver *et al*, 2011).

When domestic abuse results in maternal depression, all aspects of life can be affected: sleep can become disturbed; appetite may be lost; concentration becomes difficult; actions slow down; and many sufferers are overwhelmed by feelings of exhaustion and worthlessness. For some, life appears hopeless and they are left with little capacity to care for themselves or their children.

Children's welfare and safety may also be affected negatively when their parent is subjected to coercive control and economic abuse. The abuser may restrict or disallow all contact with family and friends. Visits to the home may be severely curtailed and trips out of the house may have to be sanctioned. As a result, a child may have little or no contact with wider family or personal friends. Restricting a parent's access to money will also affect their ability to buy food and clothes for the children, school trips may be prohibited, and toys and other treats become impossible.

As already noted, domestic violence and abuse are frequently associated with substance misuse, poor mental health and poverty, factors that will compound the difficulties parents experience in meeting the needs of their children. Research has shown that the coexistence of these issues may have a serious impact on every aspect of children's lives (Cleaver *et al*, 2007).

CHILDREN AS INNOCENT BYSTANDERS?

> *My mum and her boyfriend were, like, in the living room downstairs … and I could hear like, screaming and objects being thrown…and then like, I went downstairs and obviously I was like, traumatised and everything … and then … I just didn't know what to do and if like, I was older, I could've like, done something. If I was like, a different age then, I could've like … done something … not like, get in between them, but I could've called like the police or something.*
>
> (14 year-old girl, quoted in Children's Commissioner, 2018, pp.5–6)

Research has suggested that one child in five in the UK witnesses or is exposed to domestic abuse during childhood (Radford et al, 2011), a finding supported by research from CAADA (2012), which found that two-thirds of women who were experiencing domestic violence and abuse had children.

Most people living in an abusive relationship wish to shield their children, but they are rarely successful. McGee (2000) found that three-quarters of children in her sample of children exposed to domestic abuse had witnessed the assault of their mother and 10 per cent her rape. Children may experience domestic abuse indirectly by hearing the abuse from another room or finding damage to their home such as broken furniture.

With the majority of the violence and abuse being directed towards women, most children will have witnessed the abuse of their mother. However, as already discussed, domestic abuse does not always follow this pattern and men may be the victims, or in some cases the physical violence is mutual (Whitaker et al, 2007). As a consequence, some children will have witnessed their father being victimised, or the aggression of both parents towards each other.

DOMESTIC ABUSE AND CHILD PROTECTION

Information on the association between domestic abuse and child abuse and neglect can be obtained from a number of sources, including Government and crime statistics, overviews of safeguarding reviews, and academic research data.

The Crime Survey for England and Wales (ONS, 2020b) provides information on the concurrence of child abuse and domestic abuse within the general population. The survey estimates that one in five adults had experienced at least one form of child abuse before the age of 16 years and practically half the group had also witnessed domestic abuse.

Figures supplied by police forces in England and Wales to Her Majesty's Inspectorate of Constabulary and Fire & Rescue Services, as part of their annual inspections, also provide some information on the association between domestic abuse and child protection. For the year ending March 2018, there were 201,656 child protection referrals as a result of domestic abuse-related incidents (ONS, 2018a). It is more difficult to gain a UK-wide perspective. Domestic abuse data in England and Wales are not comparable with Scotland's data due to differences in definition.

Research by CAADA (2014) identified a significant overlap between direct harm to children and domestic abuse. Almost two-thirds (62%) of children exposed to domestic abuse had also been directly harmed in one or more ways, either physically, sexually or emotionally or had been neglected. In 91 per cent of the cases, the same person as was responsible for the domestic abuse had also abused the child; this was most commonly the child's father (64%) or mother's male partner (25%).

A further source of information is the Department for Education. Their data for 2017/18 show that domestic abuse was a factor in 246,720 child protection assessments across England, more than half of all child protection assessments (51%) (DfE, 2018a). Government statistics for Scotland show a similar pattern. For the 2,654 children on the child protection register in 2020, the most common concerns identified were domestic (43%) and emotional abuse (38%), neglect (42%), and parental substance misuse (43%) (Gov.Scot, 2020).

National analyses of serious case reviews in England have consistently shown that domestic violence and abuse are a common feature in approximately half the families where a child had died or had been seriously injured. For example, domestic abuse was identified in 59 per cent of the reviews included in Marion Brandon and colleagues' (2020) triennial study. The rapid reviews, submitted to the Child Safeguarding Practice Review Panel, identified high levels of domestic abuse in the lives of 35 per cent of the 538 serious child-safeguarding incidents they had received (Child Safeguarding Practice Review Panel, 2020a).

It is not known what proportion of fostered or adopted children have been exposed to domestic abuse prior to coming into care. This is because currently such information is not routinely recorded in relation to children who become looked after by the local authority. The latest Government statistics reveal that, in the majority of cases (63%), children became looked after because they were at risk of abuse or neglect, or were living in a family where the parenting capacity was chronically inadequate (DfE, 2020). The Department for Education data also show that:

> *Domestic violence (including that directed at children, the parent/carer or other adults in the household) remains the most common factor identified at end of assessment…*
>
> (DfE, 2019a, p.12)

A further data source is the information recorded in care applications. A study by CAFCASS (2012) looked at a sample of 343 (61%) of the 562 care applications received during the period 11 to 30 November 2011. These 343 cases involved 600 children. The study found that 'a parent had been the victim of domestic violence in 60.1 per cent of cases and the perpetrator of domestic violence in 40.3 per cent of cases' (Cafcass,

2012, p.21). It also identified a similar rate of parental drug and alcohol misuse to be a contributing factor.

CHILDREN MOST AT RISK OF SIGNIFICANT HARM

Regardless of their age, any child can be vulnerable to the impact of domestic abuse, including the unborn child. The findings from a UK study illustrate this point. It explored 251 police notifications of incidents of domestic abuse (involving 460 children) to children's services. The study identified that nearly one-half of the sample of children were under the age of five, and almost three-quarters under the age of 11 (Stanley *et al*, 2010).

There is little known about the length of time children are exposed to domestic abuse before coming into care. However, on average, high-risk female victims live with domestic abuse for over two years and medium-risk victims for three years before getting help, a finding which suggests that children are likely to have lived with violence for some considerable time (SafeLives, 2015).

Research has also suggested that children most at risk of suffering significant harm are those whose parents face a combination of stressors, the most relevant being the presence of domestic abuse (Daniel *et al*, 2009; Brandon *et al*, 2010; Cleaver *et al*, 2011). Domestic abuse is associated with all forms of child abuse: physical, sexual, emotional and neglect. The analysis of serious case reviews in England showed that domestic abuse was noted to be a feature in 64 per cent of families where the cause for concern was child neglect (Brandon *et al*, 2020). In Scotland the Care Inspectorate's analysis of 25 significant case reviews identified domestic abuse as an issue in 10 cases (Care Inspectorate, 2019). Children may be physically hurt when they try to intervene to prevent verbal abuse or violent assaults. There is also evidence to show that fathers and father figures who are violent and abusive to the mother are more likely to sexually abuse the children (Humphreys and Stanley, 2006).

Simply to witness parental distress and suffering, particularly physical violence and abuse meted out by one parent to the other, can have a devastating impact on children's mental and emotional health:

> *The psychological aftermath of exposure to DV [domestic violence] can include fear of harm or abandonment, excessive worry or sadness, guilt, inability to experience empathy or guilt, habitual lying, low frustration tolerance, emotional distancing, poor judgement, shame, and fear about the future.*
>
> (Edwards, 2019, para. 4)

The impact of domestic abuse can have long-term consequences for the health and wellbeing of children. McGee (2000) reports that they can experience:

> ... fear, powerlessness, depression or sadness, impaired social relations, impacts on the child's identity, impacts on extended family relationships and their relationship with their mother, effects on educational achievement and anger, very often displayed as aggressive behaviour.
> (McGee, 2000, p.69)

The reports of 567 people aged 18 to 34 years, participating in a recently published poll on exposure to domestic abuse as children, showed that the experience had led to:

- 59 per cent experiencing anxiety, depression or PTSD;
- 55 per cent having trust issues in relationships;
- 42 per cent having experienced exclusion from school or low academic performance;
- 34 per cent having self-medicated with alcohol or substance misuse;
- 27 per cent experiencing low attainment in their employment.

(Hestia, 2019)

Children are at most risk of significant harm when domestic abuse is accompanied by parental mental ill health, substance misuse, learning disability, and where income is inadequate (Cleaver *et al*, 2011). The negative consequences for children are exacerbated when they witness the abuse, are drawn into participating in the abuse of a parent, or into colluding in the secrecy and concealment of assaults. Children may not speak out about what is happening at home because they are frightened, embarrassed or do not trust anyone:

> *Don't be telling anyone...whatever happens in the house stays in the house.*
> (11-year-old girl, quoted in the report of the Children's Commissioner, 2018, p.18)

Each child will be affected by domestic abuse in different ways. Even those in the same family will react differently depending on their age, sex, relationship to the abuser, and role in the family. Children are less likely to suffer significant harm when:

- domestic abuse is not associated with poor parental mental health, substance misuse or learning disability;
- there is the presence of a non-abusive partner in the household;
- other responsible adults such as grandparents are involved in child care;
- the abused parent is receiving ongoing support;

- the home is stable and there are adequate finances;
- the child has a friend, relative or other responsible adult in whom they can confide;
- one parent has the capacity to act effectively in relation to themselves and their children;
- the child regularly attends pre-school or school;
- there is a positive school climate and sympathetic, empathic and vigilant teachers;
- the child belongs to organised out-of-school activities including homework clubs;
- an adult acts as a champion for the child.

(Cleaver *et al*, 2011)

The extent to which children may be shielded from the worst effects of domestic abuse will also depend on their ability to develop the necessary strengths and resilience. This may be particularly difficult for children growing up in abusive households because, as Rutter (2007) notes, resilience is related to a child's:

- sense of self-esteem and self-confidence;
- belief in one's self-efficacy and ability to deal with change and adaptation;
- repertoire of social problem-solving approaches.

These are attributes that many children growing up with domestic abuse may fail to acquire. Moreover, some of the strategies that children develop to cope with what is happening to them are not always positive. For example, detachment, avoidance and withdrawal, or aggression may help a child get through the experience of domestic abuse, child abuse and neglect, but have long-term negative consequences for future relationships.

THE IMPACT ON CHILDREN OF DIFFERENT AGES AND STAGES OF DEVELOPMENT

In order to provide support to those caring for children who have experienced domestic abuse, it is essential to understand the impact it may have on a child's health and development and its influence on their consequent behaviour patterns. Although there are factors that make children more or less vulnerable to the experience of domestic abuse, the effect and the strategies they develop will be related to their age and stage of development.

The following chapters examine the impact on children aged less than five years including the unborn child, those in middle childhood, and finally, adolescents. To provide a context to the child's behaviour, each section is introduced with a discussion of the expected development for the specific age group. The possible consequences of being exposed to domestic abuse and any co-existing parental issues are then explored in relation to the child's health, education, emotional and behavioural development, self-care skills, identity and social presentation, and family and social relationships.

TO SUM UP

- No one is immune to domestic abuse, although women are most at risk of being abused or killed by their male partner. In contrast, men in gay or bisexual relationships are more likely than men in heterosexual relationships to be abused. A number of factors increase women's risk of domestic abuse, including age, poor socio-economic conditions, ethnicity, disability and pregnancy.

- Domestic abuse is fundamentally about controlling another person. It can include physical and sexual assaults, controlling and coercive behaviour, economic abuse, psychological and emotional abuse, and the abuse of pets.

- Domestic abuse rarely exists in isolation and is often associated with poor parental mental health, alcohol and drug misuse, and poverty. These issues may apply to both perpetrator and victim.

- The experience of domestic abuse may affect all aspects of parenting. It can impact on a parent's capacity to keep the children safe and meet their basic needs for emotional warmth and stimulation. Although parents often wish to shield their children from what is happening in the home, this is rarely successful.

- There are no data to identify what proportion of fostered and adopted children and those in other forms of alternative care have previously been exposed to domestic abuse. Information drawn from child protection referrals and care applications suggest that this may be as high as 60 per cent.

- Children most at risk of suffering significant harm are those in families in which domestic abuse is associated with poor parental mental health, substance misuse, poverty, and when the child directly witnesses, or is made to participate in, the abuse of a parent.

- Children are less likely to suffer significant harm if there are no compounding factors associated with the domestic abuse, and if there is a family member who consistently and appropriately responds to their developmental needs.
- Growing up in an abusive household can have long-term consequences for a child's mental health and education; no child can be fully protected.

Chapter 3
Impact of domestic abuse on children under five years

This chapter explores the impact of domestic violence and abuse on children under five years. The initial focus is on the unborn child, before moving on to examine how babies and infants can be affected by living in a violent and abusive household.

THE UNBORN CHILD

Nourishment and a safe environment are basic to the healthy development of the unborn child. To achieve this, the expectant mother must have an adequate diet and refrain from: smoking, recreational drugs, drinking alcohol, and an overuse of prescription medication. The environment in which she lives will also affect the growing foetus. Physical impacts, bumps and blows may damage the placenta and maternal stress can increase the release of cortisol, which may also harm the foetus.

Pregnancy can trigger the start of physical violence and abuse within a relationship or increase its severity and frequency (Humphreys and Houghton, 2008). Pregnant women exposed to abuse sustain poor health outcomes for themselves and their unborn child when the violence includes punches and kicks directed at the woman's swelling abdomen and breasts. There is substantial research that shows such assaults are associated with an increased rate of miscarriage, stillborn and premature birth, foetal brain injury, and fractured placental separation. Domestic abuse during pregnancy is also linked with poor outcomes at birth, including foetal distress, low birth weight, and foetal and baby death (see for example, Mezey and Bewley, 1997; Meuleners *et al*, 2011).

A mother's emotional condition can affect her unborn baby. Domestic abuse creates a stressful, unpredictable and dangerous environment for pregnant women. It may include acute traumatic events and chronic anticipation of abusive behaviours (Martinez-Torteya *et al*, 2017). The body responds to high levels of stress through the neuroendocrine release of cortisol. Usually the placenta protects the unborn baby from the mother's cortisol but when the mother is very stressed, this works less well. When cortisol permeates the placenta, it has been shown to be linked adversely to the development of the baby's amygdala, an area of the brain involved in emotional and social development in childhood (Stoye *et al*, 2020).

Unborn babies exposed to high levels of cortisol are more likely to develop behaviour problems and have lower cognitive development at 18 months (Herba and Glover, 2021). Research has shown an association between prenatal exposure to domestic abuse and 'birth outcomes including low birth weight, stress response alterations, temperamental difficulties, and internalising (e.g. sad, inhibited) and externalising (e.g. oppositional, aggressive, rule-breaking, impulsive) behaviours during infancy and childhood' (Martinez-Torteya *et al*, 2017, p.40). Danya Glaser (2000) provides a comprehensive review of research on the effects of abuse and neglect, particularly the role of stress responses to trauma, on early brain development, and on attachment patterns in infancy.

Exposure to domestic abuse can result in an expectant mother experiencing poor mental health and post-traumatic stress, leading to an overuse of alcohol, prescription or illicit drugs; issues that may affect adversely the unborn child (Phillips, 2004). Drug use may harm a developing foetus via multiple mechanisms depending on the stage of pregnancy. Very early in pregnancy, the foetus is susceptible to structural damage whereas drugs taken later can affect growth or cause neonatal addiction (Julien, 1995; The Conversation, 2014).

The impact on the unborn child of drinking during pregnancy is related to the amount and pattern of alcohol consumed by the mother (Forrester, 2012). Excessive drinking is associated with an increased rate of miscarriage and can cause foetal alcohol syndrome disorder (FASD). The alcohol, which passes through the placenta, damages cells in the baby's brain, spinal cord and other parts of the body, and can result in miscarriage. Babies that survive may be left with lifelong problems, including difficulties in impulse control as well as behaviour and learning difficulties. A survey by Adoption UK (2020) of nearly 5,000 adopters in the UK found that one-quarter of the adopted children had been affected by parental drinking during pregnancy; eight per cent had been diagnosed with FASD; and a further 17 per cent were suspected of having FASD.

For three years, Harriet Ward and colleagues (2012) followed 57 children who had been subject to a core assessment or s.47 enquiry before their first birthday. They found that when babies had been exposed to domestic abuse in utero, the abuse continued following their birth, as the following example illustrates:

> *The police were called several times during incidents in which Nathan was held up and used as a shield between his parents.*
>
> (Ward *et al*, 2012, p.127)

The unborn child may be at risk of poor development due to the difficulties women may have in attending antenatal appointments. This could be the result of controlling and coercive behaviour, such as when an abusive partner restricts the pregnant woman's movements. For other women, the link may be indirect. For example, the experience of abuse may leave a woman with such low self-esteem and depression that she fails to look after her own and the unborn child's physical needs, including attending antenatal clinic (Peckover, 2001). Irregular attendance at antenatal clinic has been shown to be associated with pregnancy complications such as pre-eclampsia and eclampsia, both pregnancy-related high blood pressure disorders, and with anaemia. It is also linked with higher adverse birth outcomes including preterm birth, low birth weight and stillbirth (Abbas *et al*, 2017).

Finally, there is evidence that the experience of domestic abuse weakens the bond between an expectant mother and her unborn child. Women who are victims of domestic abuse have been shown to be more likely to have a lower attachment to their unborn child when compared with non-abused women (Zeitlin *et al*, 1999; Pires de Almeida *et al*, 2012).

In some cases, the effects of domestic abuse on an expectant mother and her unborn child may be mitigated. Protective factors include good, regular antenatal care, and a network of alternative, safe and supportive people.

INFANT DEVELOPMENT (UNDER FIVE YEARS)

In supporting kinship and foster carers, adopters and special guardians to meet the needs of a baby or infant who has been exposed to domestic abuse, an understanding of the underlying issues is essential. The remainder of this chapter describes the expected health and development of infants, before examining the possible impact of domestic abuse.

HEALTH

Expected developmental progression

Fundamental to the health and development of an infant is a caring adult who can meet their needs for love and affection, adequate food, and a safe environment.

Newborn babies learn from the first days of life and can habituate to repeated stimulation. Present from the beginning are their individual cycles of sleeping, waking, crying, eating and defecating. Although babies differ, they generally sleep 16 to 18 hours a day and feed perhaps 10 times. There are significant variations in their general activity rate, restlessness, irritability and cuddliness (Bee, 2000). To ensure the baby's health and development, parents need to be able to adapt to these differences.

Most babies achieve their milestones within the anticipated timeframe. They develop motor skills by repetitively performing a limited range of movements and, in order to do so, need a home that provides adequate stimulation, safety and protection. By 15 months many infants can walk unassisted and by 24 months their gross motor control has developed sufficiently to enable them to climb onto furniture. A child's gross motor control continues to develop, so that by four years most children would be expected to succeed in catching, kicking, throwing and bouncing a ball and to enjoy climbing-frames.

Fine motor control should have developed to the stage where, by 24 months, children are able to feed themselves and pick up tiny objects. By three years, they would be expected to be able to use a pencil and draw a person as a head with legs and arms coming out of it, and by four years to copy some letters.

Babies should be taken regularly to clinics for immunisations and developmental reviews and, when babies and infants are ill, it is essential that they receive prompt medical attention.

A UK study that took place between July and November 2020 explored the impact of the Covid-19 pandemic on children aged 0 to 2 (Reed with Parish, 2021). Their findings identified that, during the first phase of lockdown, support services for this age group were highly depleted. The majority of services did not "bounce back" quickly as the lockdown eased. Evidence of harm to very young children emerged in five overlapping areas:

- *An increased likelihood of exposure to traumatic experiences*
- *Indirect health risks from time confined indoors and reduced contact with health services*
- *Risks of harm to development from restricted social interaction*
- *Risk of increased parental stress, less responsive parenting and harms to caregiving relationships*
- *Increased likelihood of hunger or material deprivation*

(Reed with Parish, 2021, p.14)

Possible impact of domestic abuse

It is an ultimate irony that at the time when the human is most vulnerable to the effects of trauma – during infancy and childhood – adults generally presume the most resilience.

(Perry *et al*, 1995, p.271)

The widely-held assumption that babies and very young children are unaware of, and consequently can be shielded from, the impact of domestic abuse has now been debunked (Glaser, 2000; Humphreys and Houghton, 2008). Very young children exposed to domestic abuse may have been the unintended victims of both physical and emotional harm. They are particularly vulnerable to suffering injury, illness and neglect because they are unable to avoid danger or defend themselves. Most obvious are injuries that can occur when the baby or toddler is caught in the crossfire between parents, as can happen when held in a mother's arms during a physical assault. In other cases, a baby or infant may be deliberately targeted:

> *He'd think nothing like, you know, when [daughter] was three or that he would think nothing of coming in from the pub and I suppose to save myself I would always pick her up. Yeah, I did that, but that was the only protection I had and if he had hit her in any way I definitely would have done something about it ... he would get in over her some way and she would be crying and screaming, like, just leaning over her and busting me in the side of the head, you know what I mean, he's a very violent man.*
> (Hogan and O'Reilly, 2007, p.28)

Very young children are in danger because an abusive relationship is driven by the need to control and dominate. The arrival of a baby can result in intense jealousy and new mothers may be acutely aware that the time spent breastfeeding can act as a trigger to renewed abuse. In an attempt to control the abuse, mothers may prioritise the man's needs at the expense of those of her baby. Consequently, the baby may receive irregular feeds and little attention or affection when the perpetrator is present.

Regular sleep patterns may also be difficult to establish. Research has shown that babies who live with domestic abuse are subject to poor sleeping habits and excessive screaming (Humphreys and Houghton, 2008):

> *Ariel, an 11-month-old who was present when her mother was attacked by her boyfriend, kept waking up at night screaming.*
> (National Child Trauma Stress Network, 2010, p.3)

When babies cry and are not easily soothed, perpetrators of domestic abuse can become extremely frustrated and may attempt to stop the crying and control the behaviour through shaking or violence.

Young children may be harmed because domestic abuse affects a mother's mental health, leaving her in a state of apathy, with impaired concentration. This can have dangerous consequences for her infant because lack of attention may result in accidental injuries, such as when babies are left alone in the bath or infants are sent out on to the street to play unsupervised. For example, children under five years who live with domestic abuse and violence are at increased risk of having to attend a medical service because of burn injuries. This age group accounts for up to 70 per cent of children who attend UK medical services and the most common risk factors are prior injury, parental mental health problems and domestic abuse (Nuttall *et al*, 2020).

A more insidious way in which babies and toddlers may be harmed is through their day-to-day experiences and interactions with their parents. Infancy is potentially the most vulnerable period in childhood because it is the time of greatest post-natal brain development. For example, between the ages of 6 and 18 months, the orbitofrontal cortex matures – an area of the brain involved in the cognitive process of decision-making. It is thought to be the location for social and emotional interactions, attachment development, and internal working models (Archer and Gordon, 2006). When the predominant early experiences are fear and stress, these can have significant and enduring effects on how the brain develops. The advancement of neuroimaging in the 1990s has enabled the identification of an association between witnessing physical familial abuse and morphologic changes in infants' brains (Tsavoussis *et al*, 2014).

Extreme stress and trauma are also associated with enduring changes in the secretion and processing of cortisol, a hormone found to cause disrupted neural development, resulting in emotional, social and cognitive impairment in very young children (Enlow *et al*, 2013; Cairns and Cairns, 2016; Clements *et al*, 2019). The experience of trauma in infancy increases the brain structures involved in vigilance and can result in a constant state of arousal, numbing or avoidance (SAMHSA, 2014).

EDUCATION: COGNITIVE AND LANGUAGE DEVELOPMENT

Expected developmental progression

Soon after birth, babies respond to sound and voices and can almost immediately distinguish their mother (or regular caregiver) from others on the basis of smell, sight or sound (Murray and Andrews, 2000). By nine months, the vast majority of babies enjoy communicating with sound and can shout for attention or scream with rage. Generally, at about one year, infants say their first words and new words are added quickly, typically names for things or people. By two years, infants are able to follow simple instructions, and by three and four years, most can concentrate well and, although enjoy playing by themselves, are beginning to be able to "take turns".

Hearing can be a serious issue for some children. Each year around 840 babies in the UK are born with a significant hearing impairment (Claridge, 2006). There are a number of approaches that can help deaf babies to acquire language (Humphries *et al*, 2012) but regardless of the method, all these babies will need additional stimulation and help.

To progress and develop, young children need adults who listen to their verbalisations and encourage them to interact. Looking at pictures and reading to a child helps to develop their vocabulary, knowledge and understanding of words and language. A safe environment enables the toddler and infant to explore their surroundings and thus develop their cognitive skills.

Possible impact of domestic abuse

The first years of life are a critical period for cognitive and language development. An analysis of the findings from a longitudinal twin study of five-year-olds, carried out in England and Wales, found that exposure to domestic abuse was associated with children's delayed intellectual development (Koenen *et al*, 2003). Research by Dan Anderberg and Gloria Moroni (2020), in line with these findings, showed that exposure to domestic abuse during the pre-school years had a significant negative effect on a child's cognitive skills. This can result from parents being preoccupied with their own feelings and emotions, and failing to notice their child's feelings or wishes or to respond appropriately. In other cases, feelings of exhaustion, depression and a lack of self-confidence and self-worth, factors associated with the experience of domestic abuse, may result in a parent not having the capacity to engage and stimulate their infant. As a result, infants and very young children may show significant delays in their language and general understanding, and start nursery and school from an unfavourable position.

Growing up in a violent and chaotic household has been shown to be associated with children who show little or no interest in their environment (Humphreys and Mullender, 1999). If children are not sure of their parents' behaviour and fear triggering a violent reaction, they may lack the courage to explore and consequently inhibit their natural inquisitiveness. Pre-school facilities, such as a nursery or playgroup, can compensate for a lack of stimulation at home and provide an opportunity to interact with other children and adults. Sadly, when parents are in a violent and abusive relationship, they often fail to take their children on a regular basis to such a facility. This may result from an abusive and controlling partner preventing the parent and child leaving the house, or because the abused parent is experiencing poor mental health. Finally, poverty and the chaotic lifestyle of some families affected by domestic abuse can mean that getting a child ready on time to attend a preschool facility is impossible.

EMOTIONAL AND BEHAVIOURAL DEVELOPMENT

Expected developmental progression

The emotional and behavioural development of an infant depends on the parental bond with the child and the child's attachment to the parent (Bowlby, 1973; Schofield and Beek, 2018). The formation of this relationship is based on the opportunity for parent and infant to 'develop a mutual, interlocking pattern of attachment behaviours, a smooth "dance" of interaction' (Bee, 2000, p.320):

> *The baby signals his needs by crying or smiling; he responds to being held by quieting or snuggling; he looks at the parents when they look at him…(The parents in turn)…pick the baby up when he cries, wait for and respond to his signals of hunger or other need, smile at him when he smiles, gaze into his eyes when he looks at them.*
>
> (Bee, 2000, p.320)

This "dance" of interaction will be influenced by the baby's temperament, which in turn will affect the parent's reactions. Key to a good outcome will be the parent's capacity to adapt and respond appropriately to their baby's emotional and developmental needs (Belsky et al, 1998).

During the second year of life, attachment experiences influence the development of a child's working model of how people are likely to behave towards them. The child develops an awareness of others and the capacity to empathise. It is a period when emotions are difficult to regulate and moods can fluctuate greatly. How infants learn to manage their moods depends upon the relationship between parent and child.

By three or four years, children are usually friendly and helpful, although outbursts of frustration and temper, both verbal and physical, are not unusual. It is an age when children are plagued by irrational fears, and key to managing these is the presence of a consistent adult who is able to reduce their anxiety and reassure them.

Statistics for England, based on high quality assessments with a random sample, found that one in 18 (5.5%) pre-school children were identified with at least one mental disorder. Behavioural disorders were evident in 2.5 per cent of preschool children. At this age, boys were more likely than girls to have a disorder (NHS Digital, 2018).

Possible impact of domestic abuse

Mothers who are abused can 'become numb, uncommunicative, unresponsive and unable to cope', while violent fathers are 'negative,

controlling, authoritarian and punitive in their behaviour, and see fatherhood in terms of their rights rather than the child's needs.
(Lewis, quoted in Guy *et al*, 2014, p.47)

The experience of domestic abuse can leave parents emotionally unavailable and unresponsive to their infants, and create in very young children a primal fear and a host of other raw, complex and unresolved emotions (Edwards, 2019). The lack of emotional availability will impact negatively on the 'interlocking pattern of attachment behaviour'. The process of attachment may be interrupted as a result of the violent partner being arrested or if the abused parent and infant escape an abusive home. As a result, infants may experience several unplanned moves, separations, or the loss of a parent figure. This could leave them with feelings of extreme anxiety, which they may express through bed-wetting, sleep disturbance, rocking and head-banging.

The child's emotional development may also be impeded in less obvious ways. It has been argued that an infant must experience nurture and affection in order 'for the limbic nuclei, relevant for the regulation of emotion, to develop normally' (Ironside, 2004, p.40). Sadly, for many children exposed to domestic abuse, neither parent is able to consistently provide such an environment. Research using data from a UK longitudinal study found that a mother's exposure to domestic abuse was strongly negatively associated with an infant's socio-emotional skills, an infant being defined as aged between birth and three years (Anderberg and Moroni, 2021).

In the early years, an infant's emotions and behaviours generally mirror the moods and actions of those who are caring for them. The apathy, despair and feelings of worthlessness many victims of domestic abuse experience can leave them emotionally unavailable to their infants and incapable of showing any warmth. When children have not experienced love and affection, they feel unloved, unlovable and unwanted (Cleaver *et al*, 2011). As a result, children become "touch hungry" and show no discrimination between their parent and strangers; they may be unduly clingy and fearful.

When infants have heard and watched arguments and fighting, they may be flooded with unpleasant emotions: sadness, anger, fear, confusion, grief and loneliness. With a limited ability to verbalise their emotions, they may act out, cry, resist comfort or become despondent (Baker and Cunningham, 2009). Research by Alytia Levendosky and colleagues (2002a) found that pre-school children living with domestic abuse suffered symptoms of post-traumatic stress disorder (PTSD). Mothers described the children's symptoms in terms of 'argues a lot', 'can't sit still, restless, or hyperactive', and 'fears certain animals, situations or places'. No differences were found in the PTSD symptomatology between boys and girls.

A report by UNICEF (2006) identified behavioural changes for young children exposed to domestic abuse that included:

- excessive irritability;
- sleep problems;
- emotional distress;
- fear of being alone;
- immature behaviour;
- problems with toilet training; and
- language development.

When domestic abuse starts some months after birth, a young child may regress to earlier behaviour patterns, such as inconsolable crying, loss of toilet training, and asking for a bottle. Children may show increased aggression and act out in play the events they have witnessed (National Child Trauma Stress Network, 2010). The volatile environment and the inconsistency in parental reactions harm infants' ability to trust adults. It reduces their exploratory behaviours, which is a necessary element for the development of autonomy.

IDENTITY AND SOCIAL PRESENTATION

Expected developmental progression

Children's understanding of who they are develops during their first years of life. By the age of three and four years, most children recognise their parents and siblings and have a sense of who belongs to their immediate family. It is a time when children gain a sense of ownership; an understanding of "me" and "mine". At this stage in their development, children's sense of identity is concrete and based on visible characteristics, such as whether they are a girl or boy, the colour of their hair, and what they are good at doing (Bee, 2000). The hypothesis that early childhood trauma is associated with gender dysphoria is unproven (see, for example, Malone, 2017 and Giovanardi et al, 2018).

Infancy is the stage when children integrate the "good" and "bad" parts of self, through adults telling them how to behave. It is by integrating these two aspects of themselves that children come to understand 'they are good people who sometimes do "not good" things' (Fahlberg, 1994, p.74). Infants who receive sufficient love and attention develop a positive view of self and are relatively confident and able to take pride in their achievements. Consequently, they expect adults to like them and, in turn, see adults as dependable and trustworthy. Parents generally take pride in their children and ensure that they are clean and appropriately dressed.

Possible impact of domestic abuse

When domestic abuse has led to poor parental mental health or substance misuse, the abused parent may lack the capacity to care about their own and/or their child's appearance. Children may be neglected and basic hygiene ignored; they may be left unwashed, with infested hair and dressed in inadequate and filthy clothes. Some children of four years are to a very limited degree able to look after themselves, but younger ones are not. How a child looks and smells will influence how others react to them and also how they feel about themselves.

Domestic abuse that is associated with poor parental mental health can result in a child being shown little warmth and being physically and emotionally rejected. Over time, children can develop negative and distorted beliefs about themselves and lose confidence in the ability of adults to look after and protect them.

Particularly damaging to a child's sense of identity is the belief, which many hold, that in some way they are to blame for the abuse in the home: 'it's my fault'. Infancy is the time for egocentric and magical thinking (believing that thoughts or actions can influence the course of events). This can result in unrelated events being linked together in a child's mind. For example, children may associate their mother's reproof for not putting away their toys earlier in the day with the subsequent domestic violence and abuse directed at her (Baker and Cunningham, 2009).

Children, even from a very young age, may try and put things right. They may attempt to comfort the abused and distressed parent or simply wish to hold on to them, fearing the external world:

> *Whenever he saw us arguing, he used to be crying his eyes out all the time. He was 'Mummy, Mummy'. And coming to me all the time.*
> (Mother of a two-year-old boy, quoted in Humphreys and Mullender, 1999, p.8)

FAMILY AND SOCIAL RELATIONSHIPS

Expected developmental progression

Early attachment and bonding between a baby and parent (or caregiver) begin during the first year of life and this experience will influence a child's approach to all new relationships. The process is generally reciprocal; each player affects the response of the other. There are, however, some circumstances when such a complementary relationship may not be present. Research has shown that severe autism with associated learning difficulties may result in an infant failing to attach securely to their parent (Rutgers *et al*, 2004).

Fear of strangers and separation anxiety are at their height around the age of two years. When the relationship with parents is well established, such fears gradually diminish. Most children can cope well with separation by the age of three and four years, understanding that their parent continues to exist when absent, as does their relationship (Bee, 2000). This enables the parent and child to plan for brief separations, such as attending nursery school and what the child should do when frightened or needing help. However, this period of childhood is a time for irrational fears, the greatest being that parents will abandon them (Fahlberg, 1994).

Infants as young as 14 months show an interest in one another and, over the coming months, they gradually learn to establish relationships with peers and develop social skills. Pro-social behaviour emerges, such as sharing, helping or comforting, which may be directed towards a parent, sibling or unrelated child. The development of such behaviour is influenced by parental reinforcement, the modelling of altruistic behaviour, and moral exhortation (Smith and Cowie, 1993). During early childhood, siblings will spend a lot of time together. These relationships can be very volatile because infants have not developed the capacity to regulate their emotions.

Possible impact of domestic abuse

Domestic abuse and other linked parental difficulties can affect the attachment process. Children are likely to have experienced inconsistent parenting, which may leave them bewildered and frightened. They may become uncertain as to whether their needs and wishes will be met with interest and pleasure or hostility and indifference.

Children can become fearful and unnaturally vigilant, believing that danger is an ever-present feature in their lives. Infants may display excessive irritability and an increased fear of abandonment. Their inability to verbalise the powerful emotions they feel may prompt temper tantrums and aggression, crying and resisting comfort, or despondency and anxiety (Holt *et al*, 2008):

> *They see what their mother have to go through. She cry, she scream. And with me...I had to block my face when my husband start with me and I had to scream and this affect my kids a lot. I mean, my son, he was very withdrawn. He don't interact with other kids and play with them.*
> (Mother of a toddler and three-year-old,
> quoted in DeVoe and Smith, 2002, p.1085)

Children exposed to domestic abuse are shown to have more problems in playing and interacting in a sociable way with siblings and other children. They are more likely to display anger, peer aggression and behave in challenging ways, than non-exposed children (Covell and Howe, 2009). They may learn to resolve conflict with peers and siblings through mirroring what they see at home. Abused mothers in Ellen DeVoe and Erica Smith's study (2002) expressed concerns that their children were mimicking their partner's abusive behaviour. They were frustrated with their children's aggressive behaviour, as one reported:

> *He (participant's son) beat too much on his sister, oh my god. He used to hit her, and he used to bite her – he was 14 months when this all started.*
> (Mother, quoted in DeVoe and Smith, 2002, p.1086)

Some mothers feared that their children would become violent in their adult relationships. One mother reported '…he told me once, "When I get bigger, I'm gonna hit you like my dad"' (DeVoe and Smith, 2002, p.1086).

When a perpetrator controls a mother's movements, it may severely restrict their child's social life by preventing engagement with wider family, peers and extra-curricular activities. One such mother reported:

> *I just didn't go out, so then the children didn't go out. It was just school and home. So they missed out on days out, family trips, socialising with people. And they've missed out on knowing what healthy relationships are about in other families because children don't make as many friendships if you can't mix with other mums.*
> (Mother, quoted in Katz, 2016, p.53)

Children may be further traumatised as a result of family separation. Young children can experience conflicting feelings of relief and a sense of greater safety, mixed with a sense of loss. Some will yearn for continuing contact with their abusive fathers, and the intensity of the grief will vary depending on the strength of the emotional attachment (Baker and Cunningham, 2009).

TO SUM UP

Key problems for the unborn child

- Pregnancy can trigger or increase assaults on an expectant mother, including punches and kicks directed at her abdomen. Foetuses that survive such assaults may be born prematurely, suffer brain injury, foetal distress and low birth weight.

- An expectant mother may be prevented from attending antenatal appointments. Irregular attendance is associated with pregnancy complications and adverse birth outcomes.

- Expectant mothers who are subject to domestic abuse may suffer poor mental health, and some will have self-medicated with drugs or alcohol. Alcohol and drugs can affect foetal growth and result in life-long problems including impulse control, behaviour and learning difficulties. Alcohol taken later in pregnancy may lead to neonatal addiction.

- The high levels of stress experienced by an expectant mother may negatively affect the development of an unborn baby's nervous system and brain.

Key problems for children aged under five years

- The arrival of a new baby and the time spent feeding can awaken feelings of intense jealousy in an abusive partner. To counteract this, mothers may prioritise their partners' needs over those of their babies. This can result in irregular feeding and little time for affectionate interaction; bonding and attachment may be affected negatively.

- High levels of fear and stress can affect the brain development of very young infants, resulting in emotional, social and cognitive impairment.

- Infants may react to having been exposed to extreme stress and trauma with a constant state of arousal and emotional numbing.

- A young child's cognitive and language development can be delayed when parents are preoccupied with their own emotions, including exhaustion, depression, low self-confidence and self-worth. Parents may not have the capacity to engage and stimulate their child, and may react negatively or with hostility to their child's needs.

- The fear and anxiety that results from living in a violent household can inhibit children's natural instincts to explore their environment. Nurseries and pre-school facilities can compensate for delayed cognitive and language development, but an abusive partner may prevent a child's attendance.

- The key to good bonding and attachment is a parent's capacity to adapt and respond appropriately to their baby's emotional and developmental needs. Exposure to domestic abuse can leave parents emotionally unavailable. Children may react by becoming unduly clingy and fearful, excessively irritable, difficult to soothe and settle when upset, and fearful of being left alone.

- Domestic abuse can affect parents' capacity to attend to their child's physical needs, leaving children neglected and with very poor basic hygiene. Other adults and children are likely to react negatively to a child who is smelly, wearing filthy clothes and with infested hair, resulting in the child feeling rejected and unlovable.

- Many children will believe that they are at fault for the violence and abuse in their family. Such negative beliefs about themselves will be reinforced when children's efforts to please are met with rejection.

- Children who have been exposed to domestic abuse may have difficulty in regulating their emotions, resulting in frequent temper tantrums and aggression, crying but resisting comfort, and over-dependency and anxiety.

- When parental behaviour has been unpredictable and frightening, children may display symptoms similar to or be suffering from post-traumatic stress disorder.

- Children exposed to domestic abuse may have problems in playing and interacting with other children. While some may be overly aggressive to peers, others will be fearful of any interaction.

Chapter 4
Impact of domestic abuse on middle childhood

Middle childhood is the term used to refer to children aged between five and 11 years. Carers looking after a child in this age group may face greater challenges because these children are likely to have experienced domestic abuse for longer, together with any co-existing parental difficulties with all their negative effects. For some, this will be their first placement, but others may have already lived with a number of different carers, either informally or formally.

The structure of this chapter is consistent with that for the younger age group. Each developmental dimension is prefaced by what might be expected generally for the age group, followed by the possible consequences of having been exposed to domestic violence and abuse.

HEALTH

Expected developmental progression

Regular medical and dental examinations should ensure that a child's height and weight are within normal limits, and any problems with hearing and sight, physical dexterity and mobility are identified and addressed. Although during this period of childhood co-ordination is improving, at the age of five or six years children frequently overestimate their ability and injure themselves during normal play.

By middle childhood, children should have a well-developed vocabulary and communicate easily with adults and other children, unless they have speech or hearing problems or learning difficulties. In the UK, 50,000 children have hearing loss, around half from birth and the other half lose their hearing during childhood (Action on Hearing Loss, 2020). Those with a permanent hearing loss or physical disability that impacts on verbal communication should be using some form of signing.

Children may suffer other health problems. Research by the British Lung Foundation (2020) reported that 11.6 per cent of children aged 6 to 10 years were diagnosed with asthma. Boys were consistently found to be at increased risk of asthma resulting from the 'differentiated growth of lung/airway size and immunological differences' (Almqvist et al, 2007).

Children in their middle years may also develop problems with food. Although the incidence of anorexia nervosa is very low, recent research showed it to be 3.2 per 100,000 children between the ages of 8 and 12 years (Petkova et al, 2019). Obesity is also increasingly of concern: information published by the Nuffield Trust (2021) showed that, in England, one in five children aged 10 to 11 years was obese in 2019/20, an increase of 3.6 per cent since 2006/7. The study also identified a strong association between deprivation and childhood obesity.

Children may also be subject to mental health disorders. The findings from work published by the NHS in 2018 (in line with earlier research by Green and colleagues, 2005) found that 10 per cent of 5- to 10-year-olds in the UK had at least one mental disorder. Most common were behavioural and emotional disorders. For this age group, the rates of emotional disorder were similar in boys and girls. However, other types of disorder were more than twice as likely to be experienced by boys as girls: 2.6 per cent of 5- to 10-year-old boys were identified with a hyperactivity disorder compared with 0.8 per cent of girls (NHS Digital, 2018).

Children younger than eleven years rarely smoke cigarettes, and although some children will experiment with smoking, regular smoking is negligible (NHS Digital, 2019).

Possible impact of domestic abuse

Growing up in a violent household puts children at increased risk of physical injury. Like toddlers, older children can get caught in the crossfire, or injured when intervening in an attempt to protect their parent from the abuse:

> *Me and my sister would jump on his back (to stop him hurting Mum), but he would just hit you off...Then you would go flying because he was so big.*
>
> (Child, quoted in NCH, 1994, p.33)

The well-established link between domestic abuse and all forms of child abuse, outlined in Chapter 2, also puts children at risk of physical assault:

> *He hit (my son) with a leather belt. He was a very fussy eater..."You bastard, eat that dinner", and he would pick up the belt and just lash him with it. And, of course, I would go for him then, and the next thing, I would get it.*
>
> (Mother, quoted in NCH, 1994, p.30)

> *I never cried, never cried, no matter how hard he hit me…I wouldn't let myself feel it.*
>
> (Child, quoted in NCH, 1994, p.30)

There is increasing evidence to demonstrate a link between domestic abuse and elevated levels of child sexual abuse. Research suggests that approximately one-half of children who have been sexually abused were living with domestic abuse (Humphreys and Stanley, 2006; Hester *et al*, 2007). In the majority of cases, their abusive father or mother's abusive partner perpetrated the sexual abuse:

> *One night I woke up, and he was sitting on my bed … I was about 10. I'd just started to grow breasts … and he was going, 'Let me feel '… I wouldn't let him. I was trying to turn over and go to sleep.*
>
> (Child, quoted in NCH, 1994, p.31)

Research has shown that children exposed to domestic abuse are 'prone to suffer from more health problems such as delays in growth, visual or auditory problems, allergies, cutaneous [skin] infections, headaches and eating disorders' (CLIPP, 2007, p.5). Judee Onyskiw's (2003) review of 47 studies identified that children who had witnessed domestic abuse were at increased risk of:

- allergies and respiratory tract infections;
- headaches and stomach-aches;
- nausea;
- diarrhoea; and
- sleep disturbances.

In some cases, the health problems that children experience will not be dealt with promptly or adequately. The controlling parent may prevent their child from being seen by a doctor, or the abused parent not having the capacity to take the child to the clinic, or to follow systematically instructions about prescribed medication.

The experience of domestic abuse may result in children developing symptoms of post-traumatic stress disorder. They may get nightmares, flashbacks, suffer from eating and sleep disturbances, become jumpy, and have headaches and physical pains.

EDUCATION AND COGNITIVE DEVELOPMENT

Expected developmental progression

The majority of children attend school regularly. The overall absence rate in state-funded primary schools for the autumn term 2018 was 3.9 per cent (DfE, 2019b). Children see school as a place to make and meet friends and generally find the experience enjoyable and interesting (Robinson and Fielding, 2007). Teachers are usually liked and the majority of children have at least one friend.

For some children, school is a less agreeable experience. A national survey for the year 2017–18 found that approximately one-fifth (22%) of 10-year-olds reported being bullied (DfE, 2018b). The groups that were most likely to have been affected included those with special educational needs and disabilities or long-term illness; those living in deprived areas or single-parent households; and those who had truanted within the last 12 months. Sex was also relevant. More girls reported being bullied than boys.

The early school years are a time when children feel the need to win approval through specific competences, such as learning to read, doing sums and other school-based activities. If they fail to develop the necessary skills, it can result in a loss of self-confidence. At times, children aged five and six years may aspire to do more than they can achieve and become frustrated. Children have an increasing ability to concentrate and are able to screen out distractions and focus on a single issue. At the age of six years, children would be expected to concentrate for 12–18 minutes, and by 10 years this should have increased to 20–30 minutes (Brain Balance, 2020).

Possible impact of domestic abuse

Growing up with domestic abuse does not automatically have a negative impact on children's learning and education. For some children, school provides a place of safety and trusted adults who are able to support and value them:

> *Well, if something's happened and it's in my mind and then it affects me, when I'm learning then I go to my teacher and say I need to have a time out and then after she would come to me when I'm ready and then we'd discuss it…It does help.*
>
> (10-year-old girl, quoted in Children's Commissioner, 2018, p.21)

School may offer an escape from abuse and degradation, a place where a child can gain a sense of accomplishment. Some children from violent homes will become high achievers, throwing themselves into school life and study as a way to escape the harsh reality of their home life (Lloyd, 2018).

Nonetheless, research involving 877 children in receipt of help from domestic abuse services found that over one-third (39%) had difficulties adjusting to school (SafeLives, 2014). They were also more likely than others to show delayed intellectual and cognitive development. Delayed learning can have a multitude of causes. Separation anxiety linked to worries about their abused parent may make attending school difficult, and some will pretend illness or be disruptive during the school day in an attempt to be sent home (Lloyd, 2018).

For other children, the trauma of living with domestic abuse may dominate their thoughts and result in problems in concentration and focusing. 'His work is suffering at school...his reading is suffering... he can't concentrate' (mother quoted in NCH, 1994, p.57). Michael Silverstein and colleagues (2006) found that children in this age group who had been exposed to higher levels of domestic abuse had lower abilities in reading, mathematics and general knowledge.

Schooling may also be affected because children who have witnessed or been the victims of controlling and coercive behaviour at home are 'more likely to associate bullying as a preferred or acceptable style of communication' (McGaha-Garnett, 2013, p.2). Dominating others through physical aggression may become an accepted method of problem-solving. A survey conducted by Jennifer Chastain (2012) showed that children exposed to domestic abuse exhibited an increase in aggressive behaviours. These included fighting with peers; talking back to teachers; not adhering to school rules; and a generally negative attitude to authority figures:

> *That's what you have to do to make the bitch pay attention – she doesn't listen to me.*
> (Seven-year-old Andy explaining to the Principal why he punched his teacher in the stomach, quoted in Mullender and Morley, 1994, p.223)

A review of school exclusion heard of 'cases where children at risk of exclusion were known to have home environments where domestic abuse, drug or alcohol misuse were present...' (DfE, 2019c, p.73). Children who subsequently enter the care system were found to be more likely to experience one or more fixed periods of exclusion than any other group of children:

> *Well I did miss school, I didn't miss it as in emotionally miss it, I mean I literally missed school, a lot of it.*
> (12-year-old boy, quoted in Children's Commissioner, 2018, p.13)

Education may be affected because parents fail to support their child to attend school regularly; children may be left to take care of themselves including getting to school on time.

Jackie had to do a lot of her own care, her schooling was affected as Jackie had to get herself up and ready for school which made her late a lot.
(Mother talking about her daughter Jackie, aged eight years, quoted in Cleaver *et al*, 2007, p.212)

Finally, children's education may be disrupted because of unplanned moves when, for example, mother and child need to flee from a violent situation, necessitating a change of school.

EMOTIONAL AND BEHAVIOURAL DEVELOPMENT

Expected developmental progression

Children in middle childhood are generally affectionate, silly and curious. They trust adults and are confident in seeking comfort from them when distressed. They tend to see themselves as lovable and effective, and want to behave well.

It is a period when children learn to modulate their behaviour and manage their emotions. At the age of five and six years, concepts of ownership are not yet fully established and it is not uncommon for children to take things that belong to others. They may come home from school having "found" a small toy or pencil. Emotions are not yet fully under control and, when young children are stressed or upset, it is not unusual for them to revert to more infantile behaviours. When frustrated, temper tantrums are not uncommon.

By the age of eight and nine years, children increasingly incorporate the values of their family and consequently come to regulate behaviour through internal as opposed to external controls. It is also a time when boundaries are tested which, for most children, confirms their knowledge of the rules and their ability to manage their own behaviour (Schofield, 2006). Children of this age, when angry or frustrated, can be verbally aggressive, although actual physical aggression is not common.

Possible impact of domestic abuse

Research by SafeLives (2014) found that over one-half (52%) of the children exposed to domestic abuse in their sample had developed behavioural problems. Children talk of their distress and typically demonstrate this through conduct disorders and emotional distress, uncontrolled behaviour and fear (Cleaver *et al*, 2011). Children's accounts provide evidence of the fear and anxiety that domestic abuse can generate:

I thought that he was going to hit me too...I ran into the other room and shut the door.

(Child quoted in Joseph *et al*, 2006, p.34)

There is a significant body of research that shows middle year children exposed to domestic abuse to be significantly more likely to exhibit symptoms of post-traumatic stress than non-exposed children (see, for example, Graham-Bermann and Levendosky, 1998; Mertin and Mohr, 2002; Luthra *et al* 2009). The symptoms children may display include:

- *Hyperarousal* – child is jumpy, nervous or easily startled.

- *Re-experiencing* – child continues to see or relive images, sensations or memories of the domestic abuse despite trying to put them out of mind.

- *Avoidance* – child avoids situations, people and reminders associated with the abuse.

- *Withdrawal* – child feels numb, frozen or shut down, may feel and act as if cut off from normal life and other people.

- *Reactions to reminders* – child reacts to reminders of the domestic abuse, such as sights, sounds, smells, words or emotions.

- *Sleep problems* – child has trouble falling asleep, staying asleep or has nightmares.

- *Repetitive talk or play* – child's play centres on the domestic abuse experienced.

(National Child Trauma Stress Network, 2010)

Not all children who have been exposed to domestic abuse will display emotional and behaviour problems. Research suggests that those who have also been physically abused show the highest levels of behavioural and emotional disturbance (Devaney, 2015).

Children will have learned to react to their parent's violent, frightening and unpredictable behaviour in different ways depending on their personality, age, sex, level of self-esteem, and the opportunities open to them. Although boys and girls are equally disturbed, they are likely to show their anguish differently. Boys are more likely to express their distress outwardly, for example, by becoming aggressive, anti-social, disobedient and attention-seeking. They may start to use violence to solve problems, copying behaviour they have seen at home:

His temper just seems to have got worse...you'll say something and he'll just blow – have a full paddywhack, and then you just have to leave him to calm down.

(Mother, reported in NCH, 1994, p.51)

In contrast, girls are more likely to respond by internalising their worries and display symptoms of depression, anxiety and withdrawal (Bentovim and Williams, 1998).

Children may cope with the stress of living in an abusive home by seeking to escape. They may do this by physically withdrawing:

> *If they, my parents, are fighting then I normally go with my brother and hide upstairs and we don't feel very safe in that environment where something is going on downstairs, we're not very aware of what's happening. You can hear my mum crying, my dad shouting and screaming and sometimes you can hear whacks of my mum being hit and when my dad eventually goes to work we come downstairs knowing it's quite safe, seeing my mum in tears and having bruises all over herself.*
> (10-year-old girl, quoted in Children's Commissioner, 2018, p.14)

At other times, children may use fantasy, make-believe and wishful thinking as a palliative coping mechanism:

> *Sometimes, when my parents were raging at each other in the kitchen, Lecia and I would talk about finding a shack on the beach to live in. We'd sit cross-legged under the blue cotton quilt with a flashlight, doing parodies of their fights. "Reel Six, Tape Fifty One. Let her roll," Lecia would say...as if what we were listening to was only one more take in a long movie we were shooting.*
> (Child quoted in Karr, 1995, p.38)

Children may also take solace in particular treasured toys or with the family pet:

> *But at least I had one person who cuddled me and that was my big dog that I used to love...I'd say something [to my dog] like thank goodness that we've got someone who is going to care for me and not fight all the time.*
> (10-year-old boy, quoted in McGee, 2000, p.106)

Sadly, such attachments may result in further distress when children have to protect their pet from the cruelty meted out by a violent parent:

> *That day that my dad said he would burn my dog on the grill, I took him into my room and locked him in the closet with food and water until the next day.*
> (11-year-old girl, quoted in McDonald et al, 2015, p.120)

IDENTITY

Expected developmental progression

Middle childhood is a period when children develop a more global sense of self and self-worth. For example, by six years, instead of using concrete and discrete ways of describing themselves, such as 'I have black hair', they will use more global terms: 'I'm a clever girl'. By the age of 10, children will compare themselves with others: 'I'm the fastest runner in my class' (Bee, 2000). Through such comparisons, children develop concepts of themselves as good, adequate or failing in one thing or another, a process that will underpin the child's evolving self-esteem.

Both internal and external factors influence the development of identity. Children's temperament will affect how they view themselves and their abilities. Some will willingly try things repeatedly and are able to handle frustration and challenge. Others may become easily discouraged. Those who cope better with frustrations are more likely to see themselves as successful, resulting in higher self-esteem. In contrast, those who are easily frustrated and give up on a task are more prone to developing a poor self-image and lower self-esteem.

External factors will also affect how children see themselves. Positive feedback from parents, carers and teachers about their abilities and attempts to succeed (even if they are not always successful) will enable children to develop a positive view of self.

In middle childhood, children participate in extended social networks of friends, which are hierarchical in nature. Some children are more popular, while others struggle to be included. When peers tease, bully or shun children, it will negatively affect their sense of who they are.

Children in middle childhood come to see themselves as autonomous and separate from their parents. In general, they will be at ease with themselves, accepting their gender identity, ethnicity, culture and physical attributes. Family will be valued and children will know important members. They will expect to be liked by both peers and adults (Smith and Cowie, 1993).

Possible impact of domestic abuse

Children's experience of their family will impact on their evaluation of their self-worth and self-esteem:

> *If parents are unavailable to provide positive reinforcement of who and what their children are, celebrate their skills and express confidence*

> *in their potential, or are inconsistent in their responses, it is easy for children to feel rejected, uncertain and undermined.*
>
> (Kroll and Taylor, 2003, p.210)

Low self-esteem can result in children having a desperate need to be liked and to "fit in" with their peer group. Children may worry about how they are perceived, and consequently be subject to intense peer pressure. As a result they may do almost anything, even self-destructive things, in order to become well-regarded and sought after by other children.

When parents are unable to fulfil a child's needs for acceptance, validation and protection, children create distorted beliefs about themselves; they come to believe that something is wrong with them, and feelings of shame are internalised. A focus on the individual, for example, 'I can't believe how stupid you are', rather than on the behaviour, 'You did a stupid thing', increases feelings of shame rather than guilt (Stuewig and McCloskey, 2005; Cairns and Cairns, 2016). When parents continually reject or humiliate a child, or are excessively critical, a child's feelings of shame become entrenched. Research has found that this can have long-term consequences as children reach adolescence:

> *Shame-proneness in early adolescence was associated with symptoms of depression in late adolescence even when controlling for childhood symptoms of depression.*
>
> (Stuewig and McCloskey, 2005, p.335)

The child's existing relationship to the abusing parent will also be pertinent to the impact of domestic abuse. Research by Cris Sullivan and colleagues (2000) suggests that the effects are more traumatising when the child's biological parent or step-parent perpetrates abuse, than if inflicted by a more recent partner. The authors suggest that there 'may be something especially painful in the experience of witnessing one's own father abuse one's own mother' (Sullivan *et al*, 2000, p.598).

Children will be particularly affected if they see their parents unable to control themselves or their circumstances, an experience that may leave them feeling helpless and confused:

> *It's so unpredictable, it's just that, because you don't know what's going to happen, when it's going to happen, why it's going to happen.*
>
> (10-year-old girl, quoted in Children's Commissioner, 2018, p.6)

The sense of helplessness and low self-esteem will be compounded if the perpetrator of the abuse also targets the child:

> *He ruled the house with an iron fist, and any perceived slight or misdemeanour – something as minor as a lightbulb blowing or running out of his favourite brown sugar – would make him explode. Even when he seemed happy we knew his mood could flip at any time.*
>
> (Reflections on an abusive childhood, reported in *Metro*, 2020)

There is evidence from the work of Safia Joseph and colleagues (2006) that some of the reactions and coping strategies children use when exposed to domestic abuse are gender-specific. Boys are more likely than girls to believe that they should have physically intervened to protect their mother, as is clearly illustrated by the following: 'I want to catch him alone…and I want to hit him hard…break all his teeth…' Girls, in contrast, are more likely to manifest their feelings through crying: 'I didn't like them fighting…it made me cry…' (A 12-year-old boy and an eight-year-old girl, quoted in Joseph *et al*, 2006, p.31).

Children whose parents are violent frequently believe that it was their fault; something that they did triggered the violence. Practically two-thirds (60%) of children in the study by SafeLives (2014) felt responsible or blamed themselves for the negative events. Many children in middle childhood continue to use wishful or magical thinking (as described in Chapter 3) in an attempt to control events. Whether through magical thinking or direct interventions, a failure to stop the abuse may leave children feeling inadequate and guilty.

Domestic abuse can cause children shame and embarrassment. Children want to belong to "ordinary families" where behaviour is predictable. When families do not fit this stereotype, they may learn to restrict interaction with outsiders, whether friends, relatives or other adults, fearing bullying and discrimination:

> *…some of my friends may understand, but what if they start to act differently towards me…I'll feel awkward…this I can't cope with now…*
> (Child aged between 8 and 12, quoted in Joseph *et al*, 2006, p.35)

FAMILY AND SOCIAL RELATIONSHIPS

Expected developmental progression

The quality of the parent–child relationship is influenced by the ambiance within the family and the temperament of individuals. In general, children in middle childhood enjoy physical closeness with their parents and feel able to confide in them. Some may have difficulty talking about their feelings.

Peer friendships are increasingly important. This is the period when children develop the ability to see things from another person's point of view. They learn to empathise and thus to understand the impact that their behaviour may have on others, a skill that enables them to sustain friendships and function within a group.

Possible impact of domestic abuse

For children in their middle years, inconsistent parental behaviour resulting from the impact of domestic abuse may cause high levels of anxiety and faulty attachments. Such behaviours can leave children uncertain as to whether their parents love them.

Perpetrators often demand high levels of attention from mothers, resenting the time mothers and children spend together. This may lead to children receiving limited attention and restricting opportunities for fun and affection. Children may be left feeling undervalued, sad, annoyed and angry:

> *Lots of times when Mum was giving me attention he'd tell her to go over to him so she'd have to leave me to play by myself.*
> (Shannon, aged 10, quoted in Katz, 2016, p.51)

The volatile behaviour associated with domestic abuse may lead to aspects of children's lives being subjected to frightening and pervasive control. For example, violent parents may destroy valued toys, be cruel to a much-loved pet or threaten to kill them. Children may live with constant fear and learn to be continually alert to the next possible altercation:

> *He could have stuck a knife in her for all I know, with the door shut. And the worst thing for me was actually not knowing what was going to happen next, not knowing what was happening then and not knowing what was going to happen next. That was the most frightening thing for me.*
> (Nine-year-old girl, quoted in McGee, 2000, p.107)

The relationship between parent and child may be undermined if expectations for parental care and protection are not consistently met, leaving the child with feelings of betrayal and anger. These emotions can be intensely felt when children are coerced into witnessing their mother's physical or sexual abuse. Such an experience is likely to debase the relationship between mother and child, and have a negative impact on the child's perception of their father or father figure.

Children may experience conflicting emotions of love and hate: attachment and love for the abuser as opposed to disapproval for the abusive behaviour; feelings of sorrow and love towards the abused parent as opposed to resentment for their helplessness and inability to protect. This is likely to leave children with confused and ambivalent feelings towards both parents (CLIPP, 2007):

> *My father is okay sometimes...not when he is hitting my mother.*
> (Child aged between 8 and 12, quoted in Joseph et al, 2006, p.36)

> *It's a tense environment as the police is coming and then even though my dad does all these things I'm still really, I feel quite sorry for him,*

> *that he has to go through all this even though it is his fault but I just feel so guilty afterwards.*
> (10-year-old girl, quoted in Children's Commissioner, 2018, pp.8–9)

Boys may fear that they will grow up to be like their violent father:

> *It just gets me so muddled up. I'm frightened I'll be like it when I grow up. I know what she's going through and I want to help her.*
> (Eight-year-old boy, quoted in Mullender *et al*, 2002, p.96)

In many instances, children will have to learn to grow up fast and assume some adult responsibilities, including attempting to protect and care for an abused parent or younger siblings. The consequence of this may be a missed childhood, neglected schoolwork, erratic school attendance, and restricted social activities. Peer friendships may also be curtailed because children are afraid their abused parent might need them:

> *I hate leaving her alone with him…I never know what he is going to do…*
> (Boy aged between 8 and 12, quoted in Joseph *et al*, 2006, p.34)

Friendships are of growing importance during this stage of childhood. For some, play with peers may provide an escape from the trauma of family life:

> *…I wouldn't say anything, but when we're playing I forget all of this [the abuse] for a while.*
> (Child aged between 8 and 12, quoted in Joseph *et al*, 2006, p.32)

Not all children will have an opportunity to develop peer friendships. The coercive and controlling parent may prevent the child seeing their friends outside the school day (Callaghan *et al*, 2015). Alternatively, children may be reluctant to bring friends home, not wishing to expose their family life. This may reduce their understanding of how to interact with friends, due to a less well-developed ability to interpret body language and other subtle cues.

Children of this age are acutely aware of social stigma and sense that domestic abuse should not be talked about, even when parents have not explicitly told them not to do so (Gorin, 2004). A fear of ridicule will keep many from discussing their family with friends or relatives. As a result, some will develop ways of coping on their own.

Some children will find the presence of a sibling provides them with valuable support. However, sibling relationships are often complex. For example, older children may experience caring for younger siblings as burdensome but may also position themselves as carers and protectors, a role that may provide them with a sense of control and value. However, this can be at the expense of their own needs (Callaghan *et al*, 2017). For others, sibling relationships may be far from harmonious.

Sibling relationships may be negatively affected when parents are seen to unfairly favour one child over another (Beckett, 2021). In some families, one child may be scapegoated and held responsible for outbursts of domestic abuse. Although research on sibling violence is limited, what is available suggests that witnessing violence directed at a sibling can have a long-term negative impact on children's mental health (Teicher and Vigtaliano, 2011).

When children develop support networks, such as friends, adult siblings, wider family, teachers, and much loved family pets, these may be lost when families flee their abuser. For many, leaving home will be a significant loss and a cause for resentment resulting in mixed feelings:

> *I wanted to move but I dinae. Because I widnae be able to see my pals any more. But I wanted to move to get away from the violence in the house.*
>
> (11-year-old girl, quoted in Stafford *et al*, 2007, p.33)

The impact on children of having to separate from an attachment figure and all that is familiar to them may be unavoidable. When children are taken into care, they may have to leave behind all that is familiar and, depending on where they are placed, continued contact with wider family, school and friends can become problematic.

SOCIAL PRESENTATION AND SELF-CARE SKILLS

Expected developmental progression

In general, children in this age group will have learned appropriate social skills and can adjust their behaviour to suit a wide variety of situations.

Their increasing social awareness and a wish to be accepted and liked by their peers drives children's concerns over their physical appearance and the clothes they wear. Research by Smolak (2011) found that 40–50 per cent of six- to 12-year-olds reported that they were unhappy with the way they looked. Good hygiene underpins an attractive appearance; peers and adults alike tend to shun an unwashed and smelly child.

As children develop through middle childhood, they will increasingly be able to see to some of their own basic needs. They will learn to wash and dress themselves and, by the age of 11 years, to cook simple meals. As children progress, they are capable of assisting with household chores, and when asked can help look after younger siblings or assist in the care of sick or disabled parents.

Possible impact of domestic abuse

When domestic abuse and other parenting issues consume all their parents' energies, children can feel abandoned. Others may have to grow up fast; shouldering the responsibility for protecting younger siblings, looking after them, feeding them and making sure they are clean and ready for school:

> *We was doing stuff of our own, and she [mum] wanted us to help her clean or either get our dinner eaten.*
> (Eight-year-old girl, quoted in Children's Commissioner, 2018, p.12)

> *We would get hungry and we wouldn't be clean.*
> (Eight-year-old girl, quoted in Children's Commissioner, 2018, p.11)

For other children, the need to grow up fast was driven by their assumed role of protector:

> *When we were locked in the house and Mum was upset I would hug her and tell her it was going to be okay.*
> (Roxie, aged 11, quoted in Cafcass Cymru, 2019, p.10)

TO SUM UP

Key problems for children aged 5 to 11 years

- Children may be physically harmed. They can sustain injuries when caught in the crossfire between warring parents, or when they themselves are targets of an attack. In other cases, a child's abusive father or mother's partner may sexually abuse them.

- General health may be affected negatively. The stress of being exposed to domestic abuse can result in children experiencing a range of psychosomatic health issues including headaches and eating disorders, allergies, nausea and diarrhoea. Children may also suffer from symptoms of post-traumatic stress.

- Health problems may be left untreated. An abusive and controlling parent may prevent the child from being taken for medical treatment.

- Children's intellectual and cognitive development may be delayed. Problems at home may dominate children's thoughts and affect their ability to concentrate.

- Children's education may be interrupted. A child's aggressive and violent behaviour can result in short-term exclusions from school. Education may also be interrupted through poor school attendance or unexpected changes of school as a result of unplanned moves.

- How children react to domestic abuse will depend on their individual characteristics and circumstances. Some children will appear "old beyond their years", having assumed more responsibility than would have been expected for a child of their age. The experience will leave others with symptoms of post-traumatic stress disorder.

- Identity, age and sex affect behavioural responses. Boys are more likely to react to the stress and fear with aggression and anti-social behaviour. In contrast, girls are more likely to internalise their worries, becoming anxious and withdrawn. Some children will attempt to withdraw from the abusive situation, either physically or emotionally through fantasy and magical thinking.

- Relentless parental rejection and humiliation will entrench feelings of shame and low self-esteem. Children often blame themselves for their parents' problems. This can be compounded when the child is of the same sex as the perpetrator of the abuse.

- Children may be left uncertain as to whether they are lovable. This is aggravated when parents fail to care for or protect their children, or coerce them into participating in the abuse of a parent. Many children will experience conflicting feelings about their parents.

- Children may experience difficulty relating to peers. When an abusive parent prohibits and/or controls opportunities to interact with other children, a child may fail to understand subtle behavioural cues and how to socialise with others.

- When a parent and child must flee the abuser, there will be a significant loss of much that is familiar. This will be further compounded when a child is taken into care, whether temporarily or permanently, and has to leave everything behind.

Chapter 5
Impact of domestic abuse on adolescence

This chapter considers the impact of domestic abuse on children between the ages of 12 and 18 years. It is a period of significant change; a time when children test the boundaries and experiment with new experiences. It is also a time of uncertainty, anxiety and stress, when many teenagers struggle to adapt to their changing identity and the expectations of those around them.

These may be children who have had a long period of living with domestic abuse or who have experienced numerous placement changes and have no consistent caring adult in their lives. Others may have lived in apparent contentment with their current carers for some time.

As in the two previous chapters, the expected development for the age group is covered, followed by an exploration of the possible consequences of having been exposed to domestic abuse.

HEALTH

Expected developmental progression

The physical changes that occur during puberty can cause confusion and distress. During early adolescence, girls' body fat increases, breasts enlarge, and they will experience their first menstrual cycle. For boys it is the time when their muscle mass increases and their voices become much lower. Both boys and girls will find that their body hair starts to grow and sweat glands become more active. The hormonal changes that occur may cause acne, often creating much distress for teenagers. During later adolescence boys start to grow facial hair.

Teenagers are mainly concerned about their appearance, skin and weight, and issues associated with a developing sexuality, sexual health and contraception (Gleeson *et al*, 2002). Young people may become distressed about their body shape and try to change it. Research by Francesca Solmi and colleagues (2020) shows that, over the past 40 years, the proportion of adolescents in the UK who are overweight or obese has almost tripled, and in 2015, 'approximately 40 per cent of UK adolescents aged 13 to 15 years have an overweight or obese BMI' (p.268). Child obesity is associated with deprivation, being almost twice the rate for children living in the most deprived areas in the UK as for those living in the least deprived (National Statistics, 2018).

Research has identified that 42 per cent of 14-year-old girls and boys said that they were currently trying to lose weight (Solmi *et al*, 2020). However, restrictive eating behaviours aimed at weight loss have been shown to be ineffective at reducing body weight in young people (Brown *et al*, 2019) and 'are longitudinally associated with adverse mental health outcomes, including depression and eating disorders' (Solmi *et al*, 2020, p.268). A common eating disorder is anorexia nervosa, which usually develops during the teenage years. A national surveillance study of young people aged 8 to 17 years in contact with child and adolescent mental health services found that 23.2 girls per 100,000 and 2.4 boys per 100,000 had been newly diagnosed with anorexia nervosa in the UK in an eight-month period in 2015 (Petkova *et al*, 2019).

Children with anorexia nervosa may seek to lose weight in a variety of ways, including avoiding food, self-induced vomiting, excessive exercising and laxative abuse. Other children may suffer from bulimia nervosa, characterised by recurrent episodes of binge-eating followed by vomiting, and other methods of weight control.

Other health needs for this age group are mainly due to chronic illness and mental health problems. A 2017 survey suggested that 14.4 per cent of 11- to 16-year-olds in England had a mental health disorder: boys and girls were equally likely to experience poor mental health, although girls were more likely to have an emotional disorder and boys to exhibit behavioural disorders (NHS Digital, 2018).

Late adolescence is when children become vulnerable to early signs of psychosis. Research suggests that 9.8 per cent of children and young people have experienced psychotic episodes (Healy *et al*, 2019). The psychotic symptoms a teenager may experience will vary dependent on their particular circumstances. The most common are hallucinations, delusions, and disorganised thinking and speech (Mind, 2020).

The teenage years are also the time when many children experience their first sexual encounter. They need accurate factual information about puberty, sex and contraception. The conception rate for teenagers has been falling steadily in recent years. In 2018, there were 16.8 conceptions per 1,000 girls aged 15 to 17 years, a decrease of 60 per cent compared with 2007 (Office for National Statistics, 2020c). The majority of teenage pregnancies are unplanned and around a half end in abortion. Teenage mothers suffer significant disadvantage compared with older mothers. They are more likely to end their education early, be a single parent, live in poverty, and experience mental health problems (Nuffield Trust, 2019).

Teenagers are also more likely to experiment in other ways. For example, a survey of secondary school pupils carried out in England in 2018 found that regular smoking (defined as smoking at least one cigarette a week) increased with age among school children. While very few 11- and 12-year-olds smoked, seven per cent of 15-year-olds smoked regularly. Similar proportions of boys and girls smoked. As with cigarette smoking, the use of e-cigarettes increased with age: only two per cent of 11-year-olds used e-cigarettes compared with 11 per cent of 15-year-olds (NHS Digital, 2019).

The survey also provided information on drug use and alcohol consumption. Mirroring the patterns for pupils' smoking behaviour, gender was not relevant and consumption increased with age. Five per cent of 11-year-olds had taken drugs during 2018 compared to 31 per cent of 15-year-olds. Similarly, drinking alcohol on a weekly basis increased with age from one per cent of 11-year-olds to 14 per cent of 15-year-olds (NHS Digital, 2019).

Physical injuries are not uncommon, as many teenage children participate in sports and physical activities.

Possible impact of domestic abuse

Childhood trauma can have a profound effect on the mental health of children as they reach late adolescence. A quantitative review and meta-analysis of available literature identified that a child exposed to child maltreatment and trauma before the age of 16 years had a three-fold increased risk of psychosis. The more severe the trauma had been, the greater the risk of psychosis (Varese *et al*, 2012).

When a child's experience of home life is one of constant fear and anxiety, it can result in poor mental health. Such emotions affect sleep and concentration and may increase the likelihood of alcohol and drug use. Some children reported that they had never felt safe while living at home:

> *Constantly on edge. Never free, never safe. It was like, there was no safe [place]...being at home wasn't safe at all, it was just that's the place where you are and you're constantly alert. You don't sleep properly, you just sit there and wait for something to happen.*
> (Mona, aged 17, quoted in McGee, 2000, p.72)

The lockdown resulting from efforts to control the spread of the Covid-19 virus compounded the situation, as the following call to Childline during the pandemic illustrates:

> *I'm really scared of my dad, especially when he's been drinking. Sometimes he gets really angry and throws things at my mum. It's been getting worse since the coronavirus and I worry a lot. I have no idea what to do as I can't escape because of the lockdown.*
>
> (15-year-old boy, quoted in NSPCC, 2020a)

For some, their fear of extreme abuse was justified, as they recalled having witnessed their father's brutal assaults on their mother:

> *I had me music on, but I heard her shouting and everything downstairs, so I headed down and he got the big thing, one of them car things, do you know, where you lift up the car for taking the wheel off – a car jack – and he hit that off her. Like, I did see things, you know, and it's not nice. It's horrible, like I was just scared, horrible...agh, it was mad.*
>
> (Jennifer, aged 16, quoted in Hogan and O'Reilly, 2007, p.36)

Others described their fear of their mother's violence, not only directed at their father, but also at themselves:

> *She'd hit him around the house and he would never hit her back. Well, like, she couldn't hurt him...she was too small and thin, she was anorexic, but there was a lot of mental stuff. All kinds of name-calling, like verbal name-calling – 'You're fat' or whatever, 'whoremaster' and this kind of thing...nasty stuff. And she'd hit us like. She gave my sister an awful time. She gave her a worse time than myself. I was kind of the pet of the house. She was happy, she said, when she had me. But when she had Susan, she got post-natal depression...and then she broke down after that.*
>
> (Alex, aged 17, quoted in Hogan and O'Reilly, 2007, pp.38-39)

There are a number of other ways that domestic abuse may affect a child's health and exacerbate their confusion and distress as they reach puberty. For example, teenagers may have to cope with their worries over their changing bodies, without support, and their fears and anxiety may go unaddressed. They may have to assume responsibility for their own dental care, and checks on hearing and sight.

Children who feel rejected and unwanted often seek comfort and a sense of belonging outside the home. This may result in early unbalanced relationships and sexual exploitation. A national survey carried out in the USA found that witnessing domestic abuse increased significantly the likelihood of adolescent girls aged 14 to 17 years engaging in "risky" sexual activity (Elliott *et al*, 2002). Any subsequent sexual health problems may be missed if parents, so absorbed in their own problems, fail to ensure that teenagers attend routine medical and dental appointments.

EDUCATION AND COGNITIVE ABILITY

Expected developmental progression

During the teenage years significant changes happen to the pre-frontal cortex of the brain, the area responsible for problem solving, assessing risk, decision-making, and social interaction. 'It's as though many different parts are being remodeled to work in the more complex ways necessary in adult life' (Browne, 2017). This remodeling, along with the hormonal changes, may help to explain why normally sensible, intelligent adolescents are more likely to choose high-risk activities, express stronger emotions, and make impulsive decisions (Arain *et al*, 2013).

Adolescence also heralds a major change in children's educational environment. The majority of state educated children in the UK transfer from primary to secondary school at 11+ years. Before the transition, nearly all children have some concerns about the impending move, although for the majority these are relatively short-lived. Changing schools often means the loss of long established friendships, and brings uncertainty and worries about discipline and homework. Research has shown that 'a successful transition involved functioning well in two areas: 1) being academically and behaviourally involved in school and 2) feeling a sense of belonging to school' (Rice *et al*, 2019, p.5).

The majority of teenagers attend school regularly and absence is unusual. Government statistics show that the overall absence rate across English state-funded secondary schools in Autumn 2018/19 was 5.5 per cent, and did not increase as a result of Covid-19 (Gov.UK, 2021a).

In contrast, persistent absence, defined as a child missing 10 per cent or more of their possible sessions, increased since the pandemic, rising from 12.7 per cent in the school year 2018/19 to 16.3 per cent in 2020/21 (Gov.UK, 2021a). Pupils with a statement of special educational needs or an education healthcare plan had a higher persistent absence rate. This also rose as a result of the pandemic from 27.6 per cent in Autumn 2018/19 to 29.6 per cent in 2020/21 – practically twice the rate for pupils with no special educational needs (Gov.UK, 2021a). Absence from school can be for a variety of reasons, with illness being the most common.

School attendance is encouraged when parents and carers support the child's learning and recognise the importance of education and schooling. Their commitment to their child's education is reflected in attending school events, such as parents' evenings and meetings (Desforges with Abouchaar, 2003).

Permanent and fixed period school exclusions of secondary school children are rare (0.1 and 10.13 per cent respectively), and most commonly the result of persistent disruptive behaviour (Gov.UK, 2020). Exclusion rates generally increase with age and peak at the age of 14. Boys are three times more likely to be excluded than girls.

Children generally start course work for their GCSE exams (or equivalents) in Year 10, when aged 14 to 15 years. It is a time when homework becomes increasingly important and they need encouragement and a quiet and suitable place to study. Parents of children with special educational needs should ensure that relevant resources are available so that they are able to fulfill their potential.

Bullying is not uncommon during adolescence. The Department for Education provides a clear definition of what constitutes bullying:

> *Bullying is behaviour by an individual or group, repeated over time, that intentionally hurts another individual or group either physically or emotionally. Bullying can take many forms (for instance, cyber-bullying via text messages, social media or gaming, which can include the use of images and video) and is often motivated by prejudice against particular groups, for example on grounds of race, religion, gender, sexual orientation, special educational needs or disabilities, or because a child is adopted, in care or has caring responsibilities. It might be motivated by actual differences between children, or perceived differences.*
> (DfE, 2017a, p.8)

Data from the annual crime survey 'estimated that in the year from April 2017 to March 2018, 17 per cent of young people aged 10 to 15 in England were bullied in the previous 12 months in a way that made them frightened or upset' (DfE, 2018b, p.3). Younger children (10- to 12-year-olds), those with a long-term illness or disability, children who have been suspended or excluded, and those living in the most deprived areas are amongst the groups most likely to report having been bullied.

The experience of racism may also affect a child's education and learning. Research by the YMCA found that 95 per cent of black students in the UK heard or witnessed the use of racist language in school. Half the pupils in the study felt teachers held negative perceptions of black children, seeing them as "less capable", "unintelligent" and "aggressive" (YMCA, 2020, p.12). Pupils believed this resulted in more young black pupils being excluded, a finding that is mirrored in national data (Gov.UK, 2020). When racial bullying in schools is not dealt with satisfactorily, it may affect attendance and academic performance, and result in children moving schools or being permanently excluded.

Bullying is also a problem for lesbian, gay, bisexual and transgender (LGBT) pupils. A study by Josh Bradlow and colleagues (2017) found that nearly half (45%) of LGBT pupils reported being bullied at school because of their sexuality and/or gender identity. In most cases when such bullying occurred, school staff and other pupils did not intervene. School attendance was affected; 70 per cent of LGBT pupils reported having skipped school. A more recent study by Tessa Kaufman and Laura Baams carried out in the Netherlands, reinforces these data. Important new findings suggest that 'compared with heterosexual, cisgender adolescents, SGM [sexual and gender minority] adolescents were more likely to be bullied and harassed by teachers, other school staff, and peers' family members' (Kaufman and Baams, 2021, p.6). Victimisation often occurred in secluded locations and SGM adolescents were less likely to report being bullied than their peers.

Possible impact of domestic abuse

The experience of domestic abuse may have a serious impact on adolescents' education and learning. This could be the result of a lack of parental support, an inability to concentrate, and performing below their expected ability. Teenagers may miss school because of fears for their parents' safety, homelessness, or constant moves.

The effects of domestic abuse, alongside other issues such as parental depression or substance misuse, may leave birth parents unable to support or encourage their child's learning at home. Neglect, a factor often associated with domestic abuse and parental mental health problems (Cleaver *et al*, 2011), is related to adolescents having poorer educational engagement, conduct and achievements at school (Stein *et al*, 2009).

A small-scale study, set in Northern Ireland, showed that secondary school teachers, education welfare officers and social workers agreed that exposure to domestic abuse affected children's self-esteem, peer relationships, academic work and behaviour (Byrne and Taylor, 2007). Of particular interest is the reported dichotomy in children's reactions. School attendance either dropped off or was excellent:

> *Children I come into contact with fall into two categories, one is withdrawn, quiet, don't cause conflict with anyone, very few friendships and would be very protective of parents. Often their school attendance is not good, as they don't want to leave their parent. The other type is completely the opposite. They display violent tendencies, are loud in class and it is obvious they are not getting time at home to do their homework.*
>
> (Teacher, quoted in Byrne and Taylor, 2007, pp.6-7)

Children's accounts reveal how they acted out and got into trouble at school, sometimes bullying other children, although they may not have connected this with what was going on at home (Children's Commissioner, 2018):

> *I actually did yeah [bully another child], in Year six, I got in trouble for that, but I think that was mainly, I don't know, that had nothing to do with home...In secondary school and primary school I'd get into trouble. I*

> *think even if I didn't have a problem there's always, be, it would still be the same, it was just messing about in class and stuff and nothing crazy.*
>   (16-year-old boy, quoted in Children's Commissioner, 2018, p.10)

Others were able to make the connection between their traumatic home life and how it affected their education:

> *Teachers want me out of the lesson because they think that I'm just going to be naughty all the time. Teachers need to probably put more effort in for kids like ones who have problems with family, because if, say, a child's having problems at home, like Mum and Dad have had an argument, then you're going to be a little bit down and the teachers, they're not really bothered, they're just going to treat you the same and be like, well, end of the day, you're in my lesson and you still need to keep your behaviour the same, but like I say, I were in a bit of a stroppy mood and sir shouts at me, I'll probably shout back and then I'll get done, and then that'll affect my home and stuff like that as well.*
>   (13-year-old boy, quoted in Children's Commissioner, 2018, p.13)

For some children, school provided a safe place and a period of relief from the difficulties and stresses of home. School was the one area of their lives that was "normal", and academic or sports achievements and school friendships were seen as a form of escape:

> *I think that's the main reason I wasn't as sad as I could have been, I was being at school, seeing friends, it would be at the back of my head but I forget about it for a bit. It's six-and-a-half hours a day when I'm not at home, with friends and stuff.*
>   (16-year-old boy, quoted in Children's Commissioner, 2018, p.13)

> *[I cope] by distracting myself, so like through sport, through activities revolved around school.*
>   (14-year-old girl, quoted in Children's Commissioner, 2018, p.16)

School attendance may have suffered if children had felt impelled to stay at home or miss classes because they feared for the safety of a parent:

> *Because I was scared in case, like, he battered her and she went away and then I went home and she wasnae there and it was just me left and him. Ye ken what I mean? So I was scared.*
>   (Girl, quoted in Stafford et al, 2007, p.13)

Finally, school attendance and learning may be affected because domestic abuse can result in temporary homelessness or overcrowded accommodation, frequent re-housing, or having to live long distances away from school.

Secondary school teachers in Ali Digby and Emily Fu's (2017) study spoke of the effects of homelessness on the children with whom they worked, including a lack of space at home to study, limited access to a computer for homework, increased anxiety and stress, and living in noisy, overcrowded accommodation. Frequent unplanned moves will, in some cases, have necessitated a change of school, with the inevitable interruptions to learning and course work, and the loss of friends and wider family, teachers and community support.

The consequences of domestic abuse on teenagers' schooling, academic achievements and peer relationships can be cumulative. Multiple changes of school and limited time for interaction with peers may have resulted in self-doubt, loneliness and feelings of isolation. It will have left some with little confidence in their abilities, distrust and dislike of school and teachers, and a reluctance to commit to any school-related activities.

EMOTIONAL AND BEHAVIOURAL DEVELOPMENT

Expected developmental progression

Early adolescence is the period when children start to become independent, a time when they wish to spend more time with friends and rather less with their family. On occasion, teenagers may appear rude or short-tempered with their parents, while at others, they seek closeness and love. But on the whole, adults are seen as trustworthy.

Emotions are frequently volatile, unstable and poorly controlled. 'They can fly into a rage at short notice and burst out laughing with little provocation' (Fahlberg, 1994, p.102). As children get older, they gain greater control over their emotions and may appear undemonstrative. Physical responses to anger are less common and they are likely to resort to swearing and sarcasm. Older teenagers will become increasingly self-assured and seek to gain control over more areas of their lives.

Adolescence is thought to be a period of heightened stress and, as already noted, increased levels of mental health problems. Adolescent worries and fears tend to centre on their appearance, friendships, exams and social issues. They worry about their weight and body shape, and any minor blemishes may be interpreted as a crisis. Although anxiety and worry increase during the teenage years, most cope well with the support of caring friends and parents.

For a small proportion of teenagers, their emotions are overwhelming and they may turn to maladaptive coping mechanisms. For example, one such mechanism is self-harm, affecting 10 per cent of adolescents, and encompasses cutting, burning or non-lethal overdoses (Doyle *et al*, 2015):

> *It is a way of dealing with distress and feelings that are difficult to cope with and which the young person cannot express in any other way. The self-harm is often a way of releasing feelings of self-hatred, anger, sadness and depression.*
>
> (Mental Health Foundation, 2006, p.18)

Such behaviour provides only temporary relief because it does not address the underlying issues. Judi Kidger and colleagues' (2012) cohort study in England of 4,810 young people aged 16 and 17 years found that almost one in five (18.8%) reported that they had self-harmed, with girls being more likely to self-harm than boys (25.6% compared to 9.1%).

A rather different maladaptive behaviour is the externalising of anger and distress, conduct that may result in criminal behaviours. The rate of children being arrested in England and Wales has fallen steadily over the past 10 years. National statistics indicate that, from April 2019 to March 2020, there were 58,939 arrests of children aged between 10 and 17 years (Youth Justice Board/ Ministry of Justice, 2021). 'Black children were over four times more likely than White children to be arrested' (Youth Justice Board/Ministry of Justice, 2020, p.6). Such a disparity raises serious questions about possible prejudicial police and judicial systems and the greater disadvantages this group of children experience.

Teenage boys are the most likely group to be involved in crime, accounting for 83 per cent of first-time offenders. Few children are engaged in crime during early adolescence: most (71%) first time offenders are aged between 15 and 17 years (Youth Justice Board/ Ministry of Justice, 2021).

Possible impact of domestic abuse

The emotional instability of the teenage years means that abuse and any co-existing parental problems will have a profound impact on development. Teenagers may feel helpless, that life is chaotic and impermanent, and their emotions overwhelming:

> *It was the worst part of my life – constantly being shouted at, frightened, living in fear. You will never know what it is like, thinking that every day could be your last day.*
>
> (16-year-old girl, quoted in Mullender *et al*, 2002, p.94)

A survey in Scotland of 254 secondary school pupils who had experienced domestic abuse found that 21 per cent reported feelings of fear, 15 per cent sadness, 10 per cent felt lonely and isolated, and nine per cent reported suicidal thoughts (Alexander *et al*, 2005).

Living with constant fear of abuse and manipulation, and feelings of helplessness and inadequacy, may result in some teenagers considering suicide as a possible way out:

I would feel like killing myself because I would think it was my fault, 'cos he drilled it in my head.
(17-year-old girl, quoted by Mullender, 2006, p.59)

Other teenagers may escape or dissociate themselves from emotional pain, anxiety and anger through the use of alcohol or illicit drugs. A USA study by Merle Hamburger and colleagues (2008) found that witnessing domestic abuse was associated with early alcohol use.

Teenagers may also try to cope with their anxiety and sadness through self-harming or by severely restricting their food intake:

When I was 13 I was like really stressed, and having a lot of anxiety. I was self-harming myself, and I was trying to commit suicide and stuff...and then again, either last year or year before, I was causing myself to throw up so I was diagnosed with bulimia – and that was due to stress and not feeling confident in myself – and not feeling happy with anything that was going on – Yeah I think that was the two major things I have ever done to myself to try and cope.
(16-year-old girl, quoted in Children's Commissioner, 2018, p.9)

In contrast to those who internalise their anxiety and fears, others (particularly boys) may externalise these emotions through aggressive and violent behaviours towards their peers or younger children (McCloskey and Lichter, 2003).

Research by CAADA in 2014 identified that two-thirds of children exposed to domestic abuse were also abused and/or neglected. Finally, there is growing evidence suggesting that cumulative forms of childhood maltreatment are associated with borderline personality disorder symptoms in adolescents (Marchetti *et al*, 2021).

IDENTITY

Expected developmental progression

Put simply, our identity is "who we are". As children reach adolescence, how they define themselves broadens out from simply how they look and what they can do.

In general, young teenagers continue to identify strongly with the beliefs and values of their family, although those of their peers, teachers and other salient adults become increasingly important. Middle and older adolescents may come to oppose family rules, values and expectations, as they struggle to separate psychologically from their parents and create their own identity. This can lead to teenagers being rebellious and moody, although they still have a strong need to belong to the family and to be taken seriously (Fahlberg, 1994).

Adolescents' perceptions of themselves are influenced by their subjective age and their psychosocial maturation. There is considerable evidence to suggest that adolescents who assume greater household and financial responsibilities develop a more adult sense of identity than their seemingly more advantaged peers (Johnson and Mollborn, 2009; Benson and Elder, 2011). The reasons for assuming such responsibilities may be due to a number of issues, including living in an economically deprived family, having to look after a parent, or exposure to parental substance misuse or domestic abuse.

How teenagers choose to self-identify is also influenced by their ethnicity and culture (Umana-Taylor et al, 2014). By adolescence, children have the capacity to merge their personal sense of who they are with their reference group. Those whose parents have migrated from a country with different cultural values face the challenge of reconciling the expectations of their parents' cultural beliefs with their own wish to fit in with the resident teenage culture (Bailey, 2006).

Adolescents' perceptions of self will be affected by experiences of racism that they may have encountered in school and community settings, as well as on media platforms. In Sarah Page's (2020) study of 57 school and college pupils aged 14 to 17 years in the Midlands, the pupils reported verbal abuse, physical assaults, Islamophobic abuse, and attacks with weapons. One minority ethnic pupil reported that when 'playing football…[at school] people will kick me instead of kicking the ball' (Page, 2020, p.70). Teachers were seen as favouring white pupils when racially motivated incidents occurred. It is important to understand that racial hate is not exclusively between white and minority ethnic pupils, but also occurs between minority ethnic pupils of different origins. Pupils saw teachers' and schools' reactions to reported incidents as inadequate.

An adolescent's feelings of who they are will vary dependent on whether they consider themselves to be primarily masculine, primarily feminine, or a combination of both. Although often used interchangeably, the terms "sex" and "gender" refer to different things: sex is a constant and refers to biologically defined characteristics, whereas gender is different, as the World Health Organization (2021) explains:

> *Gender refers to the characteristics of women, men, girls and boys that are socially constructed. This includes norms, behaviours and roles associated with being a woman, man, girl or boy, as well as relationships with each other. As a social construct, gender varies from society to society and can change over time.*

Young people may experiment with a range of different identities, including their sexuality and gender. Over the last decade, there has been an increase in young people seeking help with gender dysphoria (a feeling that their gender identity is different from their biological sex). Many with gender dysphoria have a strong and lasting wish to live a life that "matches" or expresses their gender identity. They may change their appearance and behaviour, and some may want to use hormones and sometimes surgery to express their gender identity (NHS, 2020).

Regardless of the many challenges that teenagers and young people face in developing their individual sense of who they are, and these may include a rejection of family values and culture, long-lasting rifts with families are unusual (Rutter *et al*, 1976).

Possible impact of domestic abuse

The family shapes the child's sense of identity. Those who are rejected and undervalued will come to adopt these perceptions of self and develop low self-esteem.

Parents and close relatives act as role models for teenagers, and their values and beliefs are absorbed but also questioned. Teenage boys who are exposed to domestic abuse can react in different ways. Some may learn from their fathers to be violent to women and adopt a very macho identity. Many strongly reject such patterns of behaviour and develop an identity that does not include abuse, manipulation or bullying. The reactions of teenage girls to their gender identity will also be influenced by their parents' relationship. Some girls may mirror the female role demonstrated by their mother, for example, assuming a role of compliance and submission, while others may refuse such an identity and assume one of self-assertion.

Minority ethnic teenagers may experience additional difficulties in cultures where women are traditionally obliged to surrender to their husbands. For example, in most Nigerian communities, 'the domestic abuse of a female partner is widely acceptable and justified; it is therefore unquestioned and naturalised' (Nwabunike and Tenkorang, 2015, p.2).

Teenagers may blame themselves for the abuse that occurred within their family and develop a deep sense of guilt and a misplaced responsibility for not having been able to stop it:

> *Sometimes, like, I feel like it's my fault, like why did I never stop it. Like why did I never go down and…It's horrible like. It's just, what if I went down…he would have stopped and, do you know, things like I remember the feeling and I still remember like I couldn't go down downstairs. Like what if he did it to me or something. It was horrible…*
> (Jennifer, aged 16, quoted in Hogan and O'Reilly, 2007, p.36)

The experience of domestic abuse can change an adolescent's sense of who they are:

> *Yeah, I feel different and I've changed a lot. Like I used to be really soft and everything, like to other people and that, people used to boss me around and that. But now everything's happened, I've got a lot more rougher with everyone else, outside or in school and that if someone starts on me I just lash out on them.*
>
> (Tracy, aged 15, quoted in McGee, 2000, p.75)

For others, the need to support and look after their abused parent and younger siblings will advance their psychosocial development; they will have to grow up quickly and assume adult responsibilities:

> *Because of everything that was happening I kinda had to grow up quite quickly, so most of the stuff people did at my age I didn't really do as much so like having the time to go out with friends and stuff like that wasn't really an option – because I was helping out with chores and I was helping my siblings – and because I didn't want to leave my siblings alone because I didn't know what would happen so I kind of stayed at home most of the time. I don't really relax – I was always like tense – and hobbies – they have kind of faded away – anything that I liked kinda just left.*
>
> (16-year-old girl, quoted in Children's Commissioner, 2018, p.12)

FAMILY AND SOCIAL RELATIONSHIPS

Expected developmental progression

Adolescence is a critical period for the development of autonomy. It is a time when children begin to reflect on what they want from life, independent of what their parents want for them. Independence takes time to accomplish and the self-assured young teenager may quickly dissolve into tears and become stubborn and unco-operative when things do not go according to plan. Despite the commonly-held notion that adolescence is a period of *storm and stress* (a decreased level of self-control and an increased level of sensitivity), the various transformations and disruptions in family dynamics during adolescence are generally short-lived, and overall, both parents and teenagers view their relationship positively.

Friends in later adolescence become increasingly important and influential in the lives of young people, although not necessarily at the expense of their relationship with parents. These friendships differ in quality from those of middle childhood and early adolescence; they are more intimate and involve more mutual exchanges of thoughts, feelings and shared activities.

Although in early adolescence single-sex peer groups are still prominent, there is a shift as children grow older to male–female relationships. It is the age when many young people fall in love and embark on their first sexual encounter. Kaye Wellings and colleagues' (2001) survey of 11,161 young people in Britain found that nearly one-third of men (30%) and one-quarter of women (26%) first had sexual intercourse before the age of 16 years.

As we have observed, LGBT teenagers experience high levels of prejudice and bullying from their peers. A UK survey found that half of LGBT pupils (52%) heard homophobic language "frequently" or "often" at school. Practically half (45%) of transgender pupils have attempted suicide, and one in five (22%) lesbian, gay and bisexual students have done the same (Stonewall, 2017).

The first love affair for most adolescents is an important experience and its break-up causes considerable stress. Although teenagers may turn to their peers for support, few will seek help from their parents, and many cope with the stress alone.

Possible impact of domestic abuse

Domestic abuse can affect every aspect of family and social relationships. Perhaps most distressing is that, although teenagers recognise particular incidents of domestic abuse, such behaviour may have become normalised:

> *I mean I couldn't understand it – like I kinda thought maybe this is something that some other people go through as well – like this is just a normal thing – like people drink, stuff like this happens so I kinda took it upon myself that stuff happens that I can't do anything about I'm only 11/12 – however old I was – there's nothing I can really do.*
> (16-year-old girl, quoted in Children's Commissioner, 2018, p.5)

Children who have witnessed domestic abuse and violence may have learned that these are acceptable modes of behaviour. A recent study by Silke Meyer and colleagues (2021), on the intergenerational transmission of family violence, found that some mothers reported that their teenage sons had started to use violence against younger siblings or themselves:

> *I could see my son starting to be violent towards my daughter, like just going to hit her. He would not know any better. He'd go to hit her when she would not move for him…Like my son is 14 and he's pretty much getting out of control. I would say it comes back to that because of what he's grown up [with] and seen. He has no respect for me. He talks to me like I'm a dog all the time.*
> (Mother, quoted in Meyer *et al*, 2021, p.6)

Most teenagers express strong disapproval of the behaviour of their abusive parent. But anger may be directed at both parents – the abuser for perpetrating the abuse, and the abused for accepting the behaviour. However, in most cases, children continue to love their parents and are thus left with ambivalent and conflicting emotions:

> *That was tough, I'm not going to lie, that was quite hard for me, because it's weird, he was a good person, I guess, but he just had the problem and I was quite sad to go even though I definitely should have. So I found it quite tough to say goodbye because I knew I wasn't going to see him, I just felt sorry for him coming home alone, I don't know.*
> (16-year-old boy, quoted in Children's Commissioner, 2018, p.7)

McGee's (2000) research found that many children had felt unable to talk to anyone about their circumstances due to a variety of reasons. These included there being no one they trusted; they found it too embarrassing, upsetting or shameful; or they feared that speaking out would have negative consequences, thereby further damaging relationships at home. The fear that exposing their family situation would result in further problems meant that some teenagers became very wary of forming close friendships:

> *It was very rare for friends to come over, it would be mostly me going to friends' houses. Just messy, stink, dad being home for a start, that's not something you want to show my friends.*
> (16-year-old boy, quoted in Children's Commissioner, 2018, p.11)

Forming friendships may also be difficult because the experience of domestic abuse, and the secrecy and stigma that surround it, can affect young people's self-confidence and self-esteem:

> *Loss of self-confidence and self-esteem was also described by the older teenagers and young people, and an overwhelming feeling of 'being different', having 'a neon sign that told everyone what was going on', sticking out 'like a freak' were some of the feelings expressed by the older teenage group.*
> (Buckley et al, 2007, p.302)

For others, particularly teenage girls, peer friendships provided support and someone with whom they could discuss their thoughts and emotions:

> *I talk to one of my closest friends about it. But I'll be careful like who I tell things to, and then, yeah. She's been one of my closest friends ever since the beginning of secondary.*
> (14-year-old girl, quoted in Children's Commissioner, 2018, p.20)

Research in the USA involving 111 adolescents aged 14 to 16 years who had experienced domestic abuse showed that friends were a significant protective factor. Peer friendships were found to counter the negative impact of domestic abuse on young people's mental health (Levendosky *et al*, 2002b).

Teenagers may also seek to cope with the stress of domestic abuse by distancing themselves from their parents and home. They may withdraw by listening to music, playing video games, reading, or participating in virtual worlds online. Others may physically withdraw by staying in their room or spending increasing amounts of time away from home:

> *It was just bad, I just used to go out on purpose just to get away from home. Just to go round friends on purpose and me and my boyfriend would go out for walks and listen to my music really loud so I wouldn't listen to the arguing all the time and the fighting. And then just, that was it really, a really bad atmosphere…used to stay round their houses a lot and their mums, their parents used to be quite comforting and I used to talk to their parents all the time.*
> (Jackie, aged 19, quoted in McGee, 2000, p.104)

Dramatic and dangerous responses

Teenagers who blame themselves for the abuse between their parents may place themselves in danger by running away. They may believe that by removing themselves they remove the cause of the abuse. In other families, a teenager may be scapegoated for the abuse within the home, resulting in the child being "thrown out".

Research for The Children's Society found that the majority of teenagers (approximately 70%) who ran away from home believed that their parents or carers did not care about them (Rees and Lee, 2005). The pattern of going missing from home often starts early: 30 per cent of runaways reported staying away overnight before the age of 13 years. Although the majority spend time "sofa surfing" between friends and relatives, a small proportion (18%) of young people aged 14 to 16 years reported sleeping rough (Rees, 2011). Work by Marianne Hester and Lorraine Radford (1996) found that 26 per cent of homeless 16- to 25-year-olds left home due to domestic abuse. Youth homelessness is associated with an increased risk of mental health problems, as well as negatively affecting participation in education, employment or training (Quilgars *et al*, 2008).

Teenagers who feel rejected by their family and those who wander the streets are vulnerable to exploitation. Older young people and adults may seemingly offer support and friendship but, in reality, may groom them for prostitution or drug dealing. Gangs target vulnerable children and among the factors that heighten a person's vulnerability are childhood abuse and neglect, and the lack of a safe and stable home environment due to domestic abuse, parental substance misuse, mental health issues, or criminality (Home Office, 2020).

Research has shown that exposure to domestic abuse is strongly correlated with children displaying harmful sexual behaviour (Barnardo's, 2016). Emma James defines this as 'sexual behaviours expressed by children and young people under the age of 18 that are developmentally inappropriate, may be harmful to themselves or others and/or may be abusive towards another child, young person or adult' (James, 2020, p.16).

Some adolescents fear that being raised in an abusive environment will impact on their own future relationships. Young men worry about what sort of partner they may become and whether they will develop abusive behaviour patterns (NSPCC, 2018). A concern, supported by research, has shown that exposure to domestic abuse is associated with dating violence (Howell *et al*, 2016). Claire Fox and colleagues studied 1,203 13- to 14-year-old children in 13 schools in Staffordshire. They found a significant overlap of experiencing 'victimisation and witnessing abuse between adult carers/parents: 67 per cent of those 13- to 14-year-olds who had witnessed abuse at home had also experienced it in their own dating relationships, compared to 32 per cent who had not witnessed it' (Fox *et al*, 2013, p.6).

This overlap is illustrated in a report by a young person who contacted Childline:

> *I have seen my parents physically hurting each other for years. I used to cry every day and self-harm. I feel like I'm really affected by what I've seen. I have a boyfriend now and I feel like he's acting just like my dad. I feel like I can never be in a stable relationship.*
>
> (18-year-old teenager, quoted in NSPCC, 2018, p.16)

Developing a trusting relationship with a caring person, which is characterised by mutual trust and respect, can help young people to find less damaging ways to cope with family stress. For others, religious belief may offer solace and help them to develop resilience to family trauma:

> *My religion kept me going. We believe that your time on Earth is full of tests. If you survive, your patience and strength will end your suffering. These are my tests. I had to stand by my mum because she was not in the wrong. That pulled me through and made us stronger and better. We have been through a lot; we can feel for others and are better human beings.*
>
> (14-year-old boy, quoted in Mullender *et al*, 2002, p.150)

A key message from young people who have experienced domestic abuse is that talking about what is happening at home can really help:

> *I think as a teenager, yes it's hard to speak about your emotions. But I think that if you know that you need help yourself and if you know that you're struggling at home or at school or something, speak to someone*

that you know you can trust, even if that's your best friend or cousin, mum, dad, auntie, uncle, the best way, the best way in getting help is to speak out about it.

(15-year-old girl, quoted in Children's Commissioner, 2018, p.18)

SOCIAL PRESENTATION AND SELF-CARE SKILLS

Expected developmental progression

Physical appearance becomes increasingly important as children go through their adolescent years. As the onset of puberty brings changes to their appearance, teenagers become very conscious of how they look. They want to be in control of their own clothes, hair and skin care. Many older teenagers spend a considerable proportion of their disposable income on clothing and toiletries.

Early adolescents are capable of carrying out simple household tasks and they are increasingly able to prepare a meal and take care of their own basic needs. By the age of 16 years, most can cook, shop, wash-up, look after their own clothes, and generally take care of themselves. They will be able to use public transport and organise their own travel arrangements.

By early adolescence, children should feel confident in staying away from home for short periods and to cope with the routines and cultures of other households. Older young people should be able to function independently at an appropriate level to their cognitive and physical abilities. However well adolescents appear to cope and generally spurn parental advice, young people need an adult to whom they can turn for help when necessary.

Possible impact of domestic abuse

As already mentioned, domestic abuse is frequently associated with parental drug misuse, poor mental health and inadequate income. Teenagers, although increasingly capable of looking after themselves, are not immune from neglectful parenting.

One of the main problems in relation to social presentation is the lack of funds for adequate or appropriate clothing and toiletries. The report of one young man clearly illustrates how this impacted on him:

They spend all the money on drink. There's no soap in the house and all my clothes are too small. I lost my girlfriend because she said I smell. Others call me names and make fun of me.

(Paul, aged 14, quoted in Childline, 1997, p.37)

Young people are frequently under considerable pressure to "fit in" with their peer group, to wear the "right" clothes, shoes, jewellery, or to own the latest mobile or other electronic device. When families live in poverty and domestic abuse has resulted in a lack of parental guidance, teenagers may seek to avoid peer ridicule by resorting to stealing the items they perceive to be essential.

A further problem is that teenagers from violent homes may not have the opportunity to learn how to interact in an acceptable manner with adults outside the family. Violent and aggressive language and behaviour in day-to-day encounters may become normalised: aggression may be seen as an acceptable way of solving problems. However, an inability to control aggression may not only jeopardise friendships but also place school and work careers at risk through exclusion or encounters with the law.

Domestic abuse can impact on teenagers' self-care skills because they may have assumed too much responsibility both for themselves and for other family members:

> *I've never actually had that time to live and be a kid, I haven't had that time to go running about, messing with my friends or going to do my things, play football...*
> (Jodie, a participant in a young people's focus group, quoted in Stanley *et al*, 2010, p.28)

The traditional roles of parent and child may be reversed. Although many teenagers willingly shoulder this burden, in the belief that they are responsible for "making things run smoothly", coupled with the perceived necessity of remaining continually vigilant, they may curtail interaction with peers and any involvement in social activities.

TO SUM UP

Key problems for adolescents

- Childhood trauma that may result from the experience of domestic abuse and violence can significantly increase the risk of psychosis in late adolescence.

- Domestic abuse can result in teenagers taking entire responsibility for their own health and welfare. As a result, any physical or sexual health problems may not be dealt with adequately.

- For some children, school and extra-curricular activities will have provided a refuge from their traumatic home life. Such a façade of competence may make it difficult for teachers to identify the abuse with which a child is living.

- For other children, domestic abuse will affect their education. The stress of home life can impact on concentration, resulting in poor academic results and sporting achievements. The feeling of being left behind can lead to aggressive behaviour and bullying, and result in temporary or permanent exclusion. Other teenagers may miss school in order to look after younger siblings or to protect a vulnerable parent.

- Teenagers may live for years in a constant state of anxiety and fear, feeling helpless and inadequate. They will develop a range of strategies to deal with their high levels of stress. These coping mechanisms can include dissociation, withdrawal, self-harming, and/or excessive use of drugs and alcohol. Others will externalise their emotions through aggressive and violent behaviours.

- The teenage years are the period when children seek to understand who they are. When children have been constantly rejected and belittled, they will come to see themselves as unlovable and develop very low self-esteem.

- Parents act as role models for their children, and in cases of domestic abuse this can cause considerable confusion. While some teenage boys may mirror their father or father figure and develop a macho identity, others will strongly reject it.

- Many teenagers exposed to domestic abuse have to grow up quickly, not only taking responsibility for their own welfare but also for keeping younger siblings and their abused parent safe. They will appear "old beyond their years".

- Domestic abuse can have a very detrimental impact on the relationship between teenagers and their parents. In many cases, their feelings will be ambivalent – hating the abuser and despising the victim while continuing to love them both.

- In some cases, teenagers feel very isolated from peers and adults who might have been able to support them. They may fear that things will get worse if their home situation becomes known and are therefore reluctant to form close friendships. For others, friends may be an escape, and teenage girls in particular may find support through sharing their problems with a trusted friend.

- Older teenagers who have an abusive father or father figure may experience difficulty in forming romantic attachments, fearing that their relationships will come to mirror that of their parents. If domestic abuse has been normalised, this can be reflected in their own sexual relationships.

- When the atmosphere at home becomes unbearable, or when teenagers blame themselves for the violence between their parents, they may seek to escape. Some may find refuge with friends or go missing and sleep in sheds or garages or on the streets, a situation that will make them very vulnerable to exploitation.
- Growing up in an abusive household may leave teenagers with few social skills; aggressive and manipulative behaviour may become acceptable ways of interacting with both adults and peers. As a result, schooling, friendships and career prospects may be jeopardised.

Chapter 6
The right family for the right child

Domestic abuse creates a distressing, stressful and harmful environment, and the long-term consequences of this trauma can stretch into adulthood.

(Cafcass Cymru, 2019, p.2)

THE LONG-TERM CONSEQUENCES OF DOMESTIC ABUSE

As discussed in earlier chapters, the impact on children and their response to the trauma of having experienced domestic violence and abuse will depend on a multitude of factors including, but not limited to, their age, ethnicity, sex, stage of development, and whether they had a supportive adult in their lives.

When children have been exposed to an abusive home environment for prolonged periods, they are likely to have suffered long-lasting harm to many aspects of their health and wellbeing. For others, the abuse may have been of short duration, only starting with the introduction of a new adult into the household. Nonetheless, the impact of witnessing even a single very violent assault can result in post-traumatic stress disorder, the effects of which may prove difficult to overcome.

Although exposure to domestic abuse can have enduring consequences for children and adolescents, some are more resilient and better able to heal and thrive when their circumstances improve. Of particular importance will be the presence of a consistent, supportive relationship that may have helped them cope and thereby reduced their stress levels (National Scientific Council on the Developing Child, 2007). Others will always struggle to overcome the impact of their early family life.

The majority of children exposed to domestic abuse continue to live safely with a birth parent with considerable support from adult and children's services. In situations where, even with intensive support, birth parents are unable to care safely for their child, a placement within a caring family may be the best option. This applies particularly where a birth parent is still living in an abusive environment or waiting to escape to a refuge. Alesha's reflections on losing her children and now fighting to get them back is an example of how complicated it is to reunite mothers and their children:

> *Alesha is upset. Her children are in foster care. 'It was a violent, volatile relationship, and the children were removed because of it', says Anna [refuge manager]. 'Her only hope of getting her children back is not to be in that relationship.' Alesha came to the refuge in the hope of escaping her abuser. Since then, she has been fighting to get her children back...*
> (The Guardian, 2021, G2, p.7)

Sensitive alternative parenting can be an effective way of countering damaging early experiences. When children are unable to live at home, they enter a period of instability. Children must separate from their parents and may suffer multiple losses. These can include losing contact with siblings, friends, home, school, treasured pets, and much-loved belongings:

> *...all those things which contribute to the sense of self and a sense of security. The impact of changing homes, acquiring new families or carers and undergoing yet further moves inevitably make enormous demands on children and may have detrimental effects on their ability to trust.*
> (Rose, 2006, p.293)

Once children have been removed from an abusive home and are living with alternative carers, the long-term consequences of domestic abuse may not be a prominent issue during the settling-in period and can be missed in subsequent assessment and planning. This is particularly the case when children appear to settle well initially. However, there is considerable evidence to suggest that the impact has profound and long-term consequences for children, even when their circumstances change for the better. For example, the trauma may have overwhelmed a child's capacity to regulate emotions. They may have been left to struggle with a state of intense fear and helplessness, resulting in high levels of stress. For very young infants, high stress levels are associated with changes in neural development, leading to lifelong difficulties in learning, behaviour, and physical and mental health (Clements *et al*, 2019).

PLANNING FOR CHILDREN

The circumstances that lead to children and young people becoming looked after vary greatly and result in a wide range of needs. An effective care plan, called the child's plan in Scotland, should be informed by an assessment that identifies the specific needs of an individual child and the support that the child and their prospective carers require. The purpose of the plan is to safeguard and promote the interests of the child, prevent drift, and focus on achieving permanence. For some children, this may include planning for return to living with a birth parent or parents. The care plan is about now and the future, and must be explicit about:

- the desired outcomes and the actions and services expected from each agency;
- the type of placement required to meet the child's individual needs; and
- the aim and purpose of the period of accommodation or care.

The child or young person, their birth family and their carers should be clear about the purpose of care or accommodation from the beginning of a placement. Care plans should include the fundamental issues of suitability of housing and adequacy of finance, especially for unplanned kinship care of children. It will also need to consider contact arrangements with members of the child's birth family. Consequently, the care plan should be completed before a child becomes looked after and must be reviewed regularly.

The Care Planning, Placement and Case Review Regulations 2010 (England) set out that a Placement Plan must be drawn up by the social worker, in the responsible local authority, prior to placement or within five working days of the start of the placement. A planning meeting should be convened in order to facilitate an exchange of views and key information about the placement and the child. Core attendees at the meeting will include social workers, foster carers and wherever possible, parents, children and other significant people such as teachers or therapists. The objective of the Placement Plan is to provide information for the child about what day-to-day life will be like with their new family. Similarly, carers will be able to gain a detailed understanding of the child's development and interests. Elaine Dibben (2019) provides a useful guide to completing and implementing placement plans for fostering placements in England.

Planning for permanence

The objective of planning for permanence, written in the statutory guidance and regulations that accompany the Children Act 1989 (England and Wales), is to ensure:

> ...that children have a secure, stable and loving family to support them through childhood and beyond and to give them a sense of security, continuity, commitment, identity and belonging.
>
> (DfE, 2015, p.22, para 2.3)

There is a similar requirement in Scottish legislation (Swift, 2020). The Adoption and Children (Scotland) Act 2007 introduced the permanence order, which is intended to be used in situations where the local authority will continue to have responsibility for a child or young person:

> *The order is designed to remove uncertainty from a child's life and to empower his or her carers so that the daily experience of the child is of nurture and predictability; of someone being there for him or her.*
> (The Scottish Government, 2010, p.9)

Permanence is about being "part of the family", of having a sense of belonging and mutual connectedness (Biehal *et al*, 2010; Schofield *et al*, 2012). For children whose previous relationships have been characterised by adversity, placement stability will be an important element because it enables the development of high-quality relationships. But as Janet Boddy points out in her report to the Care Inquiry, 'the very diversity of looked after children means that no one route to permanence could be appropriate for all their needs' (Boddy, 2013, pp.7–8). It may include further planned moves if they are in the child's best interests.

In addition to children's traumatic experiences while living at home, the care plan must take into consideration the fact that many will have experienced instability, change and loss while in the care system. Research by Harriet Ward and Tricia Skuse (2001) showed that children growing up in care are at significant risk of experiencing multiple changes of placement, including periods of returning to live with birth parents.

When considering the best permanent placement plan, the focus must be on outcomes and issues that may affect stability, such as the child's needs for long-term support and contact with parents, siblings and wider family. Permanence and stability can be undermined if the placement is not adequately supported (Boddy, 2013).

The process of permanence planning, which is informed by multi-agency contributions, is to identity which option is most likely to meet the child's needs, to take account of their wishes and feelings, and to be in their best interests. Government guidance identifies the following range of options for permanence:

- *Successful return to the child's birth family, where it has been possible to address the factors in the home that led to the child becoming looked after.*

- *Family and friends care (kinship care), supported by a legal order such as a child arrangements order, guardianship order, or adoption.*

- *Other non-family and friends care supported by a legal order such as a child arrangements order or special guardianship order.*

- *For children who remain looked after, long-term foster care.*

- *Adoption with twin track or parallel planning.*

(DfE, 2015, p.20)

Data provided by the DfE (2020) on the placements for looked after children showed that, of the 80,080 children looked after in England on 31 March 2020, the majority (72%) lived with foster carers: 14 per cent of these foster carers were relatives or family friends.

Assessing the child's needs

A comprehensive understanding of children's needs, and how best to address them, depends on a wide-ranging knowledge of their strengths and struggles in all aspects of their health, cognitive and educational progress, as well as their emotional and behavioural development. It should also include a thorough understanding of children's circumstances and the significant relationships in their lives.

Children's experience of having lived in an abusive family may have resulted in their having little or no understanding of other forms of family interaction. Consequently, children may misinterpret carers' behaviour, viewing everything through the lens of potential danger. Children may experience difficulty in trusting carers and continue with learned behaviours, which are now inappropriate and can be very distressing for carers. For some children, the long-term impact of early exposure to domestic abuse may only emerge during adolescence.

There should be a detailed and recorded history of the child's experience of domestic abuse and trauma, to which the potential carers have access. This has implications for how information is collected and recorded by social workers from their first contact with the birth family. The information should be collated in the assessment report – the Child's Permanence Report (CPR) (Dibben *et al*, 2014a) in England and Wales or the Child's Adoption and Permanence Report (CAPR) in Scotland (Morrison, 2016) – and the findings considered in subsequent reviews of the suitability of the placement and the child's behaviour.

Involving children in placement decisions

Decisions on the most appropriate permanent placement must, wherever possible, be taken with the child's involvement. Children have a right to be listened to and taken seriously, a requirement of Article 12 of the United Nations Convention on the Rights of the Child (ratified in the UK in 1991):

> *States Parties shall assure to the child who is capable of forming his or her own views the right to express those views freely in all matters affecting the child, the views of the child being given due weight in accordance with the age and maturity of the child.*

Placing siblings together?

There is a general assumption and considerable research to show that children who are separated from their parents fare better when placed with a sibling (Jenkins *et al*, 1989; Gass *et al*, 2007). This notion is enshrined in legislation and guidance both in England and Wales, and in Scotland, and places an obligation on local authorities to endeavour to place siblings together when it is in their best interests. The definition of a sibling can vary and may include step-siblings, half-siblings, and non-related children growing up in the same household (Family Futures, 2019).

Shelagh Beckett (2021, p.7) reports that, when the views of children and young people have been sought, they 'consistently told us that their sibling relationships are important to them and should be respected'. Young people generally wish to keep in touch with their brothers and sisters when not placed together, and want social workers to:

> *Try their hardest to keep them together but if they don't, make sure they don't drift apart and become more like distant relatives than brothers and sisters.*
>
> (Beckett, 2021, p.24)

Beckett (2021) scrutinised relevant research and identified a number of benefits for siblings who have been placed together, including:

- increased chances of reunification with birth parents;
- easing the transition into care – the presence of a sibling can help in maintaining emotional stability;
- warm sibling relationships may help protect emotional wellbeing;
- boys in particular may be helped to develop relationship skills and competence.

Despite the emphasis on keeping siblings together, a survey of 152 English local authorities found that half (49.5%) of sibling groups in local authority care were split up and 37 per cent of children in care who had at least one other sibling in care were living with none of their siblings (Ashley and Roth, 2015). Similarly, research showed that only 37 per cent of children placed for adoption were placed with a sibling (Ivaldi, 2000). More recent research suggests that little has changed. Findings from two-thirds of local authorities in the UK showed that 1,375 children placed for adoption between April 2018 and November 2019 had been separated from birth siblings (Kenyon and Forde, 2020).

Separating close siblings when placed with new families can prove traumatic:

> *When Sophia was little, she told her adoptive mother she had an imaginary friend. She even had a name for her – Theighan. But it turned*

out Theighan was not imaginary at all. She was Sophia's older sister, who had been separated from her at the age of four while both girls were in care. The memory had simply faded over time. 'I just remember having the person there that I trusted and then I didn't and then I was alone', said Sophia.

(Kenyon and Forde, 2020)

There are a variety of reasons why so many sibling groups are split up. These include organisational issues, such as a lack of written policies and procedures when planning for sibling groups, staffing issues, personal beliefs of relevant professionals, and too few placements with sufficient resources to care for siblings. Factors relating to individual children are also relevant. The key factors are a sibling who is violent and/or sexually abusive; the age gap between siblings; starting to become looked after at different times; different contact needs of individual children; the wishes of birth relatives; siblings of different ethnicities; and when one child is disabled (Lord and Borthwick, 2008; Beckett, 2021).

When considering whether or not to place siblings together, it is important to consider how the trauma of living with domestic violence and abuse has affected each child and their relationship with their siblings. For some, the relationship may have provided comfort and support, while for others it may have been dysfunctional. As already discussed in earlier chapters, developmental trauma affects children differently and, as a consequence, the type and intensity of parenting that a child will require.

Whether siblings are placed together or separately is a complex clinical judgement that requires:

- *a comprehensive assessment*

- *an understanding of the impact of trauma on individual child development and its impact on the development of sibling relationships in infancy*

- *appreciation of the skills, knowledge and therapeutic support parents need to developmentally re-parent traumatised children*

(Family Futures, 2019, p.28)

The Adoption Regulations 2013, although supporting the principle of keeping siblings together, signal the need for a thorough assessment of the needs of each child and the capacity of potential carers to meet them, before such decisions are taken (see DfE, 2013, p.85, para12).

Legislation in Scotland also acknowledges the importance of keeping siblings together when placing for adoption wherever possible and when in the child's best interests. The Guidance on Looked After Children (Scotland) Regulations 2009 and the Adoption and Children (Scotland)

Act 2007 (Part VII) state: 'For a number of the children waiting for adoption the first choice is for them to be placed with siblings.'

Beckett (2021) argues for a full assessment of each child in a sibling group as well as an assessment of their relationship with one another before making decisions about sibling placements. Sibling assessments provide an in-depth analysis of their bonds and the quality of attachments. An assessment should involve the children and young people and those who know them well. It should examine the individual needs of each child and the impact of these needs on their siblings. In addition, the assessment should explore the skills, experience and support that carers are likely to need to meet both current and future needs.

Although, in most cases, siblings benefit from being placed together, there are circumstances that may indicate the need for permanent separation. These include the following destructive patterns of interaction:

- *Intense rivalry and jealousy, with each child totally pre-occupied with, and unable to tolerate, the attention their sibling/s may be getting.*

- *Exploitation, often based on gender, e.g. boys may have been seen and see themselves as inherently superior to their sisters, with a right to dominate and exploit them.*

- *Chronic scapegoating of one child.*

- *Maintaining unhelpful alliances in a sibling group and family of origin. Sibling patterns of behaviour may be strongly entrenched and may prevent re-parenting or learning new cultural norms.*

- *Maintaining unhelpful hierarchical positions e.g. the child may be stuck in the role of victim or bully.*

- *Highly sexualised behaviour with each other.*

- *Acting as triggers to each other's traumatic material and potentially constantly re-traumatising each other. The triggers may well be unconscious, unintentional and mundane.*

(Lord and Borthwick, 2008, p.22)

Such pernicious interactions between siblings may have resulted from children mirroring the behaviours they observed while exposed to domestic abuse within their birth family.

Although sibling assessments have become more common in recent years: '…there is no reference to "sibling relationship assessments" in statute and no legal requirement for an assessment to be undertaken' (Monk and Macvarish, 2018, p.32). Practice guides and tools are available to support practitioners to carry out sibling assessments, some of which are listed at the end of this Good Practice Guide.

FINDING FAMILIES FOR CHILDREN

To find alternative homes for children who can no longer live with their birth parents is the role of the fostering and adoption services. They are responsible for recruiting, assessing and approving prospective carers, as Marjorie Morrison so aptly states in her CoramBAAF guide for fostering and adoption panels in Scotland:

> *Those that provide that care within their own homes and families through fostering and adoption need to be carefully assessed and prepared before being approved for the task. For those children who are unable to return to their own parents, planning security for their future must be of the highest calibre.*
>
> (Morrison, 2018, p.3)

This also applies to kinship carers who are to become special guardians (Public Law Working Group, 2020).

Assessing potential families

Assessment is undertaken in partnership with potential carers and should enable professionals to judge whether the applicants would make suitable and safe carers. To ensure the best match between a child and their new family, the assessment of potential carers must be rigorous and explore sensitive issues, such as their motivation to care for someone else's child; their family history, including exposure to domestic abuse; their current relationship; attitudes and openness towards the child; and their culture, religion, gender identity and sexual orientation. 'The strongest potential matches are based on ensuring that the parenting capacity, skills and experience of the carer meet the assessed developmental needs of the child' (Cleaver and Rose, 2020, p.51).

Special guardians are assessed for their suitability to look after a specific child. Assessments must explore not only potential guardians' personal history and present circumstances, but also their knowledge, experience and expectations of the child/ren, as well as the relationship between them. Assessments should also seek to understand potential guardians' wishes and feelings about contact between child/ren and birth parents, with a particular focus on issues that might arise due to past domestic abuse. Experience has shown the value of early family group conferences to help identify who would best look after the child, either in the short term and/or permanently, and the support that can be offered by family members (Leeds City Council, 2014).

Assessment should also give applicants a comprehensive picture of the child's background and experiences and the likely challenges that may face them. Potential carers need to understand that, to survive, children may have developed strategies that result in them resisting adults' attempts to protect and care for them. These may include a range of controlling behaviours that help them feel in charge of their own safety, but can result in upsetting those who wish to nurture them.

Parenting these children will require empathy, patience and good listening skills; perseverance and resilience when things get tough; flexibility and adaptability; and a willingness to work with other people in the child's life such as birth parents, separated siblings and social workers.

Preparing families

Before a child is placed with their prospective family it is essential that carers have all the relevant information about the child. Social workers and prospective carers must be fully aware of the child's circumstances within their birth family, and all subsequent placements. This should include a child's experience of direct harm, physical and sexual, and any emotional abuse or neglect. Equally important is a comprehensive understanding of the degree of exposure to domestic abuse and violence, parental drug and alcohol misuse, mental health problems, and intellectual disability. In addition, it will be important for carers to be aware of the birth family's living conditions, and the degree of isolation or support the child may have received from extended family and friends. For older children, school attendance, friendships and involvement with groups, both online and face-to-face, must also be understood.

For many special guardians, a high proportion of whom will be grandparents, the background information is also personal to them. 'They also form part of the kinship carer's own personal and familial life story, and the difficult events described involved the carer's own child' (Holt and Birchall, 2021, p.7). Social workers need to acknowledge and discuss possible ways of providing support for the additional challenges they may face. These may be structural: a high proportion of kinship care households live in poverty; are from a minority ethnic background; and the children they care for are twice as likely to have long-term health problems or disability (Wijedasa, 2015). There may also be emotional challenges: difficult relationships with the child's birth parents or other family members may be exacerbated by conflict over contact arrangements.

Many children will have already lived with alternative families. Social workers and prospective carers should be aware of the child's placement history, including returns to live with birth family. It will be important to explore the purpose and length of each placement; the child's experience while living there; the reason the placement ended; and how it affected the child's emotional and behavioural development. Prior experiences shape children's behaviour, which means that children will arrive with established behaviour patterns based on their relationships with birth family and previous carers.

Child Appreciation Days and Life Appreciation Days provide an opportunity for prospective adopters and carers to 'have as much information as possible about the child, in the hope that this will ensure a sound base for a placement, and will lessen the chance of the placement disrupting in the future' (Sayers and Roach, 2011, p.3). Such days enable prospective adopters and carers to speak with individuals who know the child, including previous carers. Although the Adoption and Permanence Taskforce highlighted the value of Child Appreciation Days in 2004, they remain the exception rather than the rule.

Prospective carers should also be aware of how children's experiences might affect both their present and future behaviour. As explored in earlier chapters, this will depend on children's age and developmental stage when exposed to domestic abuse; any history of child abuse and neglect; and any other parenting issues. It is only with a comprehensive understanding of what children have experienced and how it has affected them, that prospective carers can fully understand what they are committing to and whether this is the right thing for their family.

It is also important that social workers explore the type of support that carers may need and ensure that prospective adopters and special guardians understand that asking for help does not suggest failure on their part.

A series of focus groups involving special guardians raised concerns over the inadequacy of the preparation, information and training they received. They were also dissatisfied and frustrated with the assessment process, a key issue being the statutory duty to complete proceedings within 26 weeks (Simmonds *et al*, 2019; see also Cleaver and Rose, 2020).

Kinship carers raised similar concerns in their response to the Parliamentary Taskforce on Kinship Care (2020). These included:

- lack of sufficient information to make informed decisions;
- uncertainty over their rights in the assessment process;
- having to make decisions with little time to prepare; and
- not having sufficient information about the legal options to make informed decisions.

Written evidence submitted by Coram Children's Legal Centre to the Taskforce also highlighted this issue:

> *It is not uncommon for prospective carers to have a poor understanding of what is being proposed, what is being assessed, what the process entails, what it is that is being asked of them – how long the placement*

is intended to last, why personal and/or intimate questions are being asked, including the family history and background information.
(Evidence from Coram Children's Legal Centre, quoted in Parliamentary Taskforce, 2020, p.53)

To address some of these concerns, the Public Law Working Group has made a number of recommendations with regard to special guardianship assessments and support plans, preparation and training for special guardians, and renewed emphasis on parental contact (Public Law Working Group, 2020, pp.27–30).

Making a good match

Key to the stability and permanence of alternative care is the match between child and carers, which research suggests is often dependent on the "chemistry" between them (Sinclair, 2005; Schofield *et al*, 2012). One adoptive mother in Julie Selwyn and colleagues' study illustrates the importance of getting the right match. Her response to the question 'whether they would have done anything differently' was:

> *Not adopted her. I should have insisted on an older child ... I should have relied more on my instincts than being swayed by other people. I would have insisted on liking a child and knowing a child before adopting ... they do not make it easy for you to meet any child. They find a child, they match the child, they say, 'This is the child for you'.*
(Selwyn *et al*, 2014, p.212)

For social workers to enable a good match, it is critically important to have a sufficient pool of foster carers and adopters, as well as identifying friends and family willing and able to cater for the varied needs of children. The challenge of finding the most suitable family has become more difficult due to increasing numbers of children looked after and a shortage of approved foster placements (Ofsted, 2020), a situation that has been exacerbated by the Covid-19 pandemic in 2020–21 (Barnardo's, 2020).

Checklist for recommending a match

Morrison (2018) provides the following checklist for adoption and fostering panels in Scotland to consider before making a recommendation about a match – this would apply equally to panels elsewhere in the UK and is also relevant to placement with kinship carers.

- *The child's needs – updated information about the child's progress; further work done in understanding the child's wishes and feelings; any other work recommended when the plan was made at panel;*

- *The assessment of the family – any change in circumstances; any significant development in the views of the family post approval, including training undertaken; other children considered or other work recommended at the time of approval;*

- *The views of the birth family – updating information about their view of the plan; if they agree, their view of the family chosen; if they disagree, what action they have taken; any other members of the birth family who are significant in the placement of the child;*

- *The linking process – issues arising from the linking report; any other work recommended prior to the panel; summary of the process and opportunities provided to ensure that the family had time to explore all the relevant information; their understanding of the child's needs;*

- *The strengths, vulnerabilities and abilities of the family as they relate to the needs of the child/ren;*

- *Preparation for the impact of the placement – other children in the family/other family members, practical preparation;*

- *Contact – the child's contact needs, the ability of the family to meet these and how this will be implemented;*

- *The support plan – confirmation that any immediate support services required will be available from the outset; a longer-term support plan; confirmation that adopters understand how to access support at any stage; adoption allowances or other financial supports recommended;*

- *The legal route – any issues arising from the current legal position; any requirement for the panel to make a recommendation about the legal route;*

- *Readiness to proceed – any further work recommended to prepare the child or family prior to introductions.*

(Morrison, 2018, p.121)

MAKING THE MOVE TO A PERMANENT FAMILY

A child's reaction to a forthcoming move will be based on past experiences of abandonment, rejection and loss. The definition of a placement move provided by Family Futures (2009) illustrates the complexity of the process:

> *... the movement of a child who is traumatised but has grown to feel safe in their foster home into a permanent home with a new "Mum" and "Dad" (or equivalent) who are inevitably strangers to this child is another trauma which is made more difficult for the child because their internal working model of parent figures is predicated on their previous relationship with their birth parents.*

(Family Futures, 2009, p.3)

An important role of foster carers is to help the child lower their levels of anxiety and fear. When children leave their care to return home or to move to a more permanent placement, a transition plan must be developed. The aim of such a plan is to transfer the source of safety and security from the current foster carer to the birth family or long-term carer. The extent to which children can be involved in deciding the type of family they would like to live with will depend on their age and understanding. It will also depend significantly on the fact that they have been traumatised and will probably have little concept of what it means to live in a family that is not dysfunctional or violent.

When children leave temporary carers for a permanent placement, carers may perceive a child's move as a positive event. In contrast, the association for a child of concepts such as "new mums and dads" or "a forever family" may be highly emotive of past events. Children's experiences of domestic abuse, trauma and chaotic living are likely to have left them very anxious about any forthcoming move, however well planned. Those who have experienced previous separations will see the move to be a repetition of past abandonments and rejections. Social workers and carers will need to acknowledge that the move will be a very stressful event for the child. Simply providing information, such as showing them photographs and sharing information about the prospective family, may generate more anxiety. Consequently, Family Futures (2009) recommends:

> *If the child meets the prospective adopters and has a positive experience of being with these real people it will be easier for the child to associate these new people with positive feelings and experiences.*
> (Family Futures, 2009, p.9)

The first meeting between the prospective long-term carer and the child should take place in the child's own territory, an environment that is comfortable for them. The presence of the current carers and social workers should ensure that the child is provided with support and reassurance. It is important that children understand and believe that their prospective long-term carers accept and value them. This is likely to take longer the older the child is. Social workers should be guided by how comfortable the child appears to be in the presence of their prospective long-term carers, and how competent and confident carers appear to be in relating to the child. Careful thought should be given to possible continuing contact with former carers.

When the time comes for the child to move, as much as possible of the child's world should accompany them. The child needs the reassurance of familiar sights, sounds and smells. Family Futures (2009) suggests that one example:

> *...would be to take the child's current bedding unwashed to the new home so that there is a familiar texture, smell and sight of sheets, pillows, etc, that are familiar. The same applies to clothing.*
>
> (Family Futures, 2009, p.10)

SUPPORT AVAILABLE FOR CARERS

All families caring for children who have been exposed to domestic violence and abuse are likely to need support at some time. Research suggests that approximately one-half of children placed with adopters (47%), kinship carers (52%) and non-kinship foster carers (52%) had experienced domestic abuse prior to placement (Farmer, 2009; Neil *et al*, 2018). However, the level of support and oversight provided by local authorities depends on the legal status of the child.

Support for foster carers is the most comprehensive due to the underpinning legal framework. Foster carers do not have parental responsibility for the child they are looking after although they do have delegated authority:

> *Delegated authority is the process that enables foster carers to make common sense, everyday decisions about the children and young people they care for, such as allowing them to go to friends' houses for sleepovers, signing consent forms for school trips and even arranging haircuts.*
>
> (The Fostering Network, 2016)

The local authority remains the child's "corporate parent" and there is a children's social worker responsible for ensuring the child's safety and welfare. Foster carers are part of the "team around the child". The fostering services will assign a supervising social worker to foster carers and provide carers with ongoing training, advice, information and support. In addition, all foster carers receive a fostering allowance to cover the cost of looking after a child.

When a local authority has placed children with prospective adopters and special guardians, and before orders are made, carers should receive the same degree of support as foster carers, as should relative or family friend kinship carers.

Joan Hunt's (2020) overview of UK research on kinship care found that a major theme was the lack of financial and practical support received by carers. Carers were found to have incurred a substantial increase in costs, often largely or fully met by carers themselves. Many also experienced pressure on living space. The study identified shortfalls in the provision of financial support; information and advice; some form of respite care; and help with children's emotional and behavioural difficulties.

Until recently, once a special guardianship order (SGO) was granted (applicable only in England and Wales), the case was often closed by children's services. Amendments to the special guardianship regulations have resulted in local authorities being required to make arrangements for the provision of special guardianship support services. These include counselling and advice, and access to the means-tested special guardianship allowance (DfE, 2017b). Increasingly, the granting of an SGO has been accompanied by a supervision order, which has been used as the means of providing additional support although no formal plan is required. This development has raised considerable concern:

> *A proposal to make a supervision order is likely to signify a lack of confidence in the making of an SGO at that time and/or results from the inadequacy of the support and services provided for in the SGSP [special guardianship support plan]…The cases where it would be appropriate/ necessary to make a supervision order alongside a SGO are likely, in our view, to be very small in number.*
> (Public Law Working Group, 2020, p.25, para 34)

The granting of an adoption order ends all local authority oversight, although adopters may be eligible for an adoption allowance and should be offered an adoption support plan. Local authorities in England must carry out an assessment of the support needs of the child, the prospective adopter, and any other children in the adopter's household (Adoption Agencies Regulations, 2005). A recent large survey of adopters and potential adopters has found that 71 per cent of respondents in England 'said that they did not have a written adoption support plan in place' (Adoption UK, 2021, p.32). Nonetheless, in general, adopters reported that they felt well supported:

> *Respondents were largely positive about the support they were given during the early weeks, with 81 per cent agreeing that social workers were supportive, and 90 per cent sure that they knew where to go for help and support if they experienced difficulties.*
> (Adoption UK, 2021, p.30)

In England, adopters and special guardians may be able to obtain support through the Adoption Support Fund; however, this funding is discretionary (Gov.UK, 2019). In addition, many local authorities offer adopters counselling and advice on a range of issues linked to adoption, and training courses on the types of challenges they may encounter.

In Scotland, the Adoption Support Plan covers whether an adoption allowance or other payment will be paid. Adoption allowances are paid at the discretion of the local authority and cover one-off payments or a regular allowance for a specified period. The purpose is to help cover the additional costs associated with caring for a child who has particular needs.

Legislation in the UK places a duty on local authorities to safeguard and promote the welfare of children within their area who are in need. Children who are adopted or live with alternative carers under different legal orders may be "in need" and eligible for services.

Chapter 10 explores in more detail the type of support available to those caring for a child who has experienced domestic abuse and trauma.

TO SUM UP

- Exposure to domestic abuse can have long-lasting effects on children's health and development, although how children react will depend on numerous factors. While some children will have incurred long-term damage, others will be able to heal and thrive when provided with a loving, safe and supportive home.

- Local authorities have a duty to explore the possibility of placing a child with family or friends connected to the child, before considering a placement by local authority fostering services, independent fostering providers or adoption.

- Finding the best alternative homes for children who can no longer live with their birth parents is the responsibility of fostering and adoption services. Placement decisions should be based on a comprehensive assessment of the skills and parenting capacity and the expectations of potential adopters and carers.

- The development of a child's care plan will be informed by an assessment of the child's strengths and needs and by the circumstances of the carers. To prevent children drifting in the child care system, care plans must focus on the desired outcome for the child and the steps that need to be taken to achieve it. Care plans should provide a child with a sense of permanence and take into consideration the factors that might affect placement stability.

- Local authorities have an obligation to try to keep sibling groups together when placed with alternative carers. However, many are separated due to resource issues, such as staffing shortages and a lack of alternative carers willing to take sibling groups. For those siblings whose interactions with each other are destructive, separate placements may be necessary to ensure their wellbeing. Sibling assessments will support practitioners in identifying children who are likely to thrive living away from one or more of their brothers and sisters.

- The successful integration of a child within a new family will depend on the "match" between children and their carers. Getting this right relies upon a sufficiently large pool of potential carers, such as relatives and family friends, foster carers and adopters who are willing to take on such a responsibility.

- To ensure the best possible "match", adoption and fostering panels should ensure that they have all relevant information about the child; prospective carers and their views of the birth family; possible contact arrangements; support for carers and children; and any legal issues that may need addressing.

- Once children have had to leave their birth parents, each subsequent move is likely to reinforce feelings of abandonment, rejection and loss. The primary role of carers is to provide a sense of safety and to meet the child's emotional needs for love and comfort.

- Practitioners should draw up a transition plan for children who move to live permanently with a different family. The plan should be sensitive to the child's age and circumstances, particularly the anxiety and stress the prospective move is likely to engender. Children may find the move easier if they are able to take with them familiar and much loved objects. Continuing contact with birth family and previous carers should be considered where appropriate and in the child's best interests.

- The support available to carers once the child joins their permanent family depends on their legal status. When children are the responsibility of a local authority, such as when fostered or prior to adoption or guardianship orders being granted, considerable advice, support and training are available. However, once such orders are in place, the training and support for adopters and special guardians are much reduced.

Chapter 7
Looking after infants who have experienced domestic abuse

She would be very clingy, and even followed me to the toilet

This chapter focuses on the challenges of looking after children under the age of five years, who have experienced domestic abuse. It might be assumed that an infant removed from an abusive home and placed with supportive and loving carers is likely to settle quickly and develop strong attachments. However, babies may have been affected negatively during their time in utero, and even very young children cannot be fully protected.

PREPARING AND SUPPORTING FAMILIES

Social workers can help families prepare for the task of looking after infants affected by domestic abuse. Chapter 3 provides details of specific consequences for the infant's health, cognitive and language development, attachment behaviours, emotional and behavioural development, and self-confidence.

Preparation courses for foster carers and adopters can draw on this information and integrate it into the training. Prior to placing the child, social workers can help carers and prospective parents to understand what life may have been like for this infant, their existing behaviour patterns, and what their present and future needs may be. Further help can be offered and carers can be introduced to particular resources, thereby equipping them to undertake the parenting of this child.

As discussed in previous chapters, information about the infant needs to be accurately presented in the assessment report on the child. Many carers and adopters have complained about the lack of adequate and accurate information and the unfortunate consequences of this, sometimes even leading to placement breakdown.

The child's life story book should accompany the child and record significant events. Carers can be reminded of its significance, its therapeutic effectiveness, and its value in providing opportunities for the child to explore, understand and accept their history.

Effects of exposure to domestic abuse

Prenatal exposure to domestic abuse can impact on an area of the brain involved in emotional and behavioural development, the effects of which may emerge as the baby develops.

Carers may need social work help and guidance to understand the impact of domestic abuse on the baby's developing brain and subsequent attachment patterns. For example, smells, sights, sounds and body sensations, even when very young children are in a safe environment, may trigger early feelings of powerlessness, fear, guilt, anxiety, anger and worthlessness (Foxon with Argent, 2007). Carers may need to know the most effective ways to support and nurture the baby.

When very young children can no longer live safely with their birth family, a stable long-term placement is essential because the presence of a constant caring figure will be crucial to correct earlier disrupted attachment patterns and allow bonding and attachment to take place. Stability and permanency in an infant's life enable this and benefit all aspects of the child's health and development, as Vera Falhlberg explains:

> *The influence of parent–child interactions on the child's developing nervous and hormonal systems may explain why some children who are not well attached have poor cognitive development and may be delayed in terms of physical development.*
>
> (Fahlberg, 1994, p.22)

Instability and change, when children enter the care system, are not restricted to older children. Work by Ward and colleagues (2006) revealed that over one-quarter of babies in their sample had experienced three or more moves before their first birthday. In such cases, placement changes will have negatively affected the process of bonding and attachment, magnifying and exacerbating the negative consequences of having been exposed to domestic abuse.

Even very young babies are affected by moves from one family to another because they are aware of differences in their "relational world" – in temperature, sound, smell, touch and visual stimulation. Once past the age of six months, the next four years are a period when children are particularly vulnerable to the emotional distress of parental separation (Rutter, 1981).

Effects on attachment patterns

John Bowlby (1973) has contributed to our understanding of attachment and the emotional reactions, anxiety and anger that young children experience when separated from carers. Young children who have been exposed to domestic abuse may have developed insecure attachment patterns and experienced periods of separation from one or both parents prior to becoming looked after. The initial separation, when placed with a new family, will have reinforced emotions of loss, anxiety and grief. These feelings and subsequent behaviours will be exacerbated when children move on from their initial carers to live with another family, be it adopters, family and friends or special guardians.

Gillian Schofield and Mary Beek's "Secure Base" model provides a framework to help 'make the links with the caregiving likely to promote security for children in foster care and adoption...' (Schofield and Beek, 2018, p.35). As discussed in earlier chapters, domestic abuse has a profound impact on parenting capacity, leaving many children with attachment disorders. Three types of attachment disorder are identified:

> **Avoidant:**...*the infant or child learns to shut down on her feelings in order to avoid overwhelming the caregiver and provoking rejection or intrusion.*
>
> **Ambivalent:**...*the infant may simply make demands almost constantly to attract and keep the attention of the caregiver or may become rather helpless in the absence of an available strategy. Over time, the infant is likely to become a rather preoccupied, demanding, clingy but distrustful and resistant child.*
>
> **Disorganised:**...*the infant's drive to approach the caregiver for care and protection results in fear and increased rather than decreased anxiety. The absence of a strategy in infancy leads to confused and disorganised behaviours, but over time the child starts to develop controlling behaviours to enable them to feel some degree of safety. However, feelings of anxiety and fear remain unresolved and reappear at times of stress.*
>
> (Schofield and Beek, 2018, p.38)

It is obvious that exposure to parental domestic abuse during early infancy may result in one or more attachment disorders.

Contact with birth family

When children are fostered, current practice, supported by the Children Act 1989 (England and Wales) and Children (Scotland) Act 1995, assumes the principle that contact with birth family members and/or significant others is generally beneficial and should be promoted, unless it is not in the child's best interests. Contact can be direct, which includes face-to-face meetings, phone calls, or through social media. It may also be indirect, such as exchange of letters and cards, which are usually through a third person. Contact with birth parents will vary from case to case, for example, if the child is expected to return to their birth family it is likely to be frequent, although less frequent or not at all in other cases.

When children are living with special guardians, contact arrangements with birth parents are, in some cases, spelled out as part of their plan, while others are expected to make informal arrangements themselves. Contact can be a very emotional experience, as parents may struggle to accept that their child is permanently living with relatives and that the special guardian is now their child's primary carer. They may repeatedly turn up late, fail to arrive at all, or try to increase contact beyond what was agreed. It will be important for special guardians to try hard not to criticise or blame birth parents in front of the child. Family Action provides useful information for special guardians on managing contact with birth families (Family Action, 2017).

When a child is adopted there is no legal requirement for adoptive families to maintain any kind of contact with members of the child's birth family once the adoption order has gone through. Contact arrangements will be discussed prior to the child's adoption and in many cases a voluntary agreement between the two families will be arranged; in some cases the arrangements will be included in the court order. Research shows that 84 per cent of adoptive families had signed an agreement for ongoing indirect contact (such as letterbox), and a further quarter were having direct contact with birth family members, mainly siblings (Adoption UK, 2019).

Seeing or hearing from birth parents can provide children with a sense of continuity, although following contact their behaviour may show a degree of disturbance as feelings of loss, rejection and sadness are brought to the fore. It will be important to help the child settle after contact and this can be promoted by carers planning some quiet time to enable children to process difficult feelings.

Contact with previous carers

Many children who are the focus of this guide will have lived as part of a foster family prior to joining their new family. Key to children's happiness, behaviour and relationships while fostered, are warm, child-orientated carers. Just over half (51%) of the 86 adoptive families in Sarah Meakings and Julie Selwyn's (2016) study believed their child had been well cared for while living with their foster family prior to coming to live with them, as the following adoptive mother reported:

> [The foster carers] provided the first experience for my children of genuine care and love, in a way they hadn't experienced within their birth

> *family. We felt that was really important. We still do think it's important, and it's helped our children.*
>
> (Adoptive mother, reported in Meakings and Selwyn, 2016, p.512)

However, a similar proportion (49%) expressed serious misgivings about the quality of care their child had experienced pre-adoption, a factor that was shown to be associated with increased risk of adoption disruption. Adopters 'described foster carers who had provided adequate physical care, yet who were disengaged emotionally from the child, and who provided very little in the way of nurture' (Meakings and Selwyn, 2016, p.513):

> *The foster carers were really lovely...but I remember them saying to us, 'We haven't looked after him like our own children because he's moving. We wanted to save him for his adoptive family, so we haven't hugged him, kissed him, or cuddled him and paid him that sort of attention, because we wanted to save all that lovely stuff for you.'*
>
> (Adoptive mother, reported in Meakings and Selwyn, 2016, p.514)

Children coming to live with new families must resolve the grief and trauma at losing a key attachment figure, while at the same time start to form new trusting and secure relationships. 'New attachments are not meant to replace old ones. They are meant to stand side by side with existing relationships' (Fahlberg, 1994, p.160). When children move to a new family, it is essential that adults recognise that a key attachment figure has been lost and children can be left feeling abandoned. Contact with past carers may provide the infant with a sense of continuity.

A survey of 3,000 foster carers from across the UK concluded:

> *...the care system is doing little to promote fostered children's relationships when they move within or out of it and is far too often, in fact, obstructing them.*
>
> *The level of support that children receive to maintain their relationships is inconsistent. They are reliant on their adopters, foster carers or family to facilitate contact, often without training or guidance.*
>
> (The Fostering Network, 2019, p.7)

The Care Inquiry (2013) identified that high-quality relationships matter more than anything else for looked after children. Relationships serve a number of purposes. They help children of all ages to build a sense of security, understand their past, and develop confidence in their ability to sustain healthy relationships in the future. The Inquiry emphasised the importance of maintaining relationships whenever children have to make a move, either between placements whilst in care or to live with families who will provide long-term care via fostering or adoption. Unfortunately, research suggests that, when this happens, the focus on children's needs may take second place to concern for the feelings and wishes of carers. Sophie Boswell and Lynne Cudmore's study found:

> ...preoccupation with how adults were managing their feelings, it seemed difficult for them to fully keep in mind the child as a separate person who was also experiencing a great change in their lives.
>
> (Boswell and Cudmore, 2014, p.14)

The study identified that any planning was generally for the sake of the foster carers who would be missing the child. There was less concern for what it might mean for the child to see, or not see, their carer again after the move. Feelings of loss were thought to reside with the foster carers, not the child. This may be encouraged by the fact that many looked after children can appear on the surface to adapt to new situations very quickly and not express the strong emotions that might be expected when faced with a sudden change. When children have been adopted, the decision about contact with foster carers is left to the adopters. 'Most appeared uncertain about what was best for the child', while foster carers often feared that contact would upset the child and be an intrusion into their new family (Boswell and Cudmore, 2014, p.21).

When children move because the placement has disrupted, the attitudes of practitioners can also affect whether contact is encouraged. Hedi Argent and Jeffrey Coleman (2012) suggest that contact may be discouraged because professionals blame carers for 'letting the children down', or want to protect the children from further pain.

> Meryl [adoptive mother] wanted to maintain contact with Barry [aged 4] but the local authority insisted it would be too upsetting for Barry to be reminded of "the failure". At the disruption meeting, ten weeks later, the new foster carer described how Barry had kept asking to speak to Meryl and she had to explain to him that he wasn't allowed.
>
> (Argent and Coleman, 2012, p.54)

Promoting attachment

Karleen Gribble (2016) has examined the methods used to promote parent–premature infant attachment and discussed how these might be useful in promoting attachment between foster carers and very young children. Although the focus is on foster carers, the messages have relevance for all families who are caring for a very young child who is not their own. A number of interventions are identified that could assist carers to form a healthy attachment relationship with a very young child. These include encouraging close contact between carers and children to enable carers to observe their child's behaviour and get to know them.

The "fretful" child

Understanding and interpreting children's behaviour is key to meeting their needs because, unlike the majority of children, those who have experienced domestic abuse and trauma may have little trust in adults and not seek closeness to them.

Some babies and young children are constantly fretful and yet hard to soothe, requiring a great deal of physical time and emotional energy to show them that their needs will be reliably met. Others have learned to shut down cries for attention in order to survive their hostile environment. Such was the experience of the following carer:

> *When Jasminder came to me at 12 weeks old, she was completely unresponsive, not waking for feeds, not responding to me, not showing any emotion. She had just switched off. I had to stay close to her and respond to even the slightest sound or facial movement and keep talking to her and touching her. It took time, but gradually she started to show different feelings and become more responsive.*
> (Foster carer, quoted in Schofield and Beek, 2018, p.163)

When an infant rejects cuddles, carers need much patience and a careful approach such as 'sitting beside him for a feed, for instance, or stroking a hand or a foot and unobtrusively building on this' (Schofield and Beek, 2018, p.164; see also Field *et al*, 1996). However, any form of touch must take account of the child's history and requires much sensitivity in its provision.

The "independent" child

Some very young children will have had to grow up fast, assuming too much responsibility for themselves and, in a few instances, for their abused parent:

> *He smashed my head against the wall because (the baby) was making a mess. He picked up the dish and threw it at me and I was covered in baby food. I just collapsed on the floor. (The baby) was trying to pull me across the floor crying... saying 'Mummy get up'.*
> (Mother, reported in NCH, 1994, p.32)

As a result, young children may appear old beyond their years. For others, the violent and chaotic lifestyle may have resulted in their having had little or no guidance as to how to behave. The atmosphere of violence and the uncertainty of their parents' reactions will have left many wary of voicing their wishes and needs.

Carers need to be supported to interpret their child's behaviour and cues. When children appear prematurely independent and self-sufficient, carers may need to take the initiative in identifying ways they can provide care, while at the same time being prepared to accept that it may be rejected. Children need time to learn to trust a new carer sufficiently to accept their help, as the experience of the following carer demonstrates:

He found it impossible to trust me and watched my face warily all the time. I found that after nursery, if I sat with a drink for him on the settee with children's television on, he would circle the house for a long time dragging his favourite blanket and eventually end up sitting on my lap wrapped in the blanket, drinking his drink. I needed just to be there and he needed to have the confidence that I would wait for him to come to me.

(Foster carer, describing the behaviour of her four-year-old foster child, quoted in Schofield and Beek, 2018, p.167)

The "challenging" child

It is important for carers to understand that, when a child's needs are met, they may move from rejecting care to demanding it. To witness violent assaults on a birth parent or be deliberately hurt themselves can leave children very fearful, unnaturally quiet and withdrawn, or desperate to please. These feelings will have been compounded if a child perceived either of their parents as powerless, untrustworthy or violent (Cleaver, 2015).

Children may exhibit their fear of abandonment by becoming extremely clingy: 'He was terrified to be left on his own in a room and needed to be with me constantly' (Dunning, 2015, p.50). Others may react to their vulnerability and fear of abandonment by acting out, as the adoptive mother of a two-year-old boy explained:

What people saw was a "naughty boy", having tempers, swearing, hitting and kicking his parents till their equilibrium was seriously disrupted. What I felt was his terror, his fear of being lost or even deliberately left somewhere because he was so "bad".

(Rigopoulo, 2015, p.71)

Burnout can be a real problem for carers in such circumstances and, if they feel run-down, unmotivated or depressed, foster carers should be encouraged to contact their supervising social worker to work out the best way forward. Although adopters and special guardians can gain funding for therapeutic help through the Adoption Support Fund in England and Wales, this can take time. In Scotland, the Adoption Support Plan can cover additional allowances and support, or therapies that a child may need. Many find support informally, as the following adoptive father explains:

When he first came to live with us we were terrorised by Joe. We had no idea what to do with an out of control four-year-old who did not want to be loved but wanted to be in charge. We did not know what to do when the night terrors started, the sweat-soaked sheets and the uncontrollable grief. We were unable to cope. What had previously been a calm stable marriage started to fall apart...After a night on the internet we found some help. We found a music therapist. She showed us some strategies to control him. She helped us understand what was happening and how to deal with it.

(Adoptive father, quoted in Hirst, 2005, p.69)

PREPARING AND SUPPORTING THE CHILD

In preparing children to live with a new family, social workers should ensure that they have some understanding, appropriate for their age and level of development, of the aims of the placement and future plans for them. Every effort should be made to learn the child's wishes and feelings about the placement and their future, and any other significant matters. Children need to be helped to express how they feel about leaving their current carers. Preparation includes introductions to all members of their proposed new family, including any pets. They should be supported to ask any questions about their proposed carers and to express their feelings about the move. Finally, it is important that children are encouraged to bring their favourite and cherished possessions with them.

Explaining the family culture

When young children come to live with a new family, nothing will be familiar and they will not understand what is expected of them. Children will need clear messages that let them know they belong in the family, are safe, and will be cared for. A simple explanation of the forthcoming routines and events and family norms will help a young child understand what to expect.

Children's previous negative experiences of family life will influence their expectations and assumptions about their new family. When this happens, carers will need to ensure that the child understands the meaning of whatever event is causing distress and that it does not threaten their safety, as illustrated by the following foster carer:

Viv noted that Amy (4) became quiet and anxious one day when Viv and her husband were having a minor disagreement. Viv realised that Amy had previously witnessed disagreements escalating into domestic violence and that she could not predict that this would not happen in her foster family. Viv therefore took care to explain to Amy that it was OK to disagree sometimes, that the disagreement was now over and that she and her husband still loved each other.

(Schofield and Beek, 2018, p.255)

Developing self-esteem

Young children may join their new family with very low self-esteem, believing that they are "bad":

> Luca simply did not hear praise, refused to believe he was good at anything, disbelieved us...and only remembered what had gone wrong or where he had failed.
>
> (Rigopoulo, 2015, p.75)

They may have blamed themselves for their parents' interpersonal abuse, thinking that their naughty behaviour had been the trigger. Carers will need to promote positive attributes in the child through frequent praise, admiration, pride and delight:

> As for infants, particular attention may need to be given to tiny steps of progress and achievement and every opportunity taken to highlight and reinforce positives in the child's appearance, talents and development, as well as helping them to manage setbacks.
>
> (Schofield and Beek, 2018, p.211)

Supporting cognitive development

An abusive household can result in children having had little or no guidance as to how to behave, leaving them with no understanding of what is acceptable and what is not. Play is an important part of caregiving and finding an activity that both carer and child enjoy doing together may provide connecting moments that are pleasurable to both, and an opportunity for affectionate touch and eye contact (Gribble, 2016). Carers need to be alerted to the importance of play and games in enabling children to learn to co-operate, to take turns, and to savour winning while learning to cope with losing.

Some young children will have delayed speech and language as a result of not having been spoken to at home. For new carers to support their child to develop these skills, they may need the advice and help from a speech and language therapist. As one adoptive mother explained, delayed language should not be seen as an insurmountable obstacle to the development of a relationship:

> Lee's speech and language delay meant that making big gestures and facial expressions became a part of life, so there was fun in whatever we did with lots of laughter.
>
> (Dunning, 2015, p.51)

Nursery and preschool offer additional opportunities for children to explore new environments, develop speech and language, learn to co-operate and play with other children, and develop trusting relationships with adults. When children reach this stage, the challenge for carers is to manage the separation. The child needs to be confident that their carers are still there for them, even if not physically present, while at the same time be enabled and supported to transfer their trust to nursery staff. Taking a much-loved toy along with them will be a comfort to many children.

TO SUM UP

- The experience of domestic abuse may have resulted in attachment disorders for very young children. The provision of stability and permanence in the infant's life is essential for bonding and attachment to take place. Unfortunately, infants often experience a number of placement changes before finding a permanent family. Even babies are susceptible to disruptions, and young children's feelings of loss will be reinforced with every move.

- The quality of care that infants experience will affect their attachment patterns and emotional development. A change of placement means the loss of a key attachment figure. Maintaining contact with past carers can provide infants with a sense of continuity.

- To establish secure bonding and attachment with an infant is the primary challenge facing carers. To achieve this, carers must understand the infant they are caring for. For those children who have learned to shut down all emotions, much patience and a careful tactile approach will help to develop trust and form a basis for attachment.

- While some infants will appear emotionally "closed down", others can be extremely demanding and fretful. An "out-of-control" young child places enormous stress on carers and can lead to depression and burnout. When carers experience such emotions, they should seek therapeutic help.

- Contact with members of the child's birth family can provide the child with a sense of continuity. However, contact needs to be carefully managed and carers supported to ensure that it does not affect the child's welfare negatively.

- Many young children believe that any change of placement is caused by their naughty behaviour. The challenge for carers is to promote a child's self-esteem and a positive sense of self.

- To develop strong attachments, children need to feel that they belong, are safe, and will be cared for. For children to feel secure, carers should explain the family routines and culture and that they are now a valued member of the family.

- Some infants may have delayed speech and language, not having been talked to or played with while living with their birth parents. Play can provide pleasurable and connecting moments for carers and children, while also giving opportunities for learning.

- Preschool facilities offer additional opportunities for children to learn. However, they may need much reassurance to understand that attending nursery is not a sign of rejection. Many children will experience separation anxiety and need considerable support to settle in.

Chapter 8
Looking after middle years children who have experienced domestic abuse

This happened because I was bad

The chapter focuses on children aged between five and 11 (the primary school years) who have experienced domestic abuse, and the support that they and their carers may need.

These children could have lived through very different circumstances prior to coming to live with their current family. Some will have become looked after when very young and remained in their first family placement. Others, although separated early from birth parents, will have had several moves prior to their current home, a factor linked to adoption disruption (Meakings and Selwyn, 2016). Peter McParlin, a consultant psychologist and adoptive parent who was himself adopted, paints a startling picture of the numerous moves some children experience:

> *Some very young children had been moved in care up to 58 times… comparable to my own experience of 59 moves pre-adoption. My son [aged 6] also had a great many placements, as his birth family moved rapidly between cities to keep one step ahead of authorities.*
> (McParlin, 2019)

Other children may have lived with domestic abuse for several years, possibly with short periods away from home, before coming to live with their present long-term family.

PREPARING AND SUPPORTING FAMILIES

As discussed earlier, families need comprehensive preparation prior to agreeing to look after a child who has experienced domestic abuse.

Chapter 4 provides information on how children's health, education, emotional and behavioural development, identity, and relationships may have been affected.

Children in their middle years will have had a life elsewhere before joining their new family. Potential carers need to be fully aware of all that is known about what the child has gone through while living with their birth family and any subsequent placements. It will be important that they understand how such experiences may have affected the child and shaped their reactions and behaviours, and to realise that the experiences may have long-term consequences. Prospective carers need to know what help and resources are available in the future.

Accurate and comprehensive information about the child should be presented in the assessment report on the child, and the child's life story book should be a record of significant events. These will provide potential carers with the foundation to help the child understand their early life, and to respond sensitively and answer any questions that the child may ask, in an age-appropriate way.

Holding a Child Appreciation Day or a Life Appreciation Day, as discussed in Chapter 6, is an additional way of enabling prospective permanent carers to understand fully the child's history, to ask questions of those attending, and to put this information within the context of the present and future (see for example, Sayers and Roach, 2011). It enables the participants to consider how best to support the child and their permanent family by, for example, offering strategies for dealing with difficult situations or identifying additional support networks.

To promote an understanding of the child's background and what they have lived through, prospective carers, their birth children and relatives need to be included in the preparations prior to the child joining the family. This can be an extremely worthwhile and valued process, as the following permanent carer describes:

> *We thought we were all done once we were approved, we thought that was all that mattered. We never expected so much more to happen when we went ahead with Jody. It was a real eye opener hearing what other people saw in her, and how she was tied in with her birth family. It made us think about her and us, like you couldn't when it was going to be any little girl. We spent days and days seeing her social worker and foster family and going to her school and talking it all through with our own social worker before we ever met Jody. It was worth every minute we spent. When she came to live with us, we didn't have any surprises.*
> (Permanent foster carer, quoted in Argent, 2006, p.33)

This level of support and information is not always forthcoming. A survey by Adoption UK (2021) found that almost one-quarter of adopters and prospective adopters 'did not feel as though they were given all the information they needed about their child/children before they moved in' (p.30).

Joining a new family

The consequences of domestic abuse for middle years children can be various and include extreme anxiety, fear and hyper-vigilance, poor academic attainment, problematic behaviour at school, low self-esteem, faulty attachments, and difficulties in forming peer friendships. The experience of domestic abuse may also have affected children's health (Howell *et al*, 2016). They may present with a range of psychosomatic disorders including allergies, stomach and headaches, nausea, diarrhoea, and disturbed sleep – all issues that will need to be addressed with sensitivity. For some, previous negative experiences will have left them very wary of physical contact:

> *And people too easily assume that physical expression – hugging, wrestling, tickling – with children is acceptable, normal, straightforward. But no one can know what might have gone on in the past. Much better to let the boundaries stand. To keep a physical distance and wait.*
> (Reynolds with Reynolds, 2021, p.218)

Social workers will need to support carers to help children to address their feelings of loss, pain and anger. Jae Ran Kim (2009) offers families the following suggestions:

- *help your child to identify what he has lost;*
- *give voice to the ambiguity;*
- *redefine the parameters of what constitutes a family;*
- *give your child permission to grieve the loss of his birth family without guilt;*
- *create a "loss box";*
- *include birth parents and other birth family members in pictorial representations of the adoptive family tree;*
- *be conscious of how certain events – birthdays, holidays, adoption day, etc may trigger intense feelings of loss;*
- *keep your expectations reasonable;*
- *model normal, healthy responses to loss.*

Looking after a child who has experienced domestic abuse will require patience, consistency and, most importantly, the capacity to provide unconditional love. The role that foster carers, special guardians and adopters can play to improve the life chances of children is immense, and children's views about fostering are remarkably positive (Narey and Owers, 2018).

Many children will experience loss when moving to live with a new family. They may have conflicting feelings of sadness and relief when leaving abusive birth parents, and further sadness when having to move on from their foster family. Children may also be mourning lost friends, familiar schools and neighbourhoods. Each child will process their grief and loss in their own way and at their own pace. As children settle into their new homes, the grief for what has been lost may be complicated if the child believes that such feelings reflect disloyalty to their new family.

Children may not understand why they have had to leave birth or foster homes; some may blame themselves, while others may blame their birth parent or carer:

> *This happened because I was bad. I cried too much, misbehaved, soiled my diaper.*
>
> *My birth parents were irresponsible and selfish.*
>
> *What if I was kidnapped by my adoptive parents?*
>
> (Singer, 2016, p.1)

On leaving everything familiar, children enter an extremely tenuous situation, not knowing fully whether they will be reunited with their birth parents and siblings, remain in the same foster home, or move to yet another unknown family. When children experience such uncertainty they may have difficulty accepting a new family.

Maintaining relationships with significant people

A relationship between previous and current carers allows information and hands-on experience about a child to be passed on. Continuing this relationship can also have considerable value for a child. Social workers will need to stress the importance and benefits of contact when preparing families.

Relationships with previous carers

> *Fostering Services Regulations, statutory guidance and National Minimum Standards put a duty on local authorities to promote positive and constructive contact between looked after children and their parents, wider family, friends and others who are important to them, unless it is specifically decided that this is not in their best interests.*
>
> (Fursland, 2011, p.49)

For many children who have been exposed to parental domestic abuse, their foster family may have provided their first experience of consistent and safe parenting. The loss of this relationship when a child moves to a new family should be made as gradual as possible, recognising the significance of it for their emotional development (Boswell and Cudmore, 2014). When a placement disrupts, for the child 'it is another experience of abandonment', for which children commonly blame themselves (Argent and Coleman, 2012, p.57). How children react to the disruption will be related to the factors leading to it, and the way individuals respond in times of trouble. Staying in contact with previous carers can be an important factor in refuting a child's feelings of self-blame and supporting a sense of continuity.

A survey of adopters by Elsbeth Neil and colleagues (2018) found that three-quarters reported that their child had some form of contact with previous carers after they had moved to live with them. The contact could be for a short period post-placement and, in some cases, there was a long gap before contact occurred. One adopter reported:

> *We allowed him to see his foster carers so that he didn't worry or miss them – but only after six months.*
>
> (Neil *et al*, 2018, p.74)

Where contact with previous carers had occurred, the majority of adopters (74%) reported that this had had a positive effect on the child. They found that the contact eased the child's transition into their family, enabled an important relationship to be maintained, and minimised the child's experiences of loss. The account of one adopter illustrates this:

> *...it was massively important for him in settling with us ... I can't say strongly enough how the inclusion of foster carers in our life is essential.*
>
> (Neil *et al*, 2018, p.76)

One-fifth (19%) of adopters in that study reported that the effect of the contact with previous carers was neutral, and only seven per cent thought it had had a negative effect on their child (Neil *et al*, 2018).

Relationships with birth relatives

For some children, the care plan specifies that contact with birth parents will be supervised. Traditionally this is managed by monitored face-to-face contact or by telephone calls to the foster home where the carer is expected to listen in to the conversation. Contact supervisors and fosters carers have a significant role in monitoring and supporting contact and need to be clear about what is expected of them. There is a body of research that highlights the difficulties that birth parents and wider family experience during contact sessions (Ross *et al*, 2017). For example, birth parents find supervised contact makes them feel anxious and disempowered; they are immobilised 'by confusion and anger, grief and also shame ...' (Gerring *et al*, 2008, p.18). Whether or not birth family contact helps children to resolve issues around attachment, separation and loss, and identity is influenced by the pre-existing relationship between the child and birth parent. Outcomes are poorest for children who have contact with parents who maltreated them (Boyle, 2015).

Face-to-face contact can present particular challenges when carers are close relatives of the birth family as this may trigger long-standing animosity, verbal aggression, and violence directed at carers.

Technology, with the widespread use of internet and mobile phones, has changed how children and birth families keep in touch. It provides an opportunity for children, young people and their birth parents to contact each other without being monitored or supervised. Such contact may leave children confused and distressed, by reawakening old fears and anxieties; it can be emotionally abusive and undermine the placement. Eileen Fursland (2011), in her guide to social workers and foster carers on social networking, outlines the potential difficulties of online contact with family members and how foster carers and children can be supported.

Very few adopted children have any formally arranged direct contact with birth parents; indirect contact via letterbox is the most usual plan. Indirect contact agreements were in place for 97 per cent of respondents in Adoption UK's (2021) study.

Adopted children and children in care generally want contact with their siblings. This can prove difficult because the sibling networks of these children may be large, complex and fragmented. Maintaining contact can provide a source of continuity for adopted and looked after children and help to mitigate some of the loss experienced. Face-to-face contact between siblings who are living with another adoptive or foster family is more common than if siblings are with birth parents.

Although contact between siblings is more likely than contact with birth parents, nonetheless research by Neil and colleagues (2018) suggests that almost a half of adopted children had no contact whatsoever with any of their siblings, and only a quarter had been able to meet up with their brothers or sisters. The study showed that, although it had not always been possible for children to maintain links with relatives, when contact had been maintained it had generally been rewarding and helpful. In contrast, Hunt's (2020) overview of UK kinship care found that most children retained some contact with at least one of their separated siblings.

Contact enables children to understand who they are and to assist in developing their sense of identity and pride in their ethnicity and culture, as the following example illustrates:

> *After several previous disruptions, Darren, a mixed ethnicity seven-year-old child, was placed with a white English foster carer. The placement had gone very well. Darren had finally found a carer he connected with and contact was regular and positive with his African-Caribbean father.*
>
> (Selwyn *et al*, 2010, p.90)

Taking account of the child's wishes and needs is fundamental to making contact arrangements. Meeting up with birth parents, relatives or siblings may trigger difficult memories and emotions and children and carers may need considerable support. Social workers should regularly discuss the effects of contact with carers and review the arrangements on a regular basis to reflect any changes in circumstances.

Building a relationship

Children may struggle to form strong bonds with their new family, particularly those who have experienced multiple placements. The trauma of their earlier life will have left many with developmental, social and emotional difficulties. Much of the child's behaviour will be driven by a desperate need to find safety and security in what they have learned is a dangerous and unpredictable world. It will be important to enable children to discuss freely their good and bad memories of home. Children may have conflicted and unresolved feelings about their parents and need encouragement to talk about them. As discussed earlier, how children cope with the trauma they have experienced will depend on multiple factors including their age, sex, personality, self-esteem, and the support they are receiving.

Social workers should encourage carers to consider the various strategies that support the development of a positive and caring relationship with their child. These include:

- reassuring the child that any misbehaviour will not terminate their love;
- providing a routine to give a sense of control and allow the development of trust;
- allowing the child some private space to enable them to feel more comfortable in the home;
- keeping lines of communication open; and
- involving the child in family decisions.

Aggressive and violent behaviour

Perhaps most distressing for new carers is the aggressive and anti-social behaviour that many of the children may exhibit. A survey carried out by Adoption UK (2019) found that 65 per cent of adopters experienced violence or aggression from their child during 2018. Kinship carers may be more liable to experience aggression from the child they are caring for. In Holt and Birchall's (2021) in-depth study of 27 grandparent kinship carers, all reported that their grandchild displayed physical violence, often daily. The study found no apparent link between the age or sex of the child and the severity of the violence:

> *The minute that it's not her way, that will start violence which will be kicking, smacking in the face, pushing downstairs, you know, a good shoving, punching in the back, throwing things, and quite recently she's taken to biting.*
> (Kinship carer of granddaughter aged eight years, quoted in Holt and Birchall, 2021, p.9)

The impact of sustained violence from young children can be debilitating and harmful to carers' wellbeing and, unless support and help are available, may blight families:

> *My shock, as a consultant psychologist who is also an adoptive parent, is just how low the fact of a six-year-old beating you up most days for the first two years can make you feel. Not least the embarrassment of letting family and friends learn of it.*
> (McParlin, 2019)

When children behave in disturbed and disturbing ways, it is important to understand the root causes of such behaviour and the continuing legacy of domestic abuse. Carers need to be able 'to "stand in the shoes" of the child, to think flexibly about what the child may be thinking and feeling and reflect this back to the child' (Schofield, 2009, p.152). Some children will initially have settled well with their new family and emotional difficulties surface years later. The experiences of adopters of a five-year-old girl and a boy of four years, who had been exposed to domestic abuse and extreme violence, serve as an example:

> *About four years into the adoption, things became difficult with our eldest child. There were behavioural issues. We were at breaking point basically – five or six hours a night of screaming and violence, shouting and smashing things up.*
> (Adopters, recorded by BBC News Wales, 2018)

Domestic abuse can leave children traumatised. Traumatised children may be hyper-vigilant and, to reduce their stress, move rapidly to extreme anger, aggression, disobedience and attention seeking. When a child is placed with a new family, such reactions will be counter-productive. The case study quoted by Andrew Browning (2020) illustrates the difficulties carers may be faced with:

> *By the time he entered foster care, at the age of seven, L was a very disturbed child. It was very difficult for him to settle in the placement and some of his behaviours were extreme. He had severe toileting issues; he would soil himself and smear the contents on the walls. His behaviour was also highly destructive; he would rip up clothes and tear pictures from walls...His destructiveness sometimes extended to his own person, for example, tearing out clumps of his own hair. In many respects, he exhibited the outbursts of a two-year-old but from within the body of a child of seven.*
> (Browning, 2020, p.186)

Caring for a developmentally traumatised child can be draining and exhausting. Carers need to keep reminding themselves that the child's behaviours are based on fear even if they are expressed as aggression, violence and "attention seeking".

Social workers need to help carers to resist responding to such outbursts with anger and punishment because this will confirm the child's perspective of the world as an unsafe and vengeful place. Establishing firm boundaries that are understood by the child to be fair will enable the child to feel secure and less "out of control". Involving them in the rewards and consequences may help children manage angry feelings in a safer way and enable them to learn to take responsibility for their behaviour. For any strategy to work, it is important that carers remain calm and positive. Carers will need to reflect on their own emotional response to the child's behaviour.

Perhaps most disturbing is when children are cruel and abusive to carers' pets or younger children in the household. Carers will need to understand that this behaviour may be a re-enactment of what children experienced or witnessed while living with their birth family. It is thought that some 30 per cent of children who have witnessed domestic violence act out a similar type of violence against pets (Johnson, 2011). A review of the literature reinforces this, suggesting that children, usually boys, who have witnessed violence and abuse between their parents are around three times more likely to abuse animals (Lee-Kelland and Finlay, 2018). Such behaviour is likely to be a symptom of a deep psychological problem and specialist help should be sought.

Supporting an aggressive child

Children learn how to react in an appropriate manner through observing the behaviour and reactions of those around them. It is important that carers model healthy relationships with their partner, other children and friends. When there are disagreements, which are an unavoidable part of life, an important lesson for children is to see that these can be resolved non-violently. For these children, the everyday stressors, such as not being able to locate something in the home or being late for an appointment, may have been met with birth parents cursing, yelling and becoming violent. Carers need to learn to model their reactions carefully to avoid reinforcing such behaviours.

Children who have difficulty controlling their anger and aggression need help to identify their feelings before they overflow. A sound understanding of a child's background, current behaviour patterns, and the issues that trigger a violent outburst can help in calming children down. The following report by an adoptive mother of a seven-year-old boy shows how she acknowledged his feelings and reacted appropriately:

> *Anja [adoptive mother] said to him: 'I can see that you feel upset and that makes you feel very cross. I think it will help you to calm down if you sit at the kitchen table with me, and colour this whole piece of paper in green.' By doing this she avoided sending him to his room, which might have felt like rejection. She gave him a simple, repetitive task to concentrate on, which was well within his capabilities, whilst also acknowledging his feelings and that he needed help to calm down rather than a punitive reaction.*
>
> (Kaniuk, 2010, p.45)

When children's rage and anger continue over long periods, it will take its toll on carers' capacity to sustain a nurturing response (Browning, 2020). Argent and Coleman (2012) found that the majority of placement disruptions occur because of children's behavioural problems and difficulties in their relationship with their carers. The plight of Marie, an adoptive mother quoted by BBC News England, illustrates this well:

> *Marie was head-butted and kicked in the stomach by her adopted daughter as well as receiving verbal abuse. She did not want to give her daughter back but said in the end she felt there was nothing else she could do.*
>
> *'I'd been fighting it for quite a while, several people suggested that would be the best option, they were saying "no-one would blame you". But I did blame myself.*
>
> *'It took me several years and treatment for post-traumatic stress disorder myself before I forgave myself for that decision,' Marie said. 'I just didn't have a choice... I just couldn't carry on'.*
>
> (Adoptive mother, quoted by BBC News England, 2019)

For placements to survive, it is important to understand the reasons why children react in this way. If these behaviours trigger overwhelming and potentially destructive reactions in foster carers, the supervising social worker should be at hand to help. Early and timely support is key to preventing placement disruption. When such crises occur, it should lead to the "team around the child" being mobilised for the requisite expertise and services to work alongside both child and carers. To gain access to similar help for adopters, special guardians or kinship carers is more difficult and families may be left struggling to cope. For example, Holt and Birchall's (2021) study of kinship carers found:

> *Grandparents reported that they did not receive a positive response and, out of all the services where they requested help (including schools, the police, CAMHS and youth offending services), they reported that they had the most difficulty in getting support from children's social care services.*
>
> (p.13)

Dissociation and withdrawal

Although some children from violent households react to stress with chaotic and violent behaviours, others turn inwards and withdraw. These children may take a long time to share their emotions and accept comfort from caregivers:

> *He can't bear to show any emotion, so he cries when he thinks you can't see him. If you see him showing emotion he clams up.*
> (Carer, quoted in Schofield and Beek, 2018, p.89)

Such children are fearful of any emotional involvement due to their history of being constantly let down and betrayed. The trauma they have experienced may have left them emotionally numb and with an inability to connect to feelings; they lack the ability to verbalise their emotions. It is important to encourage children to try and talk about what they are feeling (Jones, 2003).

Others may have survived domestic abuse through dissociating, withdrawing into their own world and ignoring what was happening around them. This coping mechanism needs careful handling, particularly when confronted with children who don't tell the truth. As Caroline Archer and Christine Gordon (2006) explain, children who dissociate may be so 'cut off from their bodies and feelings, they don't really know what the truth is' (p.107). They suggest that being sensitive, understanding and even playful, will be a much more effective strategy than criticism or anger.

Even during middle childhood, some children will have self-harmed as a way of relieving tension and stress. Such behaviours have been increasing in recent years, reflected in the rate of hospital admissions of 9- to 12-year-olds, because of self-injury, doubling in six years (BBC News, 2012). The signs to look for include wearing clothes that cover the arms (particularly in hot weather), unexplained cuts, bruises, burns or bite marks, and blood stains on clothing (NSPCC, 2020b). Social workers must ensure that carers understand that when they have concerns that a child is self-harming, they should seek professional advice.

School and education

> *These children will mostly carry their learning problems into their adoptive placements and schools, and new parents may have to cope with a lack of basic skills, slow educational progress, communication and concentration problems and to have to negotiate with schools over reports of difficult behaviour, poor relationships with peers and teachers. New parents may have to battle with the education system over obtaining psychological assessments and appropriate school*

placements, finding socially inclusive schools and educational help and advice.

(Rushton, 2004, p.97)

Data published by the Department for Education in 2014 highlighted the educational difficulties that fostered and adopted children face. The findings showed that only 45 per cent of children in care and 49 per cent of adopted and permanently placed children achieved the appropriate level in reading, writing and maths at Key Stage 2, compared with three-quarters (75%) of children living with their birth parents.

Not all children who have experienced domestic abuse will be behind in their learning and education. As noted in earlier chapters, for some children school provides a safe environment, friends and sympathetic teachers, and a way of escaping the stresses of their violent and abusive home. Others may exhibit difficulties in their learning and schoolwork, brought on by poor concentration and dissociation. They will need encouragement and some will require specialist help in order to catch up with their peers.

Children who have experienced numerous moves prior to living with their current family (for example, fleeing violence at home, living in a refuge or changing placements) may have attended many different schools. As a result, they will have had to deal with the loss of family relationships at the same time as losing friends and known and predictable adults.

Starting a new school is stressful for any child, particularly if this happens mid-term. A new pupil must find a way of breaking into existing friendship groups, negotiating unfamiliar routines and buildings, while learning the formal and informal school rules. Children who have experienced domestic abuse and trauma may find this particularly difficult due to low self-esteem, poor social skills, and delayed learning.

Many will have come to see themselves as unloved and unlovable, leaving them vulnerable to being bullied. Their vulnerability may be exacerbated because fostered or adopted children feel "different", a situation many wish to keep secret. This feeling of separateness can increase when children are of a different cultural and ethnic group from the family they are currently living with. Some may try to counteract feelings of helplessness and low self-esteem through bullying their classmates.

Learning may also be affected by previous poor attendance and short-term exclusions. Children looked after are five times more likely to have been temporarily excluded from school compared with all children (Ward, 2019). Temporary exclusion rates for adopted children are lower, but nonetheless twice the national rate (Neil *et al*, 2018). The findings conflate both primary and secondary school data; information focusing solely on primary schools is not available.

Exposure to domestic abuse will not only have affected a child's learning and education, but also their ability to cope with frustration and control their emotions and their interaction with adults and peers. One adoptive mother reported:

> *Over reacts to incidents/comments/difficulties, is hyper-vigilant, low self-esteem, and cannot "let-go".*
>
> (Adoptive mother, quoted in Neil *et al*, 2018, p.124)

Carers of children who are experiencing difficulties in school will need support. They should work with teachers to try and help all concerned to understand what triggers the child's difficult and disruptive behaviours, and so help them to adjust. Teachers possess tremendous powers and have the capacity to make a child's life miserable or enjoyable. To support and guide a child who is displaying behavioural difficulties, an understanding of attachment and how this can affect learning is essential (Geddes, 2006).

Unlike most children who engage in classroom activities, those who have learned to avoid interactions and do not seek help emotionally or academically can be easily overlooked. In contrast, aggressive and unco-operative children will not endear themselves to teachers and often come to be identified as disruptive, rather than viewed as children who need sympathy and concern.

IDENTITY

School is also an important arena for the development of children's identity. Their sense of who they are depends on a number of different aspects, including academic and sporting achievements and peer friendships. While children who deal with stress by withdrawing will become increasingly isolated from their peer group and labelled as "loners", others who have learned that aggression and violence are acceptable ways of getting what they want may gain a reputation as school bullies. Other children may be seriously developmentally delayed and unable to adjust their behaviour to cope with school life, attracting the label of "difficult", "naughty" or "stupid".

Children who are different from the majority of the population, whether because they are from minority ethnic communities, or the Traveller community, or have a disability, or are seeking asylum, may need additional support in developing a positive sense of who they are. Selwyn and colleagues (2010) found that most social workers (96%) in their study thought that children's needs were best met in an ethnically matched placement, as the following quotation illustrates:

> *I'd want an Asian family…where both partners are Asian and ideally from Pakistan and ideally Muslim, because that would have been what he was raised as.*
> (Social worker, quoted in Selwyn *et al*, 2010, p.173)

Such an ethnically matched placement may not be possible or even desirable. Some children have complex factors to be taken into account, and for children of mixed ethnicity who may have experienced an abusive parent, the ethnicity of future carers may be an important consideration. It will require sensitivity and careful assessment of what is in the child's best interests, and listening to and hearing what the child has to say about who is important to them and where they feel safe. Carers should be encouraged to ensure that the child grows up with confidence in their own identity, and understanding and pride in their cultural heritage. This may involve negotiating and facilitating contact with grandparents and older siblings living in different households or with birth parents.

The experience of domestic abuse and controlling or coercive behaviour will have left some children feeling worthless. Low self-esteem can become acute during middle childhood, reinforced by school experiences. It is essential that carers support children to believe that they are accepted and valued for who they are, regardless of behaviour. Part of this task will be to develop partnerships with teachers to work out how best to tailor their expectations and approaches to the individual child. For some children, this may involve praise and expressions of pride. However, others may be unable to tolerate praise and any attempts can trigger destructive behaviours, as the following quotation illustrates:

> *One fostered boy, on receiving notification that he was to get an award for improvement in school work, tore it up in front of the teacher and refused to attend the prize-giving ceremony. Promoting positives in ways that are acceptable in these circumstances requires additional thought and sensitivity.*
> (Schofield and Beek, 2018, p.214)

Some carers in Schofield and Beek's (2018) study found that an indirect approach was less threatening to the child. Strategies such as talking to other people (while the child was within earshot) about their achievements, or sending the child a note or card congratulating them, could have the desired effect but feel less intrusive and risky to the child.

TO SUM UP

- Children between the ages of five and 11 years, who are looked after permanently by an alternative family, may have experienced very different placement histories. To provide the support and nurture that children need to overcome the impact of domestic abuse, carers should fully understand what is known about the child's past. To promote this, prospective carers and their birth children (where appropriate) should not only spend time with the child, but also talk to those who know them well, including teachers, social workers and previous carers. Child or Life Appreciation Days provide social workers with the opportunity to bring together these key individuals.

- Contact with birth family can promote children's understanding of their background and their developing sense of who they are. Carers may need social work help and advice to ensure that this contact is managed sensitively and children are supported, because contact can reawaken painful memories and destabilise the placement.

- Some children will have formed meaningful relationships with previous carers. When this has happened, social workers need to support carers in keeping in touch with them. Staying in contact will facilitate the move, support a sense of continuity, minimise the child's loss, and refute feelings of self-blame.

- Children will process what has happened to them and develop coping strategies that reflect their personal attributes and circumstances. Many carers will, at times, experience violent and aggressive behaviour from their child. Perhaps most disturbing is when a child attacks younger children or is abusive and cruel to family pets.

- Carers need to establish firm boundaries that are understood to be fair. Learning to respond to aggressive outbursts in a calm and non-violent manner and model healthy ways of dealing with everyday frustrations and stress is fundamental. When a child's rage and anger continue over long periods, it can deplete a carer's ability to react in a nurturing way. When this happens, it is essential that carers are supported to seek access to therapeutic help.

- In contrast, other children may react to past experiences by turning inward, fearful of any emotional involvement. Carers will need considerable patience to overcome the child's fear that, if they open up, show their emotions and accept comfort, it will result in further betrayal and abandonment.

- When children come to live with their permanent family, many are likely to have delayed language development and poor educational attainment. This may be the result of a number of different factors including poor concentration, low self-esteem, previous poor relationships with teachers, frequent changes of school, poor attendance, and periods of temporary exclusion.

- Carers will need to support children's learning and school attendance and this should be done in partnership with schools and teachers. Teachers need to know the child's background in order to understand why they may react to frustrations in unacceptable ways, but this knowledge needs to be treated with great care and respect. When necessary, school staff and social workers need to support carers in obtaining specialist educational and psychological assessments for their child.

- Many children will have developed a very negative sense of who they are. They may see themselves as failures, no good at school, disliked by their peers, rejected by birth parents, and not lovable. Those who find school difficult may be labelled as "loners", "bullies", or "stupid" by peers and teaching staff. Carers should work in partnership with teachers to identify and support any interests the child may have and recognise their achievements, however small and tentative.

- Carers of children from a different cultural background need to ensure that their child grows up understanding and proud of their heritage. This may require getting in touch with older siblings and relatives or identifying relevant links within the child's cultural community. It is important that carers develop an atmosphere whereby children feel accepted and valued for who they are.

Chapter 9
Looking after adolescents who have experienced domestic abuse

| *I thought she would slap me and it would be over*

This chapter builds on the previous two and focuses particularly on the additional difficulties that transition to adolescence may bring. The experiences of families looking after adolescents (12- to 18-year-olds) will be variable. Some will have cared for the young person since early childhood, while others will be strangers. Ian Sinclair and colleagues' (2007) large-scale study of children in local authority care found that most adolescents in long-term care entered the system as young children, that is, before the age of 11 years.

For many children who enter care during adolescence, the objective is to prevent the need for long-term care, with an expectation that they will be able to return home. The small minority for whom the plan is for permanent care are likely to have been exposed to domestic abuse for long periods, have a history of previous placement breakdowns, and experience high levels of emotional and behavioural difficulties.

Planned and unplanned moves are common occurrences for teenagers in care; foster placements for adolescents have a 50 per cent chance of breaking down (Social Care Institute for Excellence, 2004). Placement moves may include periods at home interspersed with time in alternative care, often not in the same placement. A pattern of numerous moves will have consolidated feelings of insecurity and abandonment, reinforcing notions that adults cannot be trusted and nothing and no one can be relied upon. This group could pose particular challenges to carers who wish to meet the child's needs for love, support and safekeeping.

PREPARING AND SUPPORTING FAMILIES

Welcoming teenagers into the family

When adolescents come to live with a new family, whether leaving their birth family for the first time or after a number of moves, carers and social workers will be faced with many challenges. Teenagers will have developed adaptive behavioural responses to living with domestic abuse, which should be seen as understandable responses to their trauma. The challenge of building new relationships will be compounded by the many hormonal and physical changes that young people are undergoing.

Many teenagers arrive with feelings of loss and disorientation. Those who have lived with many different families, including returns to an abusive home, may have learned to keep their feelings and thoughts to themselves. Adolescents will take longer to accept their new family circumstances than younger children. 'To cope with this, foster carers will need to manage their own expectations in order not to feel disappointment or rejection' (Coleman *et al*, 2016, p.6).

Coming to join a new family, they will once again experience being 'a stranger in a strange land' (Book of Exodus 2.22). On arrival, they will have no knowledge of the house rules and norms of behaviour or the family culture. Children will not know whom to trust and whether they are safe. The confusion experienced by a teenage girl recalling her first breakfast with her foster family, serves as an illustration:

> … and then […] the table was set and I…initially I was so, so surprised because I thought, eh-ho, we have breakfast together now and then my foster mother sat there, and I have to add that she was not working. She got up in the morning just because of me. And at first I felt very uncomfortable, 'cos I thought, eh-ho, she's observing now, whether you wash your face, whether you pack your school bag and really go to school, and so on. But that was not the reason – she simply wanted to have breakfast with me. That was so strange to me. I remember I sat down and couldn't eat at all.
>
> (Young person, quoted in Reimer, 2010, p.18)

Andrea Warman (2016) considers the significance of food and argues that it can be used to welcome and encourage a sense of belonging for children who join a new household. This is most clearly evident for unaccompanied asylum-seeking children and those from cultures that are different to that of their foster family. Finding out and preparing the food to which they are accustomed is a tangible way of welcoming a young person into the family.

Many children who started to live with a new family in their teenage years 'rapidly learned to decipher the good intentions underlying the foster carers' care and attention, and even came to enjoy it' (Reimer, 2010, p.19). When disagreements arise, teenagers may seek to provoke aggression from carers because this is a response with which they are familiar. Carers may need social worker support to understand that unfamiliar and unexpected responses to behaviour or disagreements may engender feelings of uncertainty and anxiety in children. Different ways of resolving conflict can prove difficult to understand, as the following teenager explained:

> I remember when we had our first argument, I thought she would slap me and it would be over. But she didn't do that! Instead she discussed with me and I had to defend my position. I remember, I felt that she asked too much of me and I started screaming. And my foster carer kept being silent; she just said, 'I don't know why you are screaming like that, just talk to me normally'. That was completely strange. I only asked myself, 'Why doesn't she slap me and why is she sitting there, talking to me?' And I remember, I was sitting there and I thought, 'Just slap me!' but it didn't happen. It was very strange.
> (Young person, quoted in Reimer, 2010, p.19)

An experience of multiple moves will have left children with the perception that the current home will only be temporary; they will anticipate further rejection and loss. As a result, many will be wary of investing in new attachments. Some will not wish or need their carers to act as quasi-parental figures, although they still want to feel valued and cared for. Carers should strive to understand the young person's wishes for attachment and respond accordingly. Some may want a close relationship, while others may prefer to maintain greater emotional distance. Young people's ability and readiness to form new attachments to carers is influenced by their past experiences of parenting and the extent to which they have accepted that they will remain living with the family.

Adolescents may be cool, defiant and contemptuous of attempts to offer concern and care. Carers may benefit from support and advice to ensure that they avoid reinforcing the cycle of disappointment, irritation, anger and rejection. They should consider how the experience of domestic abuse might have led the teenager to adopt such defensive strategies. Schofield and Beek (2018) point out that 'years of negative experiences will have left a legacy of suppressed emotional turmoil and cognitive confusion' (p.94). They suggest that many aspects of everyday family activities offer opportunities for shared experiences and communication. Teenagers value carers who 'go the extra mile for them, stay up waiting when they are out late and demonstrate their availability' (p.94). The challenge is to provide all of the following: 'availability, sensitivity, acceptance, co-operation, and family membership' (p.148).

SUPPORTING YOUNG PEOPLE

Staying in touch with birth family

Many teenagers will remain in touch with their parents and siblings, an increasingly easy task with the widespread ownership of mobile devices and the proliferation of social media. This development has meant that social workers and carers no longer control a child's contact with their family (Fursland, 2010; Simpson and Clapton, 2020).

When teenagers have no contact with their birth family, their search for a sense of who they are may trigger efforts to locate and get in touch with lost parents and wider kin. Teenagers may not always share their curiosity with their carers because 'that's the way he operates or because he thinks they don't want to talk about it or will be angry or hurt' (Fursland, 2010, p.17). If children express an interest in finding out about their birth families, it is important that carers talk with the child about how this might be achieved. Some may go missing from home in their attempts to find members of their birth family. Carers may need to provide considerable support, particularly when attempts to get in touch with lost family fail, are rebutted, or have unforeseen negative consequences.

Carers also need to be prepared for possible approaches from birth parents, which can come via social media or another route. If this happens, carers should be supported to explore with their child their feelings about possible contact and what they want to do. Fursland (2010) provides a list of the precautions teenagers can implement to protect their privacy online (p.53).

Young people are often concerned about siblings and trace them through social networking sites. When this is successful it may result in unregulated direct or indirect contact with birth parents. In some circumstances, this enables an abusive parent to continue to manipulate their children and use them as pawns to victimise their partner. If contact is solely with a birth mother, generally the victim of domestic abuse, it can lead to enduring feelings of guilt and confused loyalties. Teenagers who are in touch with birth parents may have difficulty in committing to their new family. They will need support in learning to manage their membership of two families and gain a balanced and realistic insight into their birth family and their feelings about them.

Contact with previous carers

Children and young people are very aware of the people who are significant in their lives, both now and in the past (Cleaver, 2000). For example, Swain's (2016) survey of 179 children and young people in care and care leavers found that most (81%) thought it important to keep in touch with foster carers they have lived with. The views of foster carers were also sought and 1,106 took part in an online survey. These surveys showed that 'one third of foster carers and one third of children and young people had been prevented from having contact and over half of the children and young people in care and care leavers said that they were not supported to keep in contact with their former foster carer' (Swain, 2016, p.17).

Keeping in touch with previous carers may be highly valued as illustrated by Steve, quoted in Caroline Thomas and colleagues' study of adopted children. Steve describes how he and his brother renewed contact with their previous foster carers:

> I've heard how they looked after me. They're quite special to me...They're still very much in the picture. I'd like to keep in touch with them...I just sort of like to know them again. Like, they still remember us. They haven't heard our voices for ages. We were just little kids' voices and [when] they actually hear our voices, feel us growing up, I just thought it would be nice to get to know them again...So we just phone them up. I enjoy phoning up...As soon as I hear [my foster mother's] voice, for some reason all the memories just flood back into my mind.
> (Steve, aged 14, quoted in Thomas *et al*, 1999, p.106)

Emerging issues

Many adolescents in long-term care have been settled for years with their current family. They may be children whose earlier behavioural and emotional problems appeared to have been resolved, only for them to re-emerge years later in more worrying ways. Selwyn and colleagues (2014) describe a rapid escalation of challenging behaviour as children reach puberty. This is illustrated by the experiences of two adoptive parents. The first is a 'mother who had enjoyed a warm, loving relationship with her son until he reached puberty':

> He ran away when he was 12, we had the police out, the helicopters and when they brought him back they said, 'We're going to see more of this boy, his attitude is unbelievable'. He just turned from this lovely little kid into this very angry person ... it was like a switch.
> (Adoptive mother, quoted in Selwyn *et al*, 2014, p.146)

The second is an adoptive mother who believed that the earlier difficulties her daughter had experienced had been resolved successfully. She was to discover that, with the emergence of adolescence, problems once again erupted:

> It settled down for two to three years but then as she got older, she started to struggle again. She was probably trying to identify where she came from and she found school and making friends hard. It took the

> *adoption to nearly break down again and for her to put herself in quite a serious situation with her lifestyle for help to finally come in.*
> (Adoptive mother, quoted by BBC News Wales, 2018)

For others, existing troubles intensified or were simply more difficult to manage as children grew up, as an adoptive father explains:

> *It's always been difficult at home. Early on he was obviously much smaller so you could pick him up, but now he's a teenager, he's much larger, he's able to push his weight around, and to restrain him you have to actually use quite a lot of force.*
> (Adoptive father, quoted by BBC News, 2017)

Although most teenagers direct their aggression towards the parenting figure, some focus their distress and violence both at their carers and themselves. Self-harming reflects intense internal pain and feelings of self-loathing. A single adoptive mother explains that not only had she had been attacked by her adopted daughter, but her daughter had also tried to harm herself:

> *There were times when it didn't feel safe for either of us. She tried to jump out of an upstairs window saying she wanted to die and I was trying to restrain her. On another occasion she went to the kitchen drawer and took out a knife and asked me to kill her.*
> (Adoptive mother, quoted by BBC News England, 2019)

Young people are also aggressive towards father figures, other children in the home, as well as family pets (Selwyn *et al*, 2014). The following adopter reported the type of violence they had experienced prior to their teenage boy leaving their home:

> *From the minute he got up to the minute he went to bed he just terrorised us ... threatening us with knives ... throwing stones at us, throwing buckets of water at us, squirting us with bleach ... the TV was locked in his bedroom ... You would be walking along and he would suddenly just punch you in the back for no reason ... You couldn't even leave the dogs with him. If they were laying in here and Freddie walked in they would leave and I've known one of them to wet herself [in fear]. [Husband] was beaten round the head with a broom. I can remember one night ... we went to bed and lay there and I can remember crying and then he came in and he punched me in the back and he said, 'Yes, you cry you bitch'.*
> (Adoptive mother, quoted in Selwyn *et al*, 2014, p.150)

As some children reach adolescence, their earlier history of having lived in a dysfunctional and abusive family may trigger flashbacks, exacerbating feelings of uncertainty and fear. As with younger children, each young person has their own needs, wishes and methods of dealing with their past experience of domestic abuse and any subsequent instability and stress. Some will respond with anger and aggression, while others will internalise their emotions. These children may cope with feelings of stress through self-harming, eating disorders and/or suicidal attempts. Both types of reaction should be treated very seriously and specialist help be sought.

A few children who have experienced childhood trauma will, in later adolescence, develop symptoms of psychosis (Healy *et al*, 2019). The National Institute for Health and Care Excellence (NICE) provides a description of possible symptoms.

> *The symptoms of psychosis are usually divided into "positive symptoms", including hallucinations (perception in the absence of any stimulus) and delusions (fixed or falsely held beliefs), and "negative symptoms" (such as emotional apathy, lack of drive, poverty of speech, social withdrawal and self neglect).*
>
> (NICE, 2016, p.35)

If a child is experiencing mental health difficulties, carers should seek social work support and discuss their concerns with their GP. When a child or young person develops symptoms of possible psychosis, the child should be referred without delay to specialist mental health services, such as CAHMS, for an assessment. NICE (2016) has developed guidance for healthcare professionals on the recognition and management of psychosis in children and young people.

A 12-year survey of 689 adopted children found that approximately one-quarter of families whose children still lived at home, most of whom were teenagers, reported serious difficulties in parenting (Meakings and Selwyn, 2016). Adopters reported violence within the family, mental illness, self-harm, offending and running away. The findings from this study are, however, heartening in that they showed the rate of post-order adoption disruption was very low – just over 3.2 per cent in England and 2.6 per cent in Wales. This suggests that, with the right support, these turbulent times can be successfully weathered.

SCHOOL AND EDUCATION

Teenagers who externalise their emotions may encounter problems in school. Their behaviour patterns may be the result of mirroring the controlling and violent behaviour observed within their birth family. The lesson learned is that violence and aggression can be used successfully to get what they want from others, such as teachers and pupils. Such behaviours are difficult to accommodate in a secondary school classroom and can quickly result in school exclusion. Carers will need to work alongside teachers and the education service to try and work out a shared strategy and a planned way forward.

Although some children have used school, academic and sporting achievements as an escape from the trauma of domestic abuse, for many others school will have posed problems. Children may have had little encouragement with schoolwork and had parents who were unable or unavailable to help them when they ran into problems. Others will have had difficulty concentrating on their academic work because they were worrying about what might be happening at home. Such anxiety may have led them to skip school in order to stay at home to protect a parent from domestic abuse or to look after younger siblings. For others, the stress and distress of living with domestic abuse will have caused them to run away from home and go missing from school.

Whatever the reason learning was delayed, these teenagers will need extra help and considerable support in order to catch up academically with their peers. Like younger children, adolescents need to gain confidence that they can achieve in some way. They are not "losers", and carers should try and identify an activity in which they are interested and encourage and support them to pursue it, however diverse it might be. Small successes can be built on to provide the young person with a sense of self-worth.

IDENTITY DEVELOPMENT

Adolescence is generally the time when children seek to establish who they are and to develop their sense of identity. To do this they need to understand where they came from and what has happened to them. For many, part of their story may have been lost, or be too distressing and detrimental for the young person to contemplate.

How teenagers see themselves will be affected by their backgrounds and the prevailing youth culture. Some boys who have experienced domestic abuse will have adopted a very macho identity, viewing women and girls as existing to please men. A girl's sense of who they are may also have been negatively affected, resulting in them adopting a compliant and submissive identity. Youth culture reinforces these views to some extent. Despite a growth in more liberal attitudes, teenage boys are still regarded as sexual instigators who have sexual drives that are uncontrollable due to hormonal changes. In contrast, girls' accepted sexual identities include romantic love and sexual relationships in the context of a committed relationship (Powell, 2010).

Teenagers who have been adopted at a very young age will have few memories of their former lives. For those whose experience in care has been complex, disruptive and traumatic, they may not understand why they are in care. They may have no coherent narrative of what happened to them and be presented with conflicting stories about their earlier lives (McGill *et al*, 2018).

Establishing a positive sense of identity is more difficult when teenagers, are adopted or cared for later in life by a family that differs substantially from their birth family. For example, when carers come from a different social class, speak with a "strange" accent, or hold different beliefs, attitudes and behavioural expectations, children can become confused over their identity. Carers will need to ensure that teenagers are valued for who they are and any differences in lifestyle are accepted.

Teenagers may experience an extra challenge in establishing their identity in a family that doesn't represent their own ethnicity. To place a child with a family of a different culture can give rise to complex issues, particularly for Muslim, Hindu or Orthodox Jewish children and young people. This is because these religions define many aspects of life. For example, David Pitcher and Shabana Jaffar explain that Islam unites:

> *...all aspects of life, food, daily routines and spiritual belief. It cannot be reduced to "race", "ethnicity" or "religion".*
> (Pitcher and Jaffar, 2018, p.220)

Although fostering services seek to place children in homes that are similar ethnically and culturally to the child's birth family, this will not always be possible. For example, teenagers holding orthodox religious beliefs will, in addition to the stress of moving in with an unknown family, require the support of their social worker to help explain their basic needs in relation to diet and times for prayer.

Carers need to assist the child or young person to understand and feel positive about their own ethnicity, religion and cultural identity. Teenagers should be supported to learn about their cultural heritage and to deal with potential racism or discrimination. The guidance provided by Bristol City Council (2014) on 'Caring for a child of a different ethnicity', describes the challenge:

> *Children in transracial placements do not have the advantage of learning about their birth cultures through everyday cues and bits of knowledge, unconsciously assimilated and passed down through the years and generations, in the same way that families of the same ethnicity do.*
> (Bristol City Council, 2014, p.5)

These teenagers have an added hurdle to overcome in developing a positive sense of identity. Without support and understanding, some may come to see their abusive parents, and by extension themselves, as less worthy than the majority of society to which their carers belong. Positive racial identity is important to the overall wellbeing of a child or young person and will need effective reinforcement. It will be crucial to value and respect a child's cultural identity, heritage and religion, and develop and sustain links with their own community.

Life story work is an important tool to assist children and young people in understanding and feeling positive about their identity. A key objective is to create a secure base in order to explore the past, present and future and to celebrate children's achievements.

FORMING RELATIONSHIPS

Adolescence is the time when young people start to form romantic attachments. This can be particularly stressful for teenagers who are unsure of their own sexuality or fear "coming out" to their carers.

The ability to form healthy sexual relationships can be influenced by the child's experience of domestic abuse and violence. Some teenage boys who have observed the extreme macho and violent behaviour of their father or father figure embrace this attitude while others fear they will repeat this pattern in their own relationships. For some teenage girls, the psychological distress of domestic abuse may have left them with the belief that extreme jealousy, control and abuse are evidence of a loving and caring relationship (Cascardi, 2016). Carers are faced with having to guide and reassure teenagers that such behaviour is unacceptable, while modelling and supporting them to develop the self-confidence needed to form and sustain healthy and caring relationships.

INDICATIONS OF RISK-TAKING BEHAVIOUR

Experimental and impulsive behaviour are part of normal adolescent development. With support most teenagers are able to navigate these challenges successfully and emerge as functioning young adults. Teenagers who have experienced domestic abuse and trauma are at greater risk of being drawn into dangerous experimental and impulsive behaviours and may not always have had the support they needed. Carers and other responsible adults need to be alert to the factors that may suggest young people are in danger of harm through their risk-taking behaviour, including:

- Being aggressive or violent, isolated or withdrawn, or self-harming;
- Frequently being absent from and doing badly in school;
- Going missing, staying out late;
- Being secretive or evasive about where they are going and what they are doing;
- Taking drugs and abusing alcohol;

- Committing petty crimes;
- In a relationship with an older person;
- Having unexplained money and buying new things;
- Spending more time on social media, making more calls or sending more texts.

Going missing

Teenagers may also cope with their distress and pain by going missing. When children run away from home, they are in great danger of being physically or sexually abused or exploited. Looked after children are three times more likely to go missing compared with non-looked after children. The increased use of mobile phones and social networking sites has made it easier for perpetrators to groom and target such vulnerable children (The Children's Society, 2011). A mother of a teenage girl explained the difficulties she experienced in trying to keep her adopted daughter safe:

> *The police would bring her in through the front door, she would climb out of her window and the police would be looking for her again.*
> (Adoptive mother, quoted by BBC News England, 2019)

There are many reasons teenagers go missing: they may wish to reconnect with birth family or punish adoptive parents or carers, while others may have been seduced or coerced into gangs for illegal practices, or sought acceptance and approval from older men resulting in sexual exploitation.

Drug and alcohol misuse

> *Cassie is 13 and initially came to live with you on a short-term placement when she was 10 years old. It was hoped that she would return home quickly, but her mother's relationship with her partner is still violent and abusive. Cassie's younger brother is placed with a foster carer in the next county and they see each other every couple of months.*
>
> *Cassie is often out in the evening with her friends, who include boys, and goes to the youth disco every weekend. You overheard her and her best friend talking about "weed" and "pills" and getting "off their faces" this week.*
> (Case study provided by The Fostering Network, 2014, to National Assembly for Wales Health and Social Care Committee, 2015, pp.6–7)

Research has shown that domestic abuse is rarely a single issue and often occurs in conjunction with parental drug and alcohol misuse and poor mental health (Cleaver *et al*, 2011; Glichrist *et al*, 2019). Many children, therefore, will have been exposed to substance misuse while still living at home. Looked after young people are more likely to come into contact with drugs; in fact, those aged 11 to 19 years have been found to have a fourfold increased risk of drug and alcohol use compared to children not in care (Meltzer *et al*, 2003).

There will be a variety of reasons why young people take drugs, the most obvious being peer pressure and the enjoyment of their effects. Other reasons include rebelling against the authorities who removed them from their parents, and helping them relax and gain relief from the stress associated with not having a secure sense of belonging. Teenagers who do not value themselves and have poor self-esteem may use drugs and/or alcohol as a way of avoiding reality.

Not all children who have been exposed to alcohol and drugs within their birth family end up using substances. A minority will be very against them, having seen the damage that they caused. Others will have grown up thinking that drug taking is normal behaviour and an acceptable way to deal with the problems they may be experiencing.

Because teenagers in care are more likely to come into contact with drugs, carers need to try to provide opportunities to discuss drug and alcohol usage and their potentially harmful effects. FRANK is a Government campaign aimed at providing drugs information and support services for young people aged 11 to 21 years and their parents and carers. Their guidance to foster carers suggests that:

> ...talking about drugs can help young people in foster care to feel more independent and in control of their lives, as well as helping them to get further support and treatment if they need it.
>
> (FRANK, undated, p.2)

It may take some considerable time to develop the type of trust that allows adolescents to talk to their carers about drugs and alcohol, particularly if the young person has only recently joined the household. However, being able to discuss issues around drugs will enable them to make more informed choices with regard to their use. To help and support young people, carers need to have an understanding of the different kinds of drugs and their effects, in order to provide accurate information.

Carers must understand that, when they suspect or know the child in their care is using drugs and/or alcohol excessively, they should talk to the child's social worker as well seeking advice from their supervising social worker.

Gangs – mixing with the "wrong crowd"

The traumatic background many of these teenagers have experienced will have left them with low self-esteem and little self-worth. They will have a strong need for approbation, for love, and to be recognised and admired for who they are. Friends and friendship groups are where teenagers increasingly look for emotional support and affirmation. Being part of a friendship group is a normal part of growing up and it is important that carers distinguish these groups from what the Government describes as:

> ..."street gangs" for whom crime and violence are a core part of their identity.
>
> (HM Government, 2010, p.10)

The emotional vulnerability of adopted and looked after teenagers can leave them open to exploitation. Adopters and carers may find that, despite their best intentions, the teenagers they are caring for become drawn into dangerous, illegal and ruthless groups, as the following adopters explained:

> *She was mixing with the wrong children, she was involved with drugs, alcohol and basically she would be friends with anybody who was nice to her so there was always a concern that she was going off with the wrong people....*
>
> *She tends to think she's older than what she is but she really is quite naive. So there's always the concern about who she's with – you've seen the stories of Rotherham and places like that – and you're concerned because she's a pretty girl and there's always the risk that if the wrong person befriends her.*
>
> (Adopters, talking to BBC News Wales, 2018)

These adopters reported that they had received little support from social services, and had had to resort to paying for private counselling for their adopted daughter.

There is considerable evidence of a link between childhood experiences of domestic abuse and gang-related crimes. For example, the report of the Children's Commissioner for England (2019) found that 24 per cent of young offenders flagged as involved in gangs were known to have witnessed domestic abuse.

Domestic abuse will have left some children with many of the issues that have been identified as high-risk factors for a young person becoming involved in gangs. These include anti-social and criminal behaviour; difficulties in regulating emotions and behaviour; physical violence and aggression; school exclusion; anti-social friendship group; and substance misuse (HM Government, 2010). Children are also vulnerable to being drawn into gangs if they have run away from home. Work by The Children's Society (2011) found that girls are more likely to run away than boys and most are between the ages of 13 and 15 years. Just over one-quarter (27%) of children living with foster carers went missing from their placements during the year ending March 2019 (DfE, 2019a).

Once involved with a gang, teenagers are at risk of suffering harm from gang behaviour, either as a victim of gang violence and exploitation, or as a result of gang-involved activities. The Government's (2018) Serious Violence Strategy provides a definition of child criminal exploitation:

> *Child Criminal Exploitation occurs where an individual or group takes advantage of an imbalance of power to coerce, control, manipulate or deceive a child or young person under the age of 18 into any criminal activity (a) in exchange for something the victim needs or wants, and/or (b) for the financial or other advantage of the perpetrator or facilitator and/or (c) through violence or the threat of violence. The victim may have been criminally exploited even if the activity appears consensual. Child Criminal Exploitation does not always involve physical contact; it can also occur through the use of technology.*
> (HM Government, 2018b, p.48)

Some children from black and minority ethnic backgrounds appear to be more vulnerable to criminal exploitation (The Child Safeguarding Practice Review Panel, 2020b). Jahnine Davis and Nicholas Marsh (2020) suggest that "adultification", that is, the preconception of black children as less vulnerable and more adult-like, may lead services to 'overlook their needs and disregard their legal rights to be protected, supported and safeguarded' (p.255).

Girls and boys experience gang membership very differently. Being a member of a gang can provide girls with an alternative, compensating family structure to those who have, for example, experienced domestic abuse (Centre for Social Justice, 2018). Girls often get involved in gangs through relationships with male members. Their role is complex and multifaceted and often results in sexual exploitation, criminal behaviour, such as selling drugs and concealing weapons, or bringing other girls into the gang for sexual purposes. The following story provides an example:

> *The gang asked her to make friends with girls her age or younger. Once she had made friends with other girls, she would invite them round to her flat where roughly 20 gang members would be waiting. Each time they would rape the new girl, and film the encounter to entrap the new girls. She was often physically forced to watch the other girls she had befriended being raped.*
> (Girl X's story, as reported by Centre for Social Justice, 2018, p.15)

Henrietta Bond's (2021) booklet is aimed at foster carers and provides guidance to help them identify if a young person belongs to a gang or is in danger of being groomed by one, and how to steer them away and keep them safe.

Drugs and county lines

County lines is a term used to describe gangs and organised criminal networks involved in exporting illegal drugs into one or more importing areas [within the UK], using dedicated mobile phone lines or other form of "deal line". They are likely to exploit children and vulnerable adults to move [and store] the drugs and money and they will often use coercion, intimidation, violence (including sexual violence) and weapons.

(HM Government, 2018b, p.48)

The advent of adolescence can exacerbate feelings of inadequacy and alienation thereby leaving children vulnerable to gang membership, grooming, and manipulation into violence and drug dealing. The report by Joe Caluori and colleagues (2020) identified that 'looked after children are disproportionately represented in county lines networks' (p.7). Although the most vulnerable are teenagers placed in residential care homes and unregulated settings, fostered children are not exempt. The report identified that they are particularly at risk of exploitation in county lines drug networks 'partly due to the impact of traumatic childhood experiences which can leave many children with a desire for forms of belonging and approval, even when they are harmful in their nature' (Caluori *et al*, 2020, p.11). Children are recruited through a mixture of grooming and intimidation:

They may be lured in with gifts of money or drugs, or by the promise of attention, belonging and status. After this, they are coerced through threatened or actual violence (against the children themselves or against their family members), sexual abuse and shaming, and/or "debt bondage" (where they are forced to repay the cost of gifts from exploiters).

(Caluori *et al*, 2020, p.14)

The charity St Giles (2021) highlights the typical signs that suggest a young person is being exploited:

- *Changes in behaviour – this could include your child going missing, changes in the way they dress and speak, verbally and/or physically aggressive behaviour, anxiety and distress*

- *Changes in friends and/or peer group*

- *Coming home unusually dirty and extremely tired*

- *Not coming home at all or being away for extended periods without reason*

- *Truancy – if your child is skipping school and you cannot account for their whereabouts*

- *Signs of physical injury – these can include injuries from assaults, concealing drugs and other illicit items in their bodies and self-harming*

- *Unexplained cash or possessions – if your child is in possession of things they normally cannot afford*

HM Government (2010) guidance on safeguarding children and young people from gang activity also provides a helpful list of the potential "tell-tale" signs of gang involvement.

If carers are worried that an adolescent in their care is being exploited in this way, they should ask questions but avoid appearing judgemental. The child is likely to be extremely scared so will need to feel supported and believe that their carer is on their side. It is important for carers to understand that they should seek the help of professionals, such as their supervising social workers, teachers, and the police, as well as other people they trust.

Risks of child sexual exploitation

Child sexual exploitation is a form of child sexual abuse. It occurs where an individual or group takes advantage of an imbalance of power to coerce, manipulate or deceive a child or young person under the age of 18 into sexual activity (a) in exchange for something the victim needs or wants, and/or (b) for the financial advantage or increased status of the offender or facilitator. The victim may have been sexually exploited even if the sexual activity appears consensual. Child sexual exploitation does not always involve physical contact; it can also occur through the use of technology.

(DfE, 2017c, p.5)

Research has shown that girls aged between 14–17 years are at greatest risk of sexual exploitation. Additional factors include 'being in care, experiencing episodes of going missing, and having a learning disability' (Home Office, 2020, p.18).

Adolescents with low self-esteem and little self-worth, feelings often experienced by children who have been exposed to domestic abuse, may be in danger of sexual exploitation. One-third of adopters in Selwyn and colleagues' study (2014) had concerns about the 'inappropriate sexualised behaviours shown by their adolescent child', as the following adoptive mother reported:

She gets on the internet and she is contacting older people, adults, in their 20s, for sex. It first happened a couple of years ago. She'd have been 14 ... first it was Facebook and it was inappropriate people and from all over the country.

(Adoptive mother, quoted in Selwyn *et al*, 2014, p.153)

Sexual exploitation often starts by someone, "the groomer", building a relationship with the child or young person that may be formed online or in person. They could be a stranger or someone known to the child. Their strategy is often to develop a romantic relationship and make the young person feel they are "special" by telling them how much they are loved and by giving them gifts, alcohol or drugs. Once the relationship has been established, the groomer will aim to isolate the young person from their family and friends and make them feel dependent, before coercing them to have sex. The teenager may then be taken to a party or gathering and expected or bullied to have sex with other men (Home Office, 2020):

> *These children are particularly vulnerable because they often feel unloved, and frankly they are often unloved, so they are very susceptible to being groomed by men who tell them how much they love them, and give them gifts. It is easy to see how such children can fall into the grip of exploiters …The young person can be left feeling deeply conflicted – wanting to escape and yet being drawn to their exploiter. When a young person feels unloved they are vulnerable to someone who says, 'I love you so much I want to share you with all my friends'.*
> (Sue Berelowitz, Deputy Children's Commissioner for England, quoted in APPG, 2012, p.12)

It is not easy to recognise if a child is being groomed for sexual exploitation because the signs are not always readily distinguished from what might be considered normal teenage behaviour. The NSPCC (2020c) provides a helpful list of typical signs that might indicate that a child is being sexually groomed:

- *Being very secretive about how they're spending their time, including when online*
- *Having an older boyfriend or girlfriend*
- *Having money or new things like clothes and mobile phones that they can't or won't explain*
- *Underage drinking or drug taking*
- *Spending more or less time online or on their devices*
- *Being upset, withdrawn or distressed*
- *Sexualised behaviour, language or an understanding of sex that's not appropriate for their age*
- *Spending more time away from home or going missing for periods of time*

Raising the issue of possible sexual grooming must be handled with great care, as the young person is unlikely to know that they are being exploited. The teenager may have complicated feelings about their groomer, including loyalty, admiration and love, as well as fear, distress and confusion. The NSPCC (2020b) encourages the following responses to a child revealing such abuse: listen to what they are saying and ensure that they understand that you are taking them seriously; reassure them that they are not at fault; explain what you will do next; and report to the police as soon as possible what the child has told you.

It is important not to demonise teenagers because problems do not disappear overnight. Disciplinary techniques must not reinforce feelings of shame and rejection. The challenge is to motivate the teenager to explore what they want for the future and support them in their quest. Adopters and alternative carers need to act as advocates and champions for the young people in their care and help them to clarify their needs and access services. Therapy for the most traumatised may need to be continued for years, well into late adolescence and early adulthood.

TO SUM UP

- Most adolescents who are living with permanent alternative families will have left their birth family in early or middle childhood. Some will have settled well and difficulties may only emerge during their teenage years. The physical and emotional changes they experience may trigger flashbacks to feelings of fear and uncertainty experienced while living with domestic abuse.

- Others may have experienced considerable disruption and change in their lives, resulting from placements breaking down and failed attempts to reunite with family. To care for a teenager who has experienced domestic abuse, which has subsequently been overlaid with a life of instability and numerous perceived rejections, will be particularly challenging.

- Children who have experienced numerous moves may assume that their current home is only temporary. They may reject offers of emotional warmth and concern, wary of forming close relationships with their carers because they fear further rejection and loss. Carers will need to be sensitive to their wishes, try to reassure them, and use every opportunity to demonstrate that they are an accepted and a valued member of the family.

- As with younger children, how teenagers respond to the emotional turmoil they are experiencing will depend on innumerable factors, both personal and external. Some will respond with aggression and anger, often focused on their female carer. Others will react to the uncertainty and stress they are feeling through self-harm, disordered eating and suicidal ideation. Both types of reaction must be taken very seriously and, when necessary, specialist therapeutic help should be sought.

- With the growth of the internet and widespread use of mobile phones, an adolescent's ability to retain or gain contact with their birth families is now effectively out of the control of social workers and carers.

Teenagers who initiate contact with their parents, separated siblings or relatives may be left with very confused and distressing emotions and need considerable support to manage them.

- For a multitude of reasons, teenagers may have fallen behind with their education. School may represent academic failure and rejection from peers due to bullying behaviour or extreme temerity. Carers will need to work in partnership with schools and teaching staff to find ways to inspire and support their child's learning. They will need to develop the child's confidence in their ability to succeed through sensitive praise and encouragement. Small successes can become the building blocks for greater achievement.

- Adolescence is the period when many children seek to establish who they are. To do this, children need to understand their background and what happened to them. Life story work is an important tool that can be used to explore the past, present and future and to celebrate a child's achievements.

- Developing a positive sense of identity can be much more difficult when children are living with families with different religious beliefs, ethnicity or cultural identity. In such circumstances, the challenge for carers is to encourage the child to learn and value their cultural heritage and support them when they experience racism and discrimination.

- Romantic relationships are generally started during the adolescent years and the experience of domestic abuse can affect how teenagers behave. Boys may fear repeating the behaviour of their abusive fathers and be reluctant to form a relationship. In contrast, some boys may assume partner abuse is acceptable behaviour within a romantic and sexual relationship. Girls, on the other hand, may believe that controlling and abusive behaviour is evidence of love and affection. Carers must seek to guide their teenage children in what constitutes loving relationships and support them to develop self-respect and the confidence to negotiate with prospective partners.

- Teenagers have many reasons why they may take up using drugs and/or alcohol. Perhaps most common is peer pressure and the enjoyable effects. Others may use them to alleviate stress, to obliterate their circumstances, and rebel against society. It will take carers considerable effort and time to develop the degree of trust that will allow their teenager to talk about substance misuse. In order for carers to help their child comprehend the dangers of substance use, they will need to understand the impact of individual substances. Carers may need to consider seeking advice from their supervising social worker or other experts.

- Although membership of a friendship group is normal during the teenage years, the long-term consequences of domestic abuse may have left some children vulnerable to gang involvement. Criminal gangs who seek to groom and manipulate children into drug trafficking and criminal behaviour will take advantage of their feelings of inadequacy and alienation. Carers will need to seek out the guidance (available from Government and charities) on safeguarding children from gang activity and the signs that would suggest exploitation.

- The feelings of inadequacy, low self-esteem and self-worth also leave children open to sexual exploitation. When children believe that they are unloved and unlovable, they are easily persuaded through expensive gifts and expressions of love that their groomer really cares about them. Carers need to be particularly vigilant for signs of possible grooming, and the NSPCC provides useful guidance. Talking about possible sexual exploitation must be done with great care as the teenager may have complicated feelings towards their groomer and what is happening to them.

- When carers are aware that a teenager they are looking after has become involved in either drug-related gang activity or sexual exploitation, they must talk to the child to reassure them that they are the victims. Carers should seek the advice of relevant professionals and make a report to the police.

Chapter 10
Support for carers and their children

The incidence of domestic abuse in the histories of children living with alternative families is considerable. Research by Neil and colleagues (2018) suggests that approximately one-half of children placed with adopters (47%) had experienced domestic abuse prior to placement. Elaine Farmer's (2009) study showed similar results for children looked after: domestic abuse was the cause that had led to half of all placements with kinship (52%) and non-kinship foster carers (52%).

All families caring for children who have experienced trauma are likely to need support at some time. Where alternative carers have strong supportive networks of family members and close friends, or have the necessary financial resources, they may be able to respond to their children's distress without the need to call upon statutory children's services. Families without such resources will be dependent on the availability and quality of local authority services and value accurate information and active support.

LOCAL AUTHORITY SUPPORT

As discussed in Chapter 6, the level of support and oversight available to children and carers depends on the legal status of the child. Looked after children and their carers should be able to receive a comprehensive package of support via the "team around the child". This is a multi-disciplinary team of practitioners established to support a child. In addition, fostering services are responsible for providing foster carers with a range of formal and informal support services. While many foster carers appreciate and are satisfied with the support they receive from their supervising social worker (Brown *et al*, 2014), they are less content with the provision of other types of services (The Fostering Network, 2021).

Local authorities no longer have parental responsibility for a child once an adoption or special guardianship order is made. In two studies, most adopters are recorded as receiving some professional support, although this generally did not include therapeutic services (Selwyn *et al*, 2014;

Neil *et al*, 2018). The majority of those services were social events for the adopted children, support groups for adopters, and special needs support.

There have recently been a number of Government strategies aimed at increasing the support and access to services provided to adopters and special guardians. These include, in:

- England: the Adoption Support Fund and, from July 2021, the National Adoption Strategy;
- Scotland: the Independent Care Review 2020 recommended that adopters should have access to the support services they need;
- Northern Ireland: the delayed Adoption and Children (Northern Ireland) Bill is expected to update existing legislation for adoption; and
- Wales: the Adopting Together Service.

To access support, families need to contact their local authority, regional adoption agency or voluntary adoption agency.

Kinship carers may also be entitled to support because they are caring for a "child in need", as defined by the Children Act 1989. A child in need is one who is unlikely to achieve or maintain a reasonable level of health or development, or whose health and development is likely to be significantly or further impaired, without the provision of services; or a child who is disabled. The family of the child is defined as 'any person who has parental responsibility or any other person with whom the child has been living' (Children Act 1989, part III, s.17: 10). Local authorities in Scotland have a similar duty to provide assistance to kinship carers. This includes advice and information, counselling, financial support and other help.

THERAPEUTIC SERVICES

There is an ample body of research that shows that looked after and adopted children are at increased risk of mental health difficulties (see, for example, Meltzer *et al*, 2003; Dejong *et al*, 2015; Adoption UK, 2020). Accessing therapeutic services for these children is a challenge facing many carers. The Mental Health Foundation (2002) identified that the mental health needs of fostered children frequently went unnoticed or were ignored. Even when carers did identify children's mental health needs, there were often barriers in accessing services, such as concerns about being stigmatised, ever-changing social workers, and long waiting lists (Bazalgette *et al*, 2015).

A UK-wide survey, carried out by Adoption UK (2020), found that when adopters had contacted their agency and 'reported they were "experiencing significant difficulties" or at "crisis point", 36 per cent said that they had only been offered universal support services...They were not offered any enhanced post-adoption support, such as specific assessments or therapeutic interventions' (p.45). Therapeutic services, particularly those provided by Child and Adolescent Mental Health Services (CAMHS), were the most frequently required services that adopters never received.

The referral requirements of the mental health service do not allow those parenting a child, including kinship carers, foster carers, special guardians or adopters, to make direct referrals. As a result, carers are dependent on professionals to do this, such as health service staff, school teachers and heads, and social workers. The high turnover of social workers and frequent use of temporary agency staff by local authorities is having a damaging impact on their ability to make referrals to CAMHS.

The Care Quality Commission (2018) recognised that in many cases children and young people had to reach crisis point before gaining access to CAMHS, and delays in getting support were detrimental to their situation:

> *I would have definitely benefitted from CAMHS earlier in care and wish I had seen them when I came into care. It would have given me someone I could express my feelings to.*
> (Young person, quoted in Care Quality Commission, 2018, p.37)

Once referred to CAMHS, long waiting lists can result in services being provided only for children with very high level needs, leaving carers to manage the situation unsupported. Even when accepted by CAMHS, children and families may then experience a long wait for any service; others may even be refused a service.

The poor mental health of many adopted children and the need for carers to gain greater support has been acknowledged. The Adoption Support Fund in England was set up to help adoptive families and special guardians access support and settle into their new lives. The Fund is highly valued but only currently available until 2025. The ongoing evaluation found that 'A strongly held belief by providers was that the Fund is leading to better access to therapeutic support and better outcomes for children and families, although they acknowledge that children's outcomes are not yet being systematically measured' (The Institute of Public Care at Oxford Brookes University, 2020). In Scotland, families are assessed for adoption support services and an adoption support plan identifies the level of support needed; adoption allowances are also made available.

In 2019, specifically targeted Lottery funding was made available to Adoption UK for a programme supporting adoptive parents 'to raise traumatised children in a therapeutic way' (McParlin, 2019).

It is widely acknowledged that the Covid-19 pandemic has had a negative effect on the mental health of many children and young people. In response, the UK Government has pledged £79 million to increase mental health teams in schools and colleges. The aim is to enable children to text their mental health support team, where a health professional will respond within an hour during the school day (Gov.UK, 2021b).

The evidence suggests that many of these children and adolescents are deeply troubled and require mental health services to overcome the trauma they have experienced. Sadly, the mental health services remain under resourced and difficult to access, leaving children and carers with nowhere to turn.

EDUCATIONAL SERVICES

As described in earlier chapters, the cognitive development and education of many children who have experienced domestic abuse will have been affected negatively and they will need additional help. All children in care must have in place an educational plan that takes into account the child's overall behaviour and their academic development and lays out a course of action to help them to reach their full academic potential. It is reviewed regularly and children, schools, social workers and foster carers should all be involved in the process.

Virtual School Heads (VSHs), introduced in 2014, have a statutory role in England, Wales and Scotland to act as an educational advocate and provide the maximum opportunity for looked after children (including those placed for adoption or special guardianship) to reach their full potential. This applies to children who are in early years provision and continues through the years of compulsory education. Government statutory guidance exhorts all relevant professionals to work together to ensure appropriate education provision for a child.

Classroom teachers can play a key role in supporting children who are permanently looked after to settle into the rather formal school environment and develop the confidence required to achieve academically. Many adopters report good support from schools, especially in relation to Special Education Needs Co-ordinators (SENCo) and pastoral teams (Adoption UK, 2020).

INDEPENDENT VISITORS AND MENTORS

The placement moves that children can experience once in the care system will exacerbate feelings of abandonment and rejection. Although many will develop trusting relationships with their carers, the diversity of children's experiences may leave some without anyone with whom they can forge a personal bond, and no one they can fully trust.

Under the Children Act 1989, local authorities in England and Wales must appoint an independent visitor for looked after children if it is considered to be in their best interests. The child must be in agreement with the decision. Independent visitors are one of the support services that some organisations provide for looked after children, for example, Family Action, Barnardo's, The National Youth Advisory Service and Coram Voice. The provision of an independent visitor enables the child to build a relationship with an adult who is not their social worker or carer, and gives them someone to look to as a role model and a source of support in developing life skills:

> *An independent visitor is a volunteer who doesn't work for social care services, and is there to visit and befriend the child. Independent visitors need to be consistent and reliable in order that children can build a trusting, positive relationship with them over time. They will endeavour to become and remain a consistent adult in the child's life who doesn't change when placements or social workers change and will at all times stay child-focused.*
>
> (Gordon and Graham, 2016, p.3)

Very few looked after children are provided with an independent visitor. In 2015, only 3.2 per cent of the total children looked after population in England, approximately 2,200 children, were matched with an independent visitor (Gordon and Graham, 2016).

Research suggests that 'natural mentoring by a sympathetic non-parental adult who is part of a young person's social network may be more effective than the support provided by a formally appointed mentor who is unfamiliar to the young person' (Cosmo and Soni, 2020, p.401).

Some local authorities and many charities in the UK run mentoring schemes to support young people, including looked after children. These provide guidance for children to cope with issues in their lives in order that they may realise their full potential. In many instances, a trained youth worker provides the support. Children are assessed to identify the most appropriate programme of mentoring sessions. Some mentoring projects aim to improve outcomes for children aged 8–15 years who have missed out on their education prior to becoming looked after. Others provide support for young people leaving the care system. The aim is to match young people with a voluntary mentor and build positive, long-term friendships in order to access useful services, pursue high aspirations, and prepare for adulthood and independent living (see for example, Family Action, undated; Catch22, undated).

There is a much greater emphasis on mentoring for looked after children in Scotland, through projects aimed at ensuring that children's educational and health needs are met (Scottish Government, 2018). Susan Elsley, in her pilot work to develop a national mentoring service for looked after children, commissioned by the Scottish Government to improve educational outcomes, defined mentoring in the following way:

> *A relationship-based approach to supporting an individual (or group) by another or others. It should include both goal orientated and social aspects of mentoring, based on the intrinsic value of relationships and the consent of the child or young person. It should be undertaken formally by trained mentors, taking into account existing relationships with family members and other informal mentor-type relationships with trusted adults.*
>
> (Elsley, 2013, p.12)

The findings from this study showed that the majority of children and young people were positive about having a mentor.

Elsely's study identified that a mentor would be an independent person who would be expected to:

- *Be an active, constant and long term person in a child's life*
- *Provide encouragement and support*
- *Support a child's voice to be heard*
- *Act in a child's best interest*
- *Challenge systems and services to meet an individual child's needs*

(Elsley, 2013, p.22)

Attainment Scotland Fund, a targeted initiative focused on closing the attainment gap between the most and least disadvantaged children, now supports the MCR Pathways project, a national charity aimed at helping to close the attainment gap and addressing social challenges for "care-experienced" children and young people (Scottish Government, 2018). "Care-experienced" is a very inclusive term and 'refers to anyone who has been or is currently in care or from a looked-after background at any stage in their life, no matter how short, including adopted children who were previously looked-after' (Scottish Government, 2021). The Pathways project involves young people and mentors being matched based on shared interests.

Research suggests that children and young people are very positive about their independent visitor or mentor and value the help and support they give them (Oakley and Masson, 2000; Children's Rights Director for England, 2012; Cosmo and Soni, 2020). Interviews with young people in care and professionals, carried out by the New Economics Foundation (2014), would suggest that mentoring and befriending could make a material difference to the lives of looked after children.

The plight of children and young people in the care system can be heart-rending. Many are isolated, marginalised, lonely, depressed and have little self-esteem. 'More than anything else they want to know that somebody whom they trust, cares about them, is interested in what they do and will forgive them for minor transgressions' (Cleaver, 1996, p.26). The New Economics Foundation review of available evidence on mentors, befrienders and independent visitors, 'suggests that this provision is severely undersupplied. Funding is fragile and opportunities to expand provision are limited' (New Economics Foundation, 2014, p.3).

TO SUM UP

- Exposure to domestic abuse and violence will have had long-term consequences for children. Many will have been left traumatised which will become manifest in different maladaptive behaviours. Those who assume the responsibility for caring for them may find such behaviours extremely challenging to the point of threatening the stability of their family.

- Carers are likely to need advice, practical help and more specialist services in order to enable children to thrive and for carers' own emotional and mental wellbeing. When children's and families' needs are not recognised and resourced, there is a risk of family breakdown.

- Looked after children and their carers should receive a comprehensive package of support from both children's social work and fostering services. Local authorities have begun to develop dedicated teams to provide post-order support to adopters and special guardians. In addition, a few local authorities are developing specialist teams to support kinship carers.

- Therapeutic services, such as CAMHS, are much in demand by carers but prove difficult to access. Barriers have included young people's fear of stigmatisation, changes in social worker, and long waiting times. These issues have been aggravated during the Covid-19 pandemic.

- The additional funding for CAMHS, provided by the UK Government in response to the impact of Covid-19 on children's mental health, is aimed to make access to services quicker and simpler.

- The education of looked after children is based on their Personal Education Plan, supported by the "team around the child" including the Virtual School Head. Many adopters may also receive support from pastoral teams and Special Education Needs Co-ordinators.

- In England and Wales, looked after children have the right to the support of an independent visitor. Children value the personal and long-term support provided by independent visitors. Unfortunately, local authorities rarely appoint an independent visitor for children in their care.

- Some local authorities and a number of voluntary agencies run mentoring schemes for vulnerable children and those in care. Mentoring is generally task focused and time limited and based on an assessment of children's needs. The majority of children viewed their mentors positively.

- There is greater emphasis on mentoring in Scotland. The Scottish Government supports and funds mentoring programmes to help improve the attainment of care experienced children and young people.

Chapter 11
Epilogue: The carer's tale

This guide has explored the experience of children growing up with domestic abuse from their conception to young adulthood. Although more often than not, domestic abuse is also associated with other forms of abuse, disadvantage and deprivation, the evidence is that the impact of domestic abuse on children is profound, traumatic and quite likely to be long lasting. Throughout the guide, the voices of children and young people from many sources have vividly illustrated this. The situation is getting worse, as evidenced by the recent increase in police referrals of domestic abuse to social services in England and Wales and the 'massive leap in calls to NSPCC's [domestic abuse] helpline' (White, 2022).

The challenge is to ensure that children living in these circumstances do not fall under the radar of intervention and that they are given safety and security and provided with the support and specialist services they need. For those children unable to live with their birth family, being placed with foster carers, adopters or kinship carers who have been well assessed, prepared and trained, and who will receive support and access to therapeutic services, is imperative. As Megan Hirst (2005), whom we have quoted earlier, has said, carers need skilled and committed professionals to be available and to work alongside them and the children.

The full extent of the task for carers and the journey they will be embarking on when they welcome "hurt" children into their families can be best understood by hearing their lived experiences. Increasingly, these accounts are being told with painful honesty by carers and children, and published and broadcast in a climate of more receptive and sensitive media (see for example, Hirst (2005), Dunning (2015) and Reynolds with Reynolds (2021)). For this reason, we conclude with the story of Luca and his family, written by his adoptive parent, Melinda Rigopoulo (2005).

INVITING IN THE STORM

It's seven o'clock in the morning and I am sitting on our balcony overlooking the valley below us, all of it hidden under a blanket of fog, with the mist rising off the river and the hills peeking out above it all. It's Sunday morning, private tea-time. This is my favourite part of the day, the calm before the storm, the time I should be using to do something worthwhile and life-prolonging like yoga or jogging or something useful like emptying the dishwasher. Instead, I sit, watch and listen. After a while, my son Luca, 14, comes upstairs and sits next to me. We've been enjoying the morning for a while in utter silence when he turns to me and says:

'Mum.'

'Mmmm.'

'I haven't had my morning hug.'

It's going to be a good day.

How it all began

My husband and I had been wanting to adopt since before we knew each other, each for very personal reasons. When we first applied for a preliminary meeting to find out how to go about it, we were told we had no chance of being matched with a child as we were too young (mid-twenties) and fertile. We decided to start our family and adopt later; perhaps the child-care experience would make us better adopters.

Eight years and two children later, we decided to re-embark on the adoption route. We welcomed the assessment process and felt it was good for us to be questioning our motivation and suitability and come out feeling either prepared or unsuitable. We came out feeling prepared. We had two lovely, healthy and happy birth children, knew friends and family who had adopted, and had a reasonable support system. I had read all the books about worst-case scenarios to really test whether we knew what we might be letting ourselves in for and to get an answer to the burning question of how this decision could affect our birth children.

We had been preparing our children for this step for some time, mentioning the topic casually now and again and discussing what this might mean for them. The usual spiel about sharing toys, being the big brother and sister, the chaos of a younger sibling, and the fact that they might not always be easy or nice, and might need the support of older siblings at times and personal space at others. I do believe that our birth children were as well prepared as any very young children can be. Our lovely and experienced assessment worker Mandy thought so too.

I must admit that I did listen in to one of Mandy's assessment conversations with my son, who was four at the time and going through his 'I'm-the-dude' phase; I knew he was eager to impress anyone who would listen with his swagger. I just "happened to be passing" in the hallway when I heard her ask, 'So how would you feel about sharing your toys with a new child?' to which he responded, 'Yeah, that would be OK' (relief on my part). 'And what toy would you want to show him or her?'

(interest) 'My knife…I stole it from nursery.' I slunk away and suspected that might be the end of our assessment and the beginning of quite different social work involvement; Mandy mentioned this conversation later and we had a good laugh. Not much phased her.

Many times over the next few years, we were asked the big "W" questions: WHY had we chosen to adopt a traumatised child? WHAT were we thinking? The only honest answer I have ever been able to give to this question has been: 'Because it felt like the right thing.' Call it karma, destiny, fate, coincidence or just pure luck. So it came about that we adopted a bonny young lad of two with big brown eyes and a gorgeous smile: Enter Luca!

We didn't know much about him at the time except that he had been removed from the family at the age of six weeks following domestic violence and a non-accidental injury severe enough to put him in hospital. He'd been with the same foster carers throughout: a very busy household with one adopted and five fostered children and several pets. We were told Luca was a happy, sociable child, a good eater and good sleeper, but that he had global developmental delay as a result of his injury.

The foster carers were very supportive and co-operative during the introduction phase, which included an overnight stay at their house to get a feel for their daily routine on a 24-hour basis as well as multiple visits and a few day trips to our house to ease Luca in gradually. They even began adjusting his diet so our food would seem less strange when he came to live with us! They truly put children first in all they did. We vividly remember a videotape (good old VHS) the foster carers had made for potential adopters, which showed Luca in the family, at mealtimes, having his nappy changed, and one particularly impressive scene in which Luca and two other toddlers were crying at the same time, along with the dog who howled in solidarity. The scene deliberately lasts several minutes without intervention, with the foster carer commenting: 'And some days, this is how it can be. So I want your new parents to be prepared for this as well as your charm.'

Coming home

I distinctly remember the day Luca was brought to stay with us for good. We had insisted that he be brought by the foster carers to whom he had formed a good attachment. The aim was to avoid the "abduction scenario" to give him a sense that this was "right", although there is no doubt that it was still unsettling, confusing and frightening for him. Both foster carers arrived in their bus with a multitude of bags filled with clothing and a huge amount of toys. In order not to upset Luca they left early, clearly struggling to hold back tears.

We have stayed in touch with the foster carers, with regular visits several times a year, and we appreciate the obvious importance this relationship has for our son. Having said that, Luca's behaviour was always atrocious two days leading up to any visit and one to two days afterwards. As much as he enjoyed seeing them, he has always found each change to his routine unsettling and seemed to believe for a long time that they might, after all, be coming to take him back.

It was the same before any trip away, even if it was only for a day. It became clear that his need for safe surroundings, safe people and predictability was so great that each time we left home, he felt completely vulnerable and terrified. By acting out, he ensured that we kept him as close to us as physically possible during any journey, holding his hand and never letting him stray near his siblings, who didn't need to do much to set him off. What people *saw* was a "naughty boy", having tempers, swearing, hitting and kicking his parents till their equilibrium was seriously disrupted. What I *felt* was his terror, his fear of being lost or even deliberately left somewhere because he was so "bad". We rarely arrived at our holiday destination short of frazzled, exhausted and relieved. Luca always took several days to acclimatise to a new place; this was hugely helped by going on holiday to the same place for ten years, so he knew what to expect. The key things about holidays were:

- **Predictability:** we always had the same or similar routine.

- **Close proximity of sleeping quarters:** our rather cramped holiday homes were great for always knowing where everyone else was, especially at bedtime.

- **Water!** We spent mornings and evenings on the beach, in the sand, in the water, returning home in the noon heat. The children played together or each at their own developmental level whilst we had them all in our field of vision and could take turns playing with them or sleeping! I may even have read a page or two of a book before one of them spotted me and came to relieve me of my "boredom": 'Poor Mummy, she's all alone. I'll play with you, Mummy!' Who could resist!

Settling in

The early days, weeks, months and even years were hard work and extremely demanding, including, of course, for our birth children, especially my elder daughter, Theresa, who at nine seemed to think her role was one of co-parenting and co-responsibility for this cute but unpredictable little brother she had been blessed with. We did not see this straight away, but when we recognised the dynamics, we explained that she should not feel responsible for Luca but just enjoy him. Of course I was grateful for any support, but when she'd had enough or simply wanted to be on her own, I sent her to do her own thing and leave him to me. Years later, I asked Theresa whether she had ever resented Luca. Her response was healthy and insightful: 'Sure I did. I resented not being the centre of attention or having enough money to go on fancy holidays like some of my friends. But I felt the same about Alex (her birth brother) too, so it had nothing to do with adoption, just with sharing!' We had a good laugh and I hug her in my mind every time I think of this conversation.

Alex, aged seven, was more chilled about the added chaos to his life. He would quite happily lie on the floor and play with Luca after school or spend hours trying to synchronise the music on the multitude of electronic toys he'd brought with him. The cacophony continued for weeks before I began to feel my sanity slowly slipping away. Miraculously, the batteries on all the toys gradually began to give out and we never seemed to remember to buy new ones. It transpired that Luca actually preferred the old-fashioned cuddly toys (non-talking or -singing!), wooden building blocks, toy cars with his very own rendition of motor sounds, and the pleasantly taciturn dollies, all of which we had in abundance from our older children. He also loved stringing large beads (thank you IKEA!) and decorating us with the results or screwing together huge plastic cubes with oversized nuts and bolts to make little seats and boats in which his dolly-babies could go out and see the world. We had collected so many electronic toys, that eventually we had a car boot sale to raise funds for the school's special needs department; one that Luca used himself in the years to come!

Once Luca had settled in he began catching up on his motor skills at an astounding pace! His speech also improved steadily under our family's "speech therapy"; we talked to him, commented on what we were doing, actively encouraged him to repeat words for objects but didn't force the issue and read to him LOTS! Television and computer time was non-existent. It would be fair to say that this approach is hard work, but we did also have our older children as eager story-readers and role models and children do seem to learn best from other children! All of this was worth it to see Luca coming on so well; a consolation for the fatigue that set in every single evening once all the children were in bed.

Behaviour

Luca had developed a very clever strategy for dealing with his anxiety and fear of anything new or unknown. Within his very limited vocabulary, the flavour of the season was clearly the word 'No!'. He used this in response to any and all questions or suggestions and after some initial bafflement, we soon learned to read between the lines.

Offered peas or pasta, his clear answer is: 'No.'

My husband, incredulous in view of the speed with which both previous portions have been devoured, puts more on his plate, which vanishes instantly. An offer of pudding gets a clear: 'No'. Having gained in wisdom, we simply place the pudding before him and he finishes three portions.

Pointing out the swings in the park, Luca clearly states 'No', hesitates, then runs towards them with a huge smile of anticipation.

'Do you want to stroke the kitten?' 'No.'

'OK, I'll put her down then.' 'No!'

It became clear that 'No' was Luca's way of stalling for time whilst he tried desperately to discern:

- what it was he was being asked or offered and whether it was safe. In case it wasn't, 'No' would keep him on the safe side;
- whether this was something he could do, or whether he was bound to fail. 'No' protected him from failing by protecting him from trying.

It was amazing over the years to see what a huge difference it made to Luca's self-esteem simply to be able to do normal things for himself that other children take for granted. The road to success, however, was very rocky and frequently interrupted by major temper tantrums at the first sign of failure. Dropping his spoon onto the floor by accident produced a look of shock and alarm on his face that was quite out of proportion to the event. We learned that we had to be extremely quick not only to retrieve the spoon but to distract him at the same time; otherwise, this tiny mishap brought a major meltdown in its wake. Luca would shout and scream, cry and throw other items onto the floor deliberately and was often so beside himself that we had to physically remove him from the table and sit with him in a quiet corner until he calmed down.

We obviously had experience of toddler tantrums, but there was a different quality to Luca's rage. It was painful to see him so very angry with himself for failing at any simple task, and he remained unreceptive to reassurance or praise for years. Luca simply did not hear praise, refused to believe he was good at anything, disbelieved us, his teachers and others that he had done well, and only remembered what had gone wrong or where he had failed. It took many years of constant and continuous positive reinforcement and refocusing on his strengths, achievements and talents before Luca ever began to believe he could be good at anything.

When it came to learning to ride a bike, Luca steadfastly refused to believe that he could, and every time he sat on the patient apparatus, he shrieked, 'No, I can't do it!'.

We calmly repeated countless times, 'Luca, you've already done it. I've seen you. You cycled all by yourself. And I'm here to catch you if you fall.' Many months later, and in the customary stooped position of parents administering cycling support, we watched our son hop onto that bike and whizz off. EVERYONE was over the moon over his success and we have had many similar cycles (no pun intended) of skill attainment since.

For Luca, the basic problem with attempting anything new is:

- the complete lack of self-confidence that he might succeed;
- the utter lack of frustration tolerance if he doesn't succeed immediately.

Anything new for Luca is subconsciously perceived as a potential threat. Instead of waiting to find out what it is he is meant to be doing, he gets restless, stops listening, and tries to find a way out. This behaviour is typical of children who have been traumatised by domestic violence; they may have been neglected or threatened, abused or frightened, or they may have sustained accidental or non-accidental injuries in response to their own signals of needing attention. As a newborn infant, Luca had probably experienced that whatever he did, it might be wrong and trigger negative or violent reactions from those adults closest to him; the ones he looked to for care and protection. As a result, he was continuously on edge and watchful. He only relaxed when he felt very safe; it must be exhausting to go through life on the constant lookout for danger!

As foster carers or adoptive parents, we often do not have enough information about our children to know whether or not domestic violence is part of the picture, or whether the difficulties our children display are the result of other issues, such as learning or attachment difficulties, ADHD or physical injury. We had very little information about exactly what had gone on in the birth family prior to Luca being taken into care. We knew that there had been violence and that social workers were afraid to go into the house. It was likely from the history that there'd been violence in the birth family before the documented incident of injury. This would presumably have involved shouting, screaming and fear in Luca's birth mother. It is highly likely that this kind of stress in the home environment prevailed even before Luca was born, when he was in the womb. Non-accidental injuries rarely occur in isolation. It is sadly more common that minor episodes of violence escalate over time until the results become too obvious to hide, as in Luca's case.

Long-term continuous or recurrent exposure to high levels of stress hormones, whether before or after birth, interferes with the connections that are formed between the nerve cells within the brain. Once we understand how trauma may have affected a young brain's hard-wiring, the behaviour we see in our children suddenly makes perfect sense. It's all about survival.

A child's brain is programmed to achieve personal safety or survival. In response to trauma caused by domestic violence, the child is left with two alternatives to secure his or her safety:

- **Fight:** Rages that can be triggered even by minor events, or a low threshold for stress in general, resulting in major meltdowns even years later.

- **Flight:** Dissociation, switching off from reality, often witnessed as daydreaming, freezing or trance-like states.

Luca's behaviour seemed irrational to others, yet it was elementary to survival from his perspective. Having been neglected and left unfed and uncared for, subjected to shouting, threats and injury, his brain had linked his carers' violent behaviour to his own display of distress; whenever he cried he was either ignored or hurt. So later, when he felt uncomfortable or frightened, or was met with demands he felt he could not achieve (like learning something new), when he failed at a task or didn't know what was coming next, he took control over this frightening situation with rage. Children who have experienced trauma before they had speech literally have no words to describe what happened, just feelings. An infant's tools to protect himself are very limited. If the stress, pain or fear becomes unbearable, some infants simply take themselves away, switch off mentally and dissociate from what is happening. Luca had learned this survival tool as well.

As a young child, Luca's rages could be triggered not only by dropping a spoon, but also by having a picture go "wrong", sensing anxiety or irritation in someone close to him, or by having to wait for something to happen, which he found unbearable. We developed seismic sensitivity to when he was about to blow and needed distraction, reassurance or a walk round the block. Like Luca, we also were in continuous alarm mode. This is exhausting and can secondarily traumatise the whole family.

When Luca was in a rage he could rarely be soothed, merely contained. We took him to a safe place, stayed by him, held him if he let us, and stuck it out. Talking in a low voice had a soothing effect and we often sang softly to him; gentle children's songs and lullabies, folk songs, blues, country, soul, we tried them all and they helped not only to bring him back down to earth, but also to control ourselves whilst being hit, scratched and kicked. If the cat walked in, he stopped almost instantly; her purring and the softness of her fur soothed him and he did not want to scare her off. Unfortunately, being a cat, she didn't come to order, but ran for it when Luca was too loud! Once calm, Luca immediately forgot the incident and acted as if nothing had happened. He had spent all his energy and played quietly for the rest of the day. Another approach that worked well was getting him out of the house and doing something physical like raking leaves, taking a walk, riding his bike. Often, it was my husband who channelled Luca's anger into something constructive by spending time with him and replacing anger, fear and negativity (*I am bad*) with a sense of achievement (*I am helpful and strong*).

EPILOGUE: THE CARER'S TALE

In his rages Luca very often pushed us to the limit. It became increasingly clear that what he was trying to do was push us over the limit. He was so afraid of what might happen that he tried to provoke the violence he feared most, so he could relax when the worst had finally happened. On the occasions when he did get hurt at school or at home, even if by accident, his indignation and sheer distress at the fact that 'you HURT me!' was way out of proportion to the actual mishap. It was the existential insult to his very soul that distressed him, not physical discomfort.

Self-injuring behaviour began early with head-banging, slapping and pinching himself and threatening to throw himself out of the window. When he was nine, Luca walked across the room, opened the window of his second storey bedroom and sat on the window-sill threatening to jump. Deliberately keeping my distance I kept his attention on me: 'I don't think you really want to jump, you want a hug.' Pure auto-pilot, but I could see in Luca's eyes that the fact that he knew that I *knew* he wasn't really going to jump (did I?) gave him the sense of security and of being held that he had lost at that moment. As he shut the window, he turned to me and said, 'Why are you looking worried? You know I wouldn't really jump.' He went back to his playing and I was left feeling physically sick.

As a result of his trauma, Luca has extremely fine antennae. He will walk into a room and immediately sense if there is discord in the air, even if it has nothing to do with him directly. This state of hyper-arousal is part of his survival strategy and also his greatest vulnerability. To this day Luca is constantly looking for danger from others. He has never liked big groups, because he quite simply cannot keep abreast of everyone's emotional state at the same time, so his DANGER signals remain on. At 14, he is afraid of drugs and alcohol due to a fear of losing control; some youngsters do end up on drugs and alcohol because the stress of being constantly on the alert becomes unbearable. Luca's music teacher once told him to 'simply relax and enjoy the music'. Luca spontaneously responded: 'I can't relax. Ever.' The saying 'You snooze, you lose' has a very real and terrifying meaning for Luca, even after a decade of experiencing love, safety, personal success, popularity with peers and a sense of safety at home. To him the world outside truly is a jungle.

Luca is preoccupied with catastrophes, death and flashing lights and is obsessed with ambulances, rescue helicopters, police cars and accidents. Scenes from films or television at a friend's house cause him nightmares for weeks. He is preoccupied with the notion that a burglar might enter through his second storey bedroom window at night and hurt him. My pointing out that this burglar would need to be a combination of Spiderman and Flat Stanley is acknowledged by him rationally, but the window stays shut!

Luca has always had an intolerance of high sensory input, be it noise, light, lack of personal space, strong smells or spicy food. Particularly in the early days, one of his coping strategies in times of severe stress (loud classrooms, shopping malls, funfairs, bright lighting in shops) was to take himself away to somewhere else. You could see that he was not part of what was going on around him but focusing on one small activity to the exclusion of the rest of the world. The extreme form of this dissociation is absolutely heart-breaking to witness. When Luca was about six, another boy known for *his* rages, planted himself directly in front of him, and proceeded to shout at Luca so loudly that it could be heard across the playground. I watched Luca's facial expression change from sheer terror to a vacant stare and a frightening pallor in response to this overwhelming situation. I ran over and held him in my arms; he sat on my lap as stiff as a board, shaking like a leaf. It took several minutes for him to recover and he refused to go anywhere near the other boy for weeks.

Education

At school, Luca has never ever had his rages. He's always said, 'I wouldn't dare. I'd be afraid of what might happen.' He was and is compliant, polite, friendly and very eager to please the teachers. He is, however, easily distractible and cannot take in the content of the lessons if anything new is introduced, such as a new teacher, a change of classroom or, as has unfortunately been the case for him, a change of schools. He is so busy studying the faces and behaviours of the teachers and other students to check that he is safe and that no one is suddenly going to lose their temper or do something unexpected, that he simply cannot take in the lessons as well. We have fought long and hard to find an inclusive school to meet his special educational needs, which are linked to his emotional state. He is now in a class in which he feels safe, happy and above all, normal. He is achieving good results with support, has friends and teachers whom he trusts, and he is less easily traumatised by unexpected events. He is now secure enough to actually learn, and he loves it (well, except maths...).

With his strong sense of justice he'll stand up for others, but needs constant reassurance that when someone does something wrong, there will be consequences. To this day, he needs this in order to feel safe. When he and a friend were recently approached indecently by an adult, his friend was too embarrassed to tell his mum about it. Luca told him 'My mum said that's wrong and that I should always tell an adult.' So they did; the advantage of black-and-white thinking. Wrong is wrong and must be righted. With Mum on the case, I can relax and trust I am safe.

What's it like for the others?

So what is it like for the adoptive family of children who have witnessed or experienced domestic violence?

For the parents:

- It is draining and potentially traumatising. You need strong support systems and a partner or close family to share the front line with you.

- Be prepared to doubt your parenting skills every day for years before you begin to see the fruits of your love, determined support and refusal to give up your child to its demons. Be a good enough parent, but be aware that there will be times when you will need to be super parent – and you'll do it too!

- We all know we cannot undo the hurt someone else has done to our child. But we still try and the children know it. It is immensely reassuring to know you have Mum or Dad on your side, no matter what.

- Parenting these children takes you to your limits and shows you things about yourself you might rather not know, but it will also unearth skills and a capacity for love that you never knew you had in you.

- You really MATTER to your child. If your child is an angel for everyone else and lets rip at home, this is because he/she feels safe enough with you to do so! And if he/she lets rip at school in order to get sent home to you, maybe this is telling you something too!

For the siblings:

Living with a traumatised sibling is hard. We often worried about the effect the adoption might have on our birth children. Did they feel they'd grown through the experience or missed out? Our older two were well adjusted, self-confident and securely attached children with good wits about them, good social skills and plenty of interests and talents. But they still needed their mum and dad. Being older, they occasionally wanted to do teenage things and have uncensored teenage conversations without the constraint of having a younger sibling around. They also needed to have one-to-one time with each of us and they needed to know that they mattered just as much, even if they were (usually) not as loud as their little brother! Through it all, neither of them has ever truly questioned our decision to adopt and when asked, they each lay claim to two siblings, no distinctions made.

I regularly accompanied my older children to sports competitions and national events, leaving Luca with my husband and vice versa. We all enjoyed that! When it became too much for Theresa, she'd leave to do her own thing, which was OK. Now she comes back from uni and looks forward to seeing Luca, being a part of his life and writing and receiving fantastic letters! Luca enjoys doing "big brother" things with Alex, like trips to the skate park, bike tours, discussing the football scores and debating the merits of pop songs on the radio.

I asked Theresa to write down her memories about living with Luca:

Some of the first memories of living with him are how he loved to listen to the cat's purring; he would put his ear to its stomach, seemingly for hours. The feather duster and the vibration of the hoover were also favourites. As a ten-year-old, I didn't really understand why the tiniest things, like dropping his knife at dinner, would result in violent tantrums. To me he was an incomprehensible package of endearment, gentleness and sudden aggression. I was still a child and did not have an effective method for making sense of his behaviour, so I think I often reprimanded him harshly, which led to him hitting me every time I came into the room as all he expected from me was negativity. At the time, I was too overwhelmed to reflect on it much but in hindsight it saddens me that I did not possess the necessary insight into what he needed from me. His relationship with the world has, I think, improved over the years; however, it is clear that he will always bear the scars of his trauma. Helping him to cope with these in order to enable him to lead a fulfilling life remains a constant test alongside enjoying his company and wonderfully kind, humorous nature.

Survival tips for siblings:

- It's great to help Mum and Dad, but don't become an additional parent. You're a kid, enjoy it!

- Have hobbies, enjoy your friends.

- Try to accept your sibling as he/she is and don't judge the behaviour as you would that of a friend. Remember he/she has been hurt; when you feel hurt, you sometimes feel angry at the world and often end up hurting the people closest to you. Don't take it personally. It's probably not you, but you can help by giving your sibling space and having fun with him/her when he/she has calmed down.

- Grab Mum or Dad on their own and play a game, work in the garden, go shopping or to the cinema, or whatever!

Support, social services and friends

'Oh, how wonderful of you to adopt!' Whenever I heard that sentence I knew that I could expect no surprise visits for coffee from that person nor be invited to their summer barbecue. It was this awe and insecurity that kept many people away. My husband's memory of those early years is *isolation*. Our great thanks go to those friends who were there when we needed them, no questions asked. Whether offering to take one or more of our children along on outings or inviting us to a social event, we love you for it!

Despite being a high-risk placement, we were never seriously inconvenienced by visits from social workers. The children's worker came twice and then left the department. The replacement came 12 months later and hadn't even bothered to read the file before she came, which was a complete waste of our afternoon. Every bit of support had to be fought for by us, including the cost for Luca's therapy, which social services should have known would be on the horizon for us.

So finally, if you are brave enough to take on an emotionally hurt child, here are some tips.

Tips for settling in your child

- **Take it slowly** and be prepared to stay at home with a pre-school child for at least one year. This year of bonding with your child and giving him/her a sense of a secure space in your family is time very wisely spent in view of the years ahead.

- **Spend lots of time with your child.** Don't let the TV have all the fun of entertaining him/her!

- **Don't send a young child to nursery soon after their arrival** unless it is one they already know well and feel secure in. Children need to feel safe in your home and family before they can feel safe elsewhere.

- **Be prepared to keep school-age children off school for a while if they need it.** The emotional security that a child gains through time spent at home after a turbulent history and a recent major move will help them to be able to cope at school. Sending a child to school too soon and having to pick them up three to five times a week when the school calls you is not nice for you or the child. A new school means new surroundings, new teachers, new rules, new kids, all before we get to the curriculum! This is real stress for an emotionally wobbly child.

- **Keep the sensory input low and soothing.** Children don't need computers, TV or electronic toys. Try them with soft toys, toys made of natural materials, cushions, feathers, a sandbox, construction toys, and if possible a swing or a rocking chair – rocking soothes.

- **Reconsider before inviting all your friends**, the neighbours, Great Aunt June and her three dogs and the rest of your family over for a **welcoming party**. Your child is almost certain to be utterly overwhelmed by this. We had our first celebration a year into the placement and invited a few close friends who came and went throughout the course of a Sunday. It was relaxing and the children could play or join in as they chose.

- **Be prepared to work part-time** if your child isn't settling down after the first year. The time you spend with your child now is healing time that will reward you later!

- **Things DO get easier**, although it may take years.

Survival tips for parents

- **Expand your resources** using books (*The Boy who was Raised like a Dog*, by Bruce Perry, is a must!), or attend talks on trauma/attachment, and the educational needs of traumatised children.

- **Get help if you need it** and don't be afraid to ask; this includes therapeutic support for yourself or your child.

- **Get a life! Don't succumb to isolation.** Pursue a hobby, join a choir, meet up with a friend, get your nails done, go shopping or whatever turns you on. Once a fortnight is better than never. Invite someone over and don't tidy up!

- **5–15 minutes at the end of each day** or in between crises to have a coffee with your feet up is worth far more to your sanity than going out for a meal once every two months, when you are likely to fall asleep over the soup.

- **Don't lose sight of your partner or support person.** You are each other's best allies! Give each other breaks and be open about feeling overwhelmed and defeated when you do. Look at it this way: if you weren't doing such a grand job, it wouldn't feel so exhausting!

- **Stay true to yourself!** Be prepared to make compromises, but don't lose sight of your dreams.

- **ENJOY your children.** There are so many funny things that happen every day. Try to remember them, review the day at bedtimes (only the good things!) or keep a diary.

- **Reserve quality time for each child** already in the family.

- **If you have no family nearby, adopt a granny!** You will need your support system.

My son recently snuggled up to me and said: 'Ah, my mummy! I feel safe with you.' After all the things I am certain we did wrong, we must somehow have been *good enough parents* after all. This keeps us going!

I started with Luca and will let him finish. At 14, he is still easily uptight, but practises relaxation on his mum; from the depths of the armchair across which he is sprawled, his response to my admonitions regarding the state of his bedroom generates a drawn-out 'Aw, Mum, it's fine. Just chill!'

© Melinda Rigopoulo, 2015

This account was first published by BAAF in 2015, in *Parenting a Child Affected by Domestic Violence*, by Hedy Cleaver.

Appendix
Resources for practitioners, carers and children

This appendix provides information about resources that may be helpful and covers the following issues;
- Making the move to a new family
- Support for carers and the children of carers
- Attachment programmes
- Preparation courses
- Placing siblings – together or apart
- Life story work
- Mentoring
- Behavioural change – therapeutic services
- Traumatised children
- Self-harm
- Drugs and alcohol
- Gang involvement
- Criminal exploitation of children
- Sexual exploitation of children

The list is by no means exhaustive and presents only a selection of organisations and publications. The Appendix concludes with additional relevant CoramBAAF publications.

MAKING THE MOVE TO A NEW FAMILY

Publications for practitioners

The UEA Moving to Adoption Model
Neil et al's research-based guide (2020) aims to support adoption social workers, fostering social workers and children's social workers when children move from foster carers to adopters. The model outlines three key stages of the move:
- Getting to know each other
- Making the move
- Supporting relationships after the move

Each stage is described in terms of its aims and objectives. The principles that guide them are explored and examples provided.

Moving to Adoption: Using the UEA model to help children move from foster care to adoption
This guide, by Mary Beek et al (2021), introduces the above practice model for supporting children's moves from their foster family to their adoptive family. Drawn from a two-year practice development project, the model promotes sensitive

practice that is responsive to the child's needs.

Publications for use with children

Me and my Family
A colourful book by Jean Maye (2011) designed to help adopted children and their families to get to know each other. Through writing, drawing and other activities, children are drawn into exploring and recording the changes in their lives as they move to their new family and learn to live together.

Moving Pictures
A picture book by Hedi Argent (2012) for social workers and carers undertaking direct work with children aged four and above, to help children explore ideas of moving and permanence and spark discussion of their wishes about moving to a new family. It includes a CD-ROM with line drawings, illustrating various aspects of the move to permanence, for children to colour in, and guidelines for use.

SUPPORT FOR CARERS AND CHILDREN OF CARERS

Carers will need considerable support when offering a home to a child who has experienced domestic abuse and trauma. Existing birth children will have to share their homes and parents with new arrivals who may come with varying issues and needs. An adjustment period as well as significant parental attention may be required to help the newly arrived children settle in to their new family. Children of carers may well feel angry and resentful at having to share toys, space and their parents' love and attention.

Organisations

Adoption UK
Offers support to adopters and special guardians UK-wide. In addition to a library of resources, Adoption UK runs community groups for adopters and special guardians and holds regular support and training events, including one titled *Domestic Abuse and the Adopted Child*. Adoption UK also provides advice and suggestions from their forum users for helping birth children cope with their new adopted sibling/s.
www.adoptionuk.org

Adoption Coast to Coast
Provides information to adopters on the impact adoption may have on birth children, including a video featuring children describing their experiences.
www.adoptioncoasttocoast.org.uk

CoramBAAF
An independent membership organisation for professionals, foster carers and adopters, and anyone else working with/looking after children in or from care, or adults affected by adoption. It is a successor organisation to BAAF. It publishes resources for carers as well as for use with children in foster, adoptive and kinship families, and offers training courses for carers and adopters.
www.corambaaf.org.uk

Family Action
A UK charity with a subscription service, available to all local authorities, which allows special guardians and the professionals supporting them to access online information and guidance, a telephone helpline, and training events.
www.family-action.org.uk

Family Futures
A not-for-profit, independent adoption and fostering agency in London that specialises in providing assessment and treatment services for children who have been traumatised or have attachment difficulties.
www.familyfutures.co.uk

The Fostering Network
Provides an essential UK-wide network bringing together everyone who is involved in the lives of fostered children to ensure that these children and young people experience stable family life. It supports foster carers to transform children's lives and works with fostering services and the care sector to develop best practice.
www.thefosteringnetwork.org.uk

Kinship (formerly Grandparents Plus)
Runs support groups for kinship carers. These allow carers to share, support each other and exchange advice and coping strategies.
www.kinship.org.uk

PAC-UK
Part of Family Action, it provides a number of services for adopters and other permanent carers. It also has an advice line available on 020 7284 5879 (London office) and 0113 230 2100 (Leeds office) providing advice on all aspects of adoption and other forms of permanent care.
www.pac-uk.org

We Are Family – adoption support community
Adoption charity in England that seeks to connect people so that they can build strong relationships and support networks. It provides resources and information including webinars of relevance to prospective and approved adopters.
www.wearefamilyadoption.org.uk

Various voluntary adoption agencies and regional adoption agencies offer support of various kinds, including therapies, support networks and parenting skills groups for adopters.

Publications for carers

Kinship Care Guide for Wales
A guide developed by Children in Wales (2014) to offer information to kinship carers. 'It aims to offer a step by step guide through the process of becoming a kinship carer, signposting the services that can offer advice, support and assistance' (p.2).

We Are Fostering
A life story workbook by Jean Camis (2003) that helps children in the family who will be fostering to understand themselves and their place in their family, along with what it means to be adopted or fostered. Working through this book will help prepare children of carers to welcome new arrivals into their homes and lives.

Training programmes for carers and practitioners

Fostering Changes
A course developed by Karen Bachmann *et al* (2019) that provides practical advice and training for foster carers to develop skills in managing challenging child behaviour and forming positive relationships with their foster children. It is designed for use with carers looking after children under 12 years. Evaluation of the course shows improvements in children's behaviour and carers' confidence.

CoramBAAF Training
Offers a wide range of courses, including on running panels; making good assessments; life story work; planning for permanence, and more. Each can be specifically tailored to meet the needs of individual organisations. All courses reference the latest legislation, research and good practice, and are supported by adoption,

fostering, legal and health specialists, publications and an information archive.
www.corambaaf.org.uk

Social Care Training Solutions
Provides interactive home-based courses for foster carers, adopters and supervising social workers. Courses cover a range of subjects, including Life Story Work, Secure Base Model, Understanding the Impact of Bullying, Attachment Disorder, Trauma-Informed Practice, and PACE (stands for Playfulness, Acceptance, Curiosity, Empathy and is a model of care that helps support and form secure attachments with children).
www.socialcaretrainingsolutions.com

ATTACHMENT PROGRAMMES

Implementing the Secure Base Model
The Secure Base Model, conceived by Gillian Schofield and Mary Beek (2014), focuses on interactions between caregivers and children. Through a positive framework for therapeutic caregiving, children and young people are helped to develop greater security, confidence and competence and build resilience.

With children firmly in focus, this open course, run by CoramBAAF, provides an introduction to the Secure Base Model and related tools which enable practitioners to assess prospective carers' and adopters' parenting capacities and support needs.

Note: Secure Base training is also offered by other training providers.

Nurturing Attachments Training Resource
A group-work programme designed by Kim Golding (2013) to provide guidance to adopters, foster carers and kinship carers. It is based on attachment theory and an understanding of the impact of trauma on children's development. It provides a set of ideas for therapeutically parenting children. It is structured into three modules each with six sessions.

Foundations for Attachment Training Resource
Also by Golding (2017), this is a briefer, complementary intervention of six sessions, organised around the model of the *Nurturing Attachments* programme. It is designed specifically for those caring for children whose capacity to connect emotionally has been compromised as a result of attachment problems, trauma, loss or separation.

Publications for carers

Teenagers in Foster Care
Produced by Coleman *et al* (2016), this handbook is for carers looking after teenagers, and those that support them. The following topics are covered with "top tips" and "discussion points": start of the placement; adolescent development; attachment and foster care; effective foster care – the STAGE framework; building relationships; structure and boundaries, rules and sanctions; risk-taking; sexuality and sexual health in foster care; expectations and aspirations; co-ordination – getting the best for young people; and moving on.

PREPARATION COURSES

Preparing to Adopt
Dibben *et al* produced these programmes for trainers:
- *Preparing to Adopt – England: Trainer's Guide* (2014b)

- *Preparing to Adopt in Scotland: Trainer's guide* (2019)

These are supported by the following compilations by Shaila Shah:
- *Preparing to Adopt in England: Applicant's workbook* (2014) and
- *Preparing to Adopt in Scotland: Applicant's workbook* (2019)

Preparing to Adopt is a well-established and popular training programme. It consists of a trainer's guide, a workbook for applicants considering adoption, and supporting material, including film clips/videos, hand-outs and exercises. These two editions of *Preparing to Adopt* address the situation and regulatory framework in England and Scotland, respectively. They offer relevant, high quality and comprehensive preparation for applicants considering adoption and will equip them with sufficient knowledge to help make an informed decision.

The Skills to Foster
Developed by The Fostering Network. this is a pre-approval course designed to prepare new applicants for the challenge of fostering. A flexible resource that supports carers taking on different types of placement, including family and friends carers.
www.thefosteringnetwork.org

PLACING SIBLINGS – TOGETHER OR APART

There is no legal requirement to carry out a sibling assessment before deciding whether or not to place siblings together. However, a sibling assessment is good practice and will provide an in-depth analysis of sibling bonds, the quality of attachments, and the individual needs of each child.

Publications for practitioners
There are various practice guides and tools designed to enable practitioners to reach the most appropriate conclusion over whether or not to place siblings together. These include:
- *Ten Top Tips for Placing Siblings in Permanent Families* (Argent, 2006)
- *Beyond Together or Apart: Planning for, Assessing and Placing Sibling Groups* (Beckett, 2021)

Sibling Assessment Toolkit
Developed by Birmingham Children's Trust (undated) and designed as an aid for practitioners undertaking sibling assessments; adding to their existing assessment skills.

Siblings Together or Apart
A practice paper by Alan Burnell and colleagues (2009) that covers the practice consequences of developmental trauma in childhood for sibling placements.

LIFE STORY WORK

New innovative ways are being developed for undertaking life story work. The current objective is to start as early in the child's life as possible and continue into young adulthood.

NSPCC's Life Story Work
Provides a service for children in care. Those aged 10–17 not currently with an adoption plan can be referred for life story work. For a referral, the child must be known to children's services and social workers must obtain informed consent.
www.learning.nspcc.org.uk/services-children-families/life-story-work

Publications for carers and practitioners

There are many resources to support carers and practitioners in life story work with traumatised children. For example: Gilligan's (2001) *Life Story Work for Children and Young People in Care*. This guide for social workers also includes a number of useful references. Additionally:

- *The Child's Own Story: Life story work with traumatised children* (Rose and Philpot, 2004)
- *Model for Life-Story Work* (Cook-Cottone and Beck, 2007)
- *Digital Life Story Work* (Hammond and Cooper, 2013)
- *Life Story Work* (McMullan, 2008, updated by Dibben, 2016)
- *Life Story Work* (Ryan and Walker, 2016)
- *Life Story Work* (Peake, undated)

These are intended for all those who work with children and young people who have suffered trauma or been subject to multiple moves, including: adoption and fostering social workers; other social workers working with children and families (including in child protection); child psychologists, psychotherapists and psychiatrists; long-term foster carers, adopters and kinship carers; independent visitors and mentors; members of youth offending teams; drug workers; and barristers.

Publications for children

My Life and Me
This guide (Camis, 2002) provides a much-needed template to help children who no longer live with their birth family, to develop and record accurate knowledge of their past. Once completed, the book provides a permanent record which they, and with their permission the adults caring for them, can refer to at any time and which the child can carry through life.

Trove
A physical and digital tool that enables children to be in control of their own life story (Watson *et al*, 2018; Gray *et al*, 2020). It was co-designed with children in care, adopted children, foster carers, adopters and social workers.

MENTORING

Organisations

Chance UK
A voluntary sector organisation, based in London, aimed at early intervention to prevent crime and anti-social behaviour. It provides mentoring programmes for children between 5 and 11 years. Although it typically works with children living with parents and relatives, it also works with some who live with foster carers. The scheme is targeted to support those with specific behavioural or personal difficulties. It is time-limited and goal oriented.
www.chanceuk.com

A number of organisations provide mentoring schemes for children leaving care, such as Family Action, TACT, Catch22 and Young Lives Foundation.

Publications for practitioners

Mentoring for Looked after Children
A manual (2008) published by Rainer, the national young people's charity, in partnership with The Prince's Trust and the Mentoring and Befriending Foundation, to disseminate the findings from a national pilot for mentoring looked after children between the ages of 10–15 years. The aim is for other providers to benefit from the lessons learned.

BEHAVIOURAL CHANGE – THERAPEUTIC SERVICES

Organisations

Coram
Established the *Support Gateway* to help adoptive families and those with a special guardianship order find the services they need. Coram therapies include: art and music therapy, mentalisation-based therapy, systemic family therapy, therapeutic parenting, non-violent resistance, and trauma-focused therapy. These are provided via the Adoption Support Fund.
www.coram.org.uk

The Cornerstone Partnership
This social enterprise, based in London, aims to improve the lives of children and families touched by the care system. Cornerstone virtual reality (VR) programme is a "technology enabled behaviour change tool" designed to support the team around the child. VR material has been designed for a variety of professionals, including children's services, adoption and fostering services, schools and the legal profession. Cornerstone also provides VR-immersive therapeutic support to help children in care. Since 2018, nearly 50 local authorities, schools and independent providers have been using the VR programmes to support rapid behaviour change through improved understanding of the impact of trauma (Alexander, 2020).
www.thecornerstonepartnership.com

Partnership Projects
Offers foundation level and advanced training in *Non Violent Resistance* as well as clinical supervision. Non Violent Resistance is an innovative form of systemic family therapy, developed for parents and carers, in responding effectively to aggressive, violent, self-destructive and controlling behaviour in children and young people. Partnership Projects has adapted it to families involved with social services and for looked after children.
www.partnershipprojectsuk.com

Young Minds
A national charity that works to promote children's mental health. It has produced a range of short guides for parents and carers to help a child with specific mental health conditions, which also list where carers can get help.
www.youngminds.org.uk

A number of independent adoption support agencies, such as PAC-UK, and independent fostering providers, such as Children Always First, also provide therapeutic services for children and families.

Training courses on *Non Violent Resistance* are also provided by a number of local authorities and other agencies, including: Child & Adolescent Mental Health Services; Oxleas NHS Foundation Trust; The Child Psychology Service; and Youth Options. Guidelines and training manuals on *Non Violent Resistance* are available from, for example, Oxleas NHS (2007) and Heismann *et al* (2010, 2019 & 2020).

Publications for carers and practitioners

Child Abuse and Neglect Guideline
Produced by the National Institute for Health and Care Excellence (2017) to provide helpful guidance on therapeutic interventions that have been found to work with children who have suffered various types of maltreatment at different developmental stages.

Therapeutic Interventions for Looked After Children, Young People and their Caregivers
Produced by Child and Family Training, this introductory guide (Bentovim *et al*, 2018) takes a modular approach and includes

nine intervention guides for practitioners. Designed to meet the common patterns of parenting stresses or difficulties, the aim is to engage with children and their caregivers, establish a profile for intervention, goal setting, intervening and measuring progress.

There are also a number of intervention guides including three that focus on helping parents to develop skills in positive parenting. The authors stress that 'The approaches are relevant for foster, adoptive, kinship and residential carers working with children and young people who have suffered significant adversity, abuse and neglect' (Bentovim et al, 2018, p.7).

TRAUMATISED CHILDREN

Organisations

Beacon House
Provides evidence-based, therapeutic services for children and families who have experienced complex developmental trauma. The therapeutic goals for an individual child or young person are based on the findings from an assessment of their needs. Local authorities can refer a child under the Adoption Support Fund.
www.beaconhouse.org.uk

The Child Psychology Service
Based in Lichfield, the service has developed a *Therapeutic Parenting Programme* that offers parents and carers the means to provide a positive therapeutic environment for developmentally traumatised children.
www.thechildpsychologyservice.co.uk

Coram Creative Therapies
Works with children, young people and their families, using music and art therapy to empower them to build skills and emotional resilience. Using a range of therapeutic and multidisciplinary evidence-based approaches, they find creative ways to help young people understand and tell the stories of their lives and, where necessary, to help them develop new stories that enable them to thrive.
www.coramadoption.org.uk/coram-creative-therapies

Family Futures
Provides therapy programmes for children who have experienced trauma or attachment difficulties and are living with adoptive or birth parents, kinship carers, foster carers or special guardians.
www.familyfutures.co.uk

Publications for carers and practitioners

Adversity and Trauma-Informed Practice
Published by Rebecca Brennan *et al* (2019), this short guide is designed for frontline professionals working with children who have experienced early trauma, separation and attachment disruption.

Trauma-Informed Practice: A toolkit for Scotland
Developed by Amy Homes and Graeme Grandison (2021), to support organisations and teams across all workforce sectors in planning and developing *Trauma-Informed Services*. It includes a set of questions to guide organisations in their self-assessments, and resources to provide practical help with implementation.

What Survival Looks Like at Home
Helen Townsend, in collaboration with Beacon House, has developed a useful and insightful guide (2019) that shows how children react to trauma and what helps them feel safe again.

Working with Children and Young People: Addressing emotional and traumatic responses (Weeramantgri, 2016) and ***Working with Children and Young People: Addressing disruptive behaviour*** (Eldridge, 2016) – produced by Child and Family Training.

There are a number of charities in the USA that work to raise awareness of the impact of trauma on children and young people and how best to support them. These include, for example, the Child Mind Institute, an independent non-profit organisation dedicated to transforming the lives of children struggling with mental health and learning disorders. The Institute has produced a guide for those caring for a traumatised child which is available in the UK. Assembled by psychiatrists, psychologists and mental health experts, it provides information on how to respond and support children of different ages to cope with trauma.
https://childmind.org/guides

SELF-HARM

Publications for carers

Coping with Self-Harm
Researchers at University of Oxford have developed a guide in 2015, aimed at parents and carers of young people who are self-harming. It includes information on the nature and causes of self-harm, how to support a young person when facing this problem and what help is available.

Parents Guide to Support A-Z
YoungMinds produced a guide for parents and carers in their series *Parents Guide to Support A-Z* which provides advice and information to support children who self-harm and lists relevant resources.

DRUGS AND ALCOHOL

Organisations

FRANK
A Government campaign and service. Although there is considerable information available for parents on what to do if they suspect their child may be using alcohol or drugs (see, for example, youngminds.org.uk) there is less information designed specifically for alternative carers. FRANK provides credible drug advice and information for young people and their families.
www.talktofrank.com

Publications for carers

Drugs and Young People in Foster Care
In partnership with The Fostering Network, FRANK has produced a guide to help foster carers to support children and young people by encouraging them to talk about drugs, either with them or by contacting FRANK. The guide provides 'up-to-date facts and information about drugs – including alcohol and cigarettes – as well as guidance about how to have an open and positive conversation' (FRANK, undated, p.1).

Parents Guide to Support A-Z
YoungMinds has produced a guide for parents and carers in their series, *Parents Guide to Support A-Z*, to help them in supporting a child who is using substances. It describes the impact of different drugs and alcohol and provides guidance about addiction. The guide includes a list of relevant resources.

GANG INVOLVEMENT

Publications for carers and practitioners

Criminal Exploitation and Gangs
Advice published by the NSPCC (2021b) on how to spot signs of criminal exploitation and involvement in gangs and the support available for children and young people.

Safeguarding Children and Young People who may be Affected by Gang Activity
Guidance published by HM Government (2010) on how the child protection system can help young people at risk of gang-related harm. It is addressed 'to those who work in voluntary and statutory services across the children's workforce, social care, crime prevention, the police, prisons and probation, offender management, health, education and all others whose work brings them into contact with children and young people' (2010, p.1).

Several local authorities have written procedures for frontline professionals and their managers to safeguard children affected by gang activity and/or serious youth violence.

CRIMINAL EXPLOITATION OF CHILDREN

Publications for practitioners

Criminal Exploitation of Children and Vulnerable Adults: County lines
Guidance published by the Home Office (Gov.UK, 2020) to help those working with children and their parents and carers to understand the issue, and how to support children.

Tackling Child Exploitation: resources pack
Published by The Local Government Association (2021), this pack for local authorities informs them on the issues surrounding both child criminal and sexual exploitation and how these can be tackled.

SEXUAL EXPLOITATION OF CHILDREN

Organisations

Barnardo's
Runs specialist services in various locations across the UK, to reach out to young people at risk of, or experiencing, child sexual exploitation (CSE) and offer them confidential support in a safe environment including counselling, group work, running awareness programmes, and training professions to recognise signs of CSE.
www.barnardos.org.uk

NSPCC
Works with children aged 11–19 years who are sexually exploited or at risk of sexual exploitation. This free service provides one-to-one support to young people and their parents or carers.
www.nspcc.org.uk

Publications for practitioners

Child Sexual Exploitation
A resource pack for practitioners by Barnardo's Scotland. 'This guidance is designed to assist practitioners in preventing CSE, protecting children and young people who are at risk of abuse or are abused through sexual exploitation, and disrupting and prosecuting those who perpetrate this form of abuse' (Barnardo's Scotland, 2014, pp.8–9).

Child Sexual Exploitation
A pocket guide for healthcare staff produced by NHS England. It provides practical

information to safeguard children and young people.

What Works in Responding to Child Sexual Exploitation

Written by Sara Scott *et al* (2019), this covers the main approaches to combatting CSE, including awareness raising, outreach and community-based strategies, as well as undertaking direct work with abused young people, their parents and carers.

Publications for young people

Sexual Exploitation: Sex, secrets and lies

Jointly produced by the Welsh Government and Barnardo's Wales (2013). A colourful, easy to read booklet for young people, as well as family members and carers, to help children understand what sexual exploitation can be, and gives information to empower them to make positive choices.

CORAMBAAF PUBLICATIONS

CoramBAAF has produced a range of publications aimed at professionals and practitioners, parents and carers, and children and young people.

Although we have already cited in this appendix a number of CoramBAAF publications, the following are also important resources. Please note that these titles have not been cited in the reference list – they can be accessed at **www.corambaaf.org.uk/bookshop**.

Guides for practitioners

Good Practice Guides explore the legislative and policy framework of a variety of topics. Key to the present guide is *Dealing with Disruption* (Argent H and Coleman J, 2012; new edition forthcoming 2022).

The Ten Top Tips series provides clear and focused advice for practitioners on issues related to adoption and fostering. The following are particularly relevant:
- *Making Introductions* (Dunbar L, 2009)
- *Making Matches* (Cousins J, 2011)
- *Managing Contact* (Bond H, 2007)

There are a number of innovative and practical guides on direct work with children, the following of which are relevant to working with children affected by domestic abuse:
- *Digital Life Story Work* (Hammond SP and Cooper NJ, 2013)
- *Promoting Resilience* (Gilligan R, 2009)
- *Once Upon a Time* (Moore J, 2012)
- *Communicating Through Play* (Stringer B, 2009)

Publications on attachment provide pointers on attachment formation and helping children to feel more secure. Particularly relevant to countering the effects of domestic abuse are:
- *Attachment Handbook for Foster Care and Adoption* (Schofield G and Beek M, 2006)
- *The Secure Base Model* (Schofield G and Beek M, 2014)

There is a range of books exploring contact, a key issue when children have experienced domestic abuse. The following may be particularly useful:
- *Contact in Adoption and Permanent Foster Care* (eds Neil E and Howe D, 2004)
- *Supporting Direct Contact after Adoption* (Neil E, Cossar J, Jones C, Lorgelly P and Young J, 2011)
- *Beyond the Adoption Order* (Selwyn J, Meakings S and Wijedasa D, 2015)

Plus three reports by Eileen Fursland on the impact of social networking and one guide for children:
- *Facing up to Facebook* (2nd edn, 2013)

- *Social Networking and Contact* (2010)
- *Foster Care and Social Networking* (2011)
- *Social Networking and You* (2013)

Resources for parents and carers

A range of **training resources** focusing on practical advice and training for carers and adopters to develop skills in managing challenging behaviours in their children, including:
- *Enhancing Adoptive Parenting* (Rushton A and Monck E, 2012)
- *Safer Caring* (Cairns K and Fursland E, 2007)

The **Parenting Matters series** provides expert knowledge for carers and adoptive parents on a range of issues, including:
- *Domestic Violence* (Cleaver H, 2015)
- *Parental Substance Misuse* (Forrester D, 2012)
- *Trauma* (Hughes D, 2016)

Things foster carers need to know is a series of pamphlets by Henrietta Bond on a range of issues that carers and adoptive parents may find hard to discuss with their child. The series includes titles on sexuality; radicalisation; internet safety; self-harm; and gangs. Will enable carers to recognise if their child is exposed to problematic situations and help safeguard and support them.

Resources for children and young people

A range of picture books and stories aimed at helping children and young people understand their situation and come to terms with their history, feelings and memories. The following are of particular interest when working with young children affected by domestic abuse:
- *Spark Learns to Fly* (Foxon J, 2007)
- *Elfa and the Box of Memories* (Bell M, 2008)
- *Where is Poppy's Panda?* (Pitcher D, 2009)
- *We are Fostering* (Camis J, 2004)

References

Abbas AM, Rabeea M, Hafiz HAA and Ahmed NH (2017) 'Effects of irregular antenatal care attendance in primiparas on the perinatal outcomes: a cross sectional study', *Proceedings in Obstetrics and Gynecology*, 7:2, pp. 1–11

Action on Hearing Loss (2020) *Facts and Figures*, available at: actiononhearingloss.org.uk

Adoption UK (undated) available at: https://www.adoptionuk./pages/faqs/care

Adoption UK (2019) *The Adoption Barometer*, available at: https://www.adoptionuk.org/Handlers/Download.ashx?IDMF=fd3d3969-8138-4ede-befd-1018fe629c29

Adoption UK (2020) *The Adoption Barometer*, available at: https://www.adoptionuk.org/the-adoption-barometer

Adoption UK (2021) *The Adoption Barometer: A stocktake of adoption in the UK June 2021*, available at: https://www.adoptionuk.org/the-adoption-barometer-a-stocktake-of-adoption-in-the-uk

Aitken R and Munro VE (2018) *Domestic Abuse and Suicide*, available at: www.nspa.org.uk/wp-content/uploads/2018/08/New-Suicide-Report2c-Refuge-and-University-of-Warwick.pdf

Alexander A (2020) *Using Virtual Reality Technology to Understand the Needs of Children*, available at: www.themj.co.uk,/Using-virtual-reality-technology-to-understand-the-needs-of-children/217936

Alexander H, Macdonald E and Paton S (2005) 'Raising the issue of domestic abuse in school', *Children and Society*, 19:3, pp. 187–198

Almqvist C, Worm M and Leynaert B (2007) 'Impact of gender on asthma in childhood and adolescence: a GA2LEN review', *Allergy*, 63:1, pp. 47–57, available at: https://doi/10.1111/j.1398-9995.2007.01524.x

Anderberg D. and Moroni G (2021) 'Exposure to intimate partner violence and children's dynamic skill accumulation: evidence from a UK longitudinal study', *Oxford Review of Economic Policy*, 36:4, pp.783-815, available at: https://doi.org/10.1093/oxrep/graa052

APPG Inquiry into Children Missing from Care (2012) *Report from the Joint Inquiry into Children who go Missing from Care*, available at: https://www.becomecharity.org.k/media/1107/report-joint-appg-inquiry-missig-2012.pdf

Arain M, Haque M, Johal L, Mathur P, Nel W, Rais A, Sandu R and Sharma S (2013) 'Maturation of the adolescent brain', *Neuropsychiatric Disease and Treatment*, 9, pp. 449–461, available at: doi: 10.2147/NDT.S39776

Archer C and Gordon A (2006) *New Families, Old Scripts*, London: Jessica Kingsley Publishers

Argent H (2006) *Ten Top Tips for Placing Children in Permanent Families*, London: BAAF

Argent H (2012) *Moving Pictures*, London: BAAF

Argent H and Coleman J (2012) *Dealing with Disruption in Fostering and Adoption Placements*, London: BAAF

Ashley C and Roth D (2015) *What Happens to Siblings in the Care System?* London: Family Rights Group, available at: www.frg.org.uk/images/PDFS/siblings_in_care_final_report_january_2015.pdf

BAAF (2015) *Child's Adoption and Permanence Report (CPR) Scotland: Guidance notes for completion of CAPR*, available at: https://corambaaf.org.uk/bookshop/corambaaf-electronic-forms/adoption-and-fostering-forms-scotland

BAAF, The Scottish Government and The Fostering Network (undated) *Guidance on Looked After Children (Scotland) Regulations 2009 and the Adoption and Children (Scotland) Act 2007*, available at: https://www.gov.scot/publications/guidance-looked-children-scotland-regulations-2009-adoption-children-scotland-act-2007/documents/

Bachmann K, Blackeby K, Bengo C, Slack K, Woolgar M, Lawson H and Scott S (2019) *Fostering Changes* (3rd edn), London: CoramBAAF

Bailey S (2006) 'Adolescence and beyond: twelve years onwards', in Aldgate J, Jones D, Rose W and Jeffery C (eds) *The Developing World of the Child*, London: Jessica Kingsley Publishers

Baker L and Cunningham A (2009) 'Inter-parental violence: the pre-schooler's perspective', *Day Care and Early Education*, 37:3, pp. 199–207

Barnardo's (2016) *Now I Know it was Wrong: Report of the Parliamentary Inquiry into support and sanctions for children who display harmful sexual behaviour*, available at: www.basw.co.uk/resources/now-i-know-it-was-wrong

Barnardo's (2020) *Barnardo's declares 'State of Emergency' as Number of Children needing Foster*

Care during the Coronavirus Pandemic rises by 44%, available at: www.barnardos.org.uk

Barnardo's Scotland (2014) *Guidance on Child Sexual Exploitation: A practitioners' resource pack*, available at: https://www.south-ayrshire.gov.uk/documents/cse%20-%20practitioners%20guide%20barnardos%20and%20wos.pdf

Bazalgette L, Rahilly T and Trevelyan G (2015) *Achieving Emotional Wellbeing for Looked After Children: A whole system approach*, available at: https://www.fwsolutions.net/wp-content/uploads/2015/08/achieving-emotional-wellbeing-for-looked-after-children.pdf

BBC News (2012) *'Concerning' Rise in Pre-Teens Self-Injuring*, available at: www.bbc.co.uk/news/uk-'concerning'-rise-in-pre-teens

BBC News (2017) *We're Scared of our Adopted Son*, available at: www.bbc.co.uk /news/magazine-we're-scared-of-our

BBC News (2020) *'I didn't know it was abuse until I nearly died'*, available at: www.bbc.co.uk/'I-didn't-know-it-was-abuse

BBC News England (2019) *Adoption Breakdown: 'No support' for violent children*, available at: www.bbc.co.uk/news/uk-england-'No-support'-for-violent

BBC News Wales (2018) *'We felt abandoned as adoptive parents'*, available at: www.bbc.co.uk/news/uk-wales-we-felt-abandoned

Beckett S (2021) *Beyond Together or Apart: Planning for, assessing and placing sibling groups* (2nd edn), London: CoramBAAF

Bee H (2000) *The Developing Child* (9th edn), London: Allyn and Bacon

Beek M, Neil E and Scofield G (2021) *Moving to Adoption: Using the UEA model to help children move from foster care to adoption*, London: CoramBAAF

Belsky J, Hsief K and Crnic K (1998) 'Mothering, fathering and infant negativity at age three years: differential susceptibility to rearing experience?' *Development & Psychopathology,* 10:2, pp. 301–319

Benson JE and Elder GE (2011) 'Young adult identities and their pathways: a developmental and life course model', *Developmental Psychology*, 47:6, pp. 164–1657

Bentovim A and Williams B (1998) 'Children and adolescents: victims who become perpetrators', *Advances in Psychiatric Treatment*, 4, pp.101–107

Bentovim A, Gray J and Pizzy S (2018) *Therapeutic Interventions for Looked After Children, Young People and their Caregivers*, York: Child and Family Training, available at: https://www.childandfamilytraining.org.uk/_data/site/9/folder/126/Therapeutic_interventions_for_looked_after_children_young_people_and_their_caregivers.pdf

Bichard H, Byrne C, Saville C and Coetzer R (2020) 'The neuropsychological outcomes of non-fatal strangulation in domestic and sexual violence: a systematic review', *PsyArXiv Preprints*, October

Biehal N (2009) 'Foster care for adolescents', in Schofield G and Simmonds J (eds) *The Child Placement Handbook: Research, policy and practice*, London: BAAF, pp. 159–177

Biehal N, Ellison S, Beacon C and Sinclair I (2010) *Belonging and Permanence: Outcomes in long-term foster care and adoption*, London: BAAF

Birmingham Children's Trust (undated) *Sibling Assessment Toolkit*, available at: www.proceduresonline.com/trixcms/media/sibling-assessment-toolkit

BMA Board of Science (2014) *Domestic Abuse*, London: BMA

Boddy J (2013) *Understanding Permanence for Looked After Children: A review of research for the Care Inquiry*, available at: https://www.thefosteringnetwork.org.uk/sites/www.fostering.net/files/resources/england/understanding-permanence-for-lac-janet-boddy.pdf

Bond H (2021) *Young People and Gangs*, London: CoramBAAF

Boswell S and Cudmore L (2014) '"The children were fine": acknowledging complex feelings in the move into adoption', *Adoption & Fostering*, 38:1, pp. 5–21

Bowlby J (1973) *Attachment and Loss, Volume 11: Separation, anxiety and anger*, London: Hogarth Press

Boyle C (2015) 'What is the impact of birth family contact on children in adoption and long-term foster care?' a systematic review, *Child & Family Social Work*, 22:822–833, available at: https://doi.org/10.1111/cfs.12236

Bradley F, Smith M, Long J and O'Dowd T (2002) 'Reported frequency of domestic violence: cross sectional survey of women attending general practice', *British Medical Journal*, 324, pp. 271–274

Bradlow J, Bartram F and Guasp A (2017) *School Report: The experiences of lesbian, gay, bi and trans young people in Britain's schools in 2017*, London: Stonewall, available at: https://www.stonewall.org.uk/system/files/the_school_report_2017.pdf

Brain Balance (2020) *Normal Attention Span Expectations by Age*, available at: blog.brainbalancecentres.com /normal-attention-span

Brandon M, Bailey S and Belderson P (2010) *Building on the Learning from Serious Case Reviews:*

A two-year analysis of child protection database notifications 2007–2009: Research brief, London: DfE

Brennan R, Bush M and Trickey D with Levene C and Watson J (2019) *Adversity and Trauma-Informed Practice*, available at: https://youngminds.org.uk/media/3091/adversity-and-trauma-informed-practice-guide-for-professionals.pdf

Bristol City Council (2014) *Caring for a Child of a Different Ethnicity*, available at: www.nottinghamshire.gov.uk/media/127866/caring-for-a-child-of-a-different-ethnicity-web-version.pdf

British Lung Foundation (2020) *Asthma Statistics*, available at: www.statistics.blf.org.uk/asthma

Bronte A (1848) *The Tenant of Wildfell Hall*, Oxford: Oxford University Press (1992)

Brooks M (2020) *Male Victims of Domestic and Partner Abuse: 50 key facts*, Mankind Initiative, available at: https://www.mankind.org.uk/wp-content/uploads/2020/03/50-Key-Facts-About-Male-Victims-of-Domestic-Abuse-and-Partner-Abuse-March-2020-final.pdf

Brown K (1998) *Dispatches: 'Battered men' survey*, available at: http://www.dewar4research.org/docs/bms1.pdf

Brown HC, Sebba J and Luke N (2014) *The Role of the Supervising Social Worker in Foster Care*, available at: www.education.ox.ac.uk/wp-content/uploads/2019/05/285261.pdf

Brown F, More THM, Hooper L, Goa Y, Zayegh A, Ijaz S, Elwenspoek M, Foxen SC, Magee L and O'Malley C (2019) 'Interventions for preventing obesity in children', *Cochrane Library*, available at: doi: 10.1002/14651858.CD001871.pub4

Browne D (2017) 'The adolescent brain', *Mindmate*, available at: https://www.mindmate.org.uk/resources/the-adolescent-brain/

Browning AS (2020) 'The impact of complex and unwanted feelings evoked in foster carers by children in long-term placements', *Adoption & Fostering*, 44:2, pp.185–196

Buckley H, Holt S and Whelan S (2007) 'Listen to me! Children's experiences of domestic violence', *Child Abuse Review*, 16:5, pp. 296–310

Burnell A, Vaughan J and Williams L (2009) *Siblings Together or Apart*, available at: https://www.familyfutures.co.uk/wp-content/uploads/2015/05/Siblings-Together-or-Apart-Practice-Paper.compressed.pdf

Byrne D and Taylor BJ (2007) 'Children at risk of domestic violence and their educational attainment: perspectives of education welfare officers, social workers and teachers', *Child Care in Practice*, 13:3, pp.185–201

CAADA (2012) *A Place of Greater Safety: Insights into domestic abuse 1*, available at: www.safelives.org.uk/sites/default/files/resources/A_Place_of_greater_safety.pdf

CAADA (2014) *In Plain Sight: Effective help for children exposed to domestic abuse*, available at: www.safelives.org.uk/sites/default/files/resources/Final%20report%20In%20plain%20sight%20effective%20help%20for%20children%20exposed%20to%20domestic%20abuse.pdf

CAFCASS (2012) *Three Weeks in November...three years on...CAFCASS care application study 2012*, London: CAFCASS

CAFCASS Cymru (2019) *Impact on Children of Experiencing Domestic Abuse*, available at: https://gov.wales/sites/default/files/publications/2019-08/cafcass-cymru-impact-on%20children-experiencing-domestic-abuse.pdf

Cairns K and Cairns B (2016) *Attachment, Trauma and Resilience*, London: CoramBAAF

Callaghan JEM, Alexander JH, Sixsmith J and Fellin LC (2015) 'Beyond "witnessing": children's experiences of coercive control in domestic violence and abuse', *Journal of Interpersonal Violence*, 33:10, pp. 1551–1581

Callaghan J, Alexander J, Sixsmith J and Fellin LC (2017) 'Children's experiences of domestic violence and abuse: siblings' accounts of relational coping', *Clinical Child Psychology and Psychiatry*, 22:4, pp. 649–668

Caluori J, Corlett M and Stott J (2020) *County Lines and Looked After Children*, London: Crest, available at: https://www.crestadvisory.com/post/report-county-lines

Camis J (2002) *My Life and Me*, London: BAAF

Camis J (2003) *We Are Fostering*, London: BAAF

Care Inspectorate (2019) *Learning from Significant Case Reviews: March 2015 to April 2018*, available at: https://www.careinspectorate.com/media/3645/learning-from-significant-case-reviews-march-2015-to-april-2018.pdf

Care Quality Commission (2018) *Are we Listening? A review of children and young people's mental health services*, available at: https://www.cqc.org.uk/sites/default/files/20180308_arewelistening_qualitative.pdf

Carmo R, Grams A and Magalhaes T (2011) 'Men as victims of intimate partner violence', *Journal of Forensic and Legal Medicine*, 18:8, pp. 355–59

Cascardi M (2016) 'From violence in the home to physical dating violence victimisation: the mediating role of psychological distress in a prospective study of female adolescents', *Journal of Youth and Adolescence*, 45, pp. 777–792

Catch22 (undated) *Looked After Children and Care Leavers*, available at: https://www.catch-22.org.uk/offers/looked-after-children-and-care-leavers

Centre for Social Justice (2018) *Girls and Gangs*, available at: https://www.centreforsocialjustice.org.uk/wp-content/uploads/2018/03/Girls-and-Gangs-FINAL-VERSION.pdf

Chastain J (2012) *How Does Witnessing Domestic Violence Affect a Child's Academic as well as Behavioral Performance at School?* Trinity College Digital Repository, available at: https://digitalrepository.trincoll.edu/cgi/viewcontent.cgi?article=1097&context=theses

Child Mind Institute (2021) *Helping Children Cope after a Traumatic Event*, available at: www.childmind.org/guide/helping-children-cope-traumatic-event

Child Safeguarding Practice Review Panel (2020a) *Annual Report 2018 to 2019*, available at: www.gov.uk/government/publications/child-safeguarding-review-panel

Child Safeguarding Practice Review Panel (2020b) *It Was Hard to Escape: Safeguarding children at risk of criminal exploitation*, available at: https://assets.publishing.service.gov.uk/government/uploads/system/uploads/attachment_data/file/870035/Safeguarding_children_at_risk_from_criminal_exploitation.pdf

ChildLine (1997) *Beyond the Limit: Children who live with parental alcohol misuse*, London: ChildLine

Children Always First (undated) *Therapeutic Parenting Support*, Worcester: Children Always First

Children in Wales (2014) *Kinship Care Guide for Wales*, available at: www.childreninwales.org.uk/uploads/2014/11/Wales

Children's Commissioner (2018) *'Are they shouting because of me?' Voices of children living in households with domestic violence, parental substance misuse and mental health issues*, available at: https://www.childrenscommissioner.gov.uk/wp-content/uploads/2018/08/Are_they_shouting_because_of_me.pdf

Children's Commissioner (2019) *The Characteristics of Gang-Associated Young People*, technical report, available at: https://www.bl.uk/collection-items/characteristics-of-gang-associated children-and-young-people

Children's Rights Director for England (2012) *Independent Visitors: Children and young people's views*, Ofsted, available at: https://dera.ioe.ac.uk/15864/7/Independent%20visitors_Redacted.pdf

Claridge S (2006) *UK Hearing Loss Facts and Figures*, available at: www.hearingaidknow.com/uk-hearing-loss-facts-and-figures

Cleaver H (1996) *Focus on Teenagers: Research into practice*, London: HMSO

Cleaver H (2000) *Fostering Family Contact*, London: The Stationery Office

Cleaver H (2015) *Parenting a Child Affected by Domestic Violence*, London: CoramBAAF

Cleaver H, Nicholson D, Tarr S and Cleaver D (2007) *Child Protection, Domestic Violence and Parental Substance Misuse*, London: Jessica Kingsley Publishers

Cleaver H and Rose W (2020) *Safeguarding Children Living with Foster Carers, Adopters and Special Guardians: Learning from case reviews 2007–2019*, London: CoramBAAF

Cleaver H and Rose W (2020) *Safeguarding Children Living with Foster Carers, Adopters and Special Guardians: A guide to reflective practice*, London: CoramBAAF

Cleaver H, Unell I and Aldgate J (2011) *Children's Needs – Parenting Capacity* (2nd edn), London: The Stationery Office

Clements W, Williams LD, Wilson SL and David T (2019) 'Childhood trauma and effective empirically based interventions', *Matters of Behaviour*, 10:11, pp.17–22, available at: https://mattersofbehaviour.org

CLIPP Centre de Liaison sur l'Intervention et la Prévention Psychosociales (2007) *Children Exposed to Domestic Violence: A knowledge review* (2nd edn), Montreal: CLIPP

Coleman J, Vellacott J, Solari G, Luck N and Sebba J (2016) *Teenagers in Focus: A handbook for foster carers and those that support them*, available at: www.education.ox.ac.uk/wp-content/uploads/2019/05/Teenagers-in-Foster-Care-Handbook-1.pdf

Cook-Cottone C and Beck M (2007) 'A model for life-story work: facilitating the construction of personal narrative for foster children', *Child & Adolescent Mental Health* 12:4, pp.193–195

Coram Adoption (2021) *Support Gateway*, available at: www.coram.org.uk/adoption-support-gateway

Coram Ambitious for Adoption (2019) *Adoption Support: Accessing therapies*, available at: https://www.coramadoption.org.uk/sites/default/files/resource_files/Adoption-Support-leaflet%20-%20FINAL ONLINE.pdf

Cornerstone Partnership (undated) *Virtual Reality*, available at: www.thecornerstonepartnership.com/virtualreality

Corry CE, Pizzey E and Fiebert MS (2001) 'Controlling domestic violence against men', *Nuance*, 3, pp. 71–86, available at: citeseerx.ist.psu.edu/viewdoc/download?doi=10.1.1.544.258&rep=rep1&type=pdf

Cosmo P and Soni A (2020) 'The Mission Mentoring programme: an initiative for council employees to become mentors to looked after children', *Adoption & Fostering*, 44:4, pp. 391–412

Covell K and Howe RB (2009) *Children, Families and Violence: Challenges for children's rights*, London: Jessica Kingsley Publishers

Daniel B, Taylor J and Scott J (2009) 'Noticing and helping the neglected child: summary of a systematic literature review', *International Journal of Child and Family Welfare*, 12:4, pp. 120–133

Davis J and Marsh N (2020) 'Boys to men: the cost of "adultification" in safeguarding responses to Black boys', *Critical and Radical Social Work*, 8:2, pp. 255–259

De Graff NM, Giovanardi G, Zitz C and Carmichael P (2018) 'Sex ratio in children and adolescents referred to the Gender Identity Development Service in the UK (2009–2016)', *Archives of Sexual Behaviour*, 47:5, pp.1301–1304

DeJong M, Hodges J and Malik O (2015) 'Children after adoption: exploring their psychological needs', *Child Psychology and Psychiatry*, 21:4, pp. 536–550

Department for Education (2013) *Statutory Guidance on Adoption: For local authorities, voluntary agencies and adoption support agencies*, available at: https://assets.publishing.service.gov.uk/government/uploads/system/uploads/attachment_dat/file/270100/adoption_statutory_guidance_2013.pdf

Department for Education (2014) *Key Stage 2 Attainment for Children Recorded as Adopted from Care*, available at: https://assets.publishing.service.gov.uk/government/uploads/system/uploads/attachment_data/file/337055/key_stage_2_attainment_for_children_recorded_as_adopted_from_care.pdf

Department for Education (2015) *The Children Act 1989 Guidance and Regulations, Volume 2: Care planning, placement and case review*, available at: https://assets.publishing.service.gov.uk/government/uploads/system/uploads/attachment_data/file/441643/Children_Act_Guidance_2015.pdf

Department for Education (2017a) *Preventing and Tackling Bullying: Advice for headteachers, staff and governing bodies*, available at: https://assets.publishing.service.gov.uk/government/uploads/system/uploads/attachment_data/file/623895/Preventing_and_tackling_bullying_advice.pdf

Department for Education (2017b) *Special Guardianship Guidance*, available at: https://assets.publishing.service.gov.uk/government/uploads/system/uploads/attachment_data/file/656593/Special-guardianship_statutory_guidance.pdf

Department for Education (2017c) *Child Sexual Exploitation: Definition and a guide for practitioners, local leaders and decision makers working to protect children from child sexual exploitation*, available at: https://assets.publishing.service.gov.uk/government/uploads/system/uploads/attachment_data/file/591903/CSE_Guidance_Core_Document_13.02.2017.pdf

Department for Education (2018a) *Characteristics of Children in Need: 2017 to 2018 England*, available at: https://assets.publishing.service.gov.uk/government/uploads/system/uploads/attachment_data/file/762

Department for Education (2018b) *Bullying in England, April 2013 to March 2018*, available at: https://assets.publishing.service.gov.uk/government/uploads/system/uploads/attachment_data/file/919474/Bullying_in_England_2013-2018_1_.pd.pdf

Department for Education (2019a) *Characteristics of Children in Need: 2018 to 2019 England*, available at: https://assets.publishing.service.gov.uk/government/uploads/system/uploads/attachment_data/file/843046/Characteristics_of_children_in_need_2018_to_2019_main_text_pdf

Department for Education (2019b) *Pupil Absences in Schools in England, Autumn Term 2018*, available at: https://assets.publishing.service.gov.uk/government/uploads/system/uploads/attachment_data/file/805047/Absence_autterm_201819_maintext.pdf

Department for Education (2019c) *Timpson Review of School Exclusion*, available at: https://assets.publishing.service.gov.uk/government/uploads/system/uploads/attachment_data/file/807862/Timpson_review.pdf

Department for Education (2020) *Children Looked After in England Including Adoptions*, available at: https://explore-education-statistics.service.gov.uk/find-statistics/children-looked-after-in-england-including-adoptions/2020

Department of Health, Department for Education and Employment and Home Office (2000) *Framework for the Assessment of Children in Need and their Families*, London: The Stationery Office

Desforges C with Abouchaar A (2003) *The Impact of Parental Involvement, Parental Support and Family Education on Pupil Achievements and Adjustment: A literature review*, available at: https://www.nationalnumeracy.org.uk/sites/default/files/the_impact_of_parental_involvement.pdf

Devaney J (2015) 'Research review: the impact of domestic violence on children', *Irish Probation Journal*, 12, pp. 79–94

DeVoe ER and Smith EL (2002) 'The impact of domestic violence on urban preschool children', *Journal of Interpersonal Violence*, 17:10, pp. 1075–1101

Dibben E (2019) *Devising a Placement Plan: A guide to gathering information to complete and implement a placement plan for fostering placements (England)*, London: CoramBAAF

Dibben E with Bugarski L, Probert N and Wilson J (2014a) *Completing a Child's Permanence Report*, London: BAAF

Dibben E, Fursland E and Probert N (2014b) *Preparing to Adopt – England: Trainer's guide*, London: CoramBAAF

Dibben E, Fursland E and Probert N (2019) *Preparing to Adopt in Scotland: Trainer's guide*, London: CoramBAAF

Digby A and Fu E (2017) *Impacts of Homelessness on Children: Research with teachers*, available at: https://england.shelter.org.uk/__data/assets/pdf_file/0011/1474652/2017_12_20_Homelessness_and_School_Children.pdf

Donovan C, Hester M, Holmes J and McCarry M (2006) *Comparing Domestic Abuse in Same Sex and Heterosexual Relationships*, available at: www.equation.org.uk/wp-content/uploads/2012/12/Comparing-Domestic-Abuse-in-Same-Sex-and-Heterosexual-Relationships.pdf

Doyle L, Treacy MP and Sheridan A (2015) 'Self-harm in young people: prevalence, associated factors, and help-seeking in school-going adolescents', *International Journal of Mental Health Nursing*, 24:6, pp. 485–495

Dunning H (2015) 'Can we break the cycle?', in Cleaver H, *Parenting a Child Affected by Domestic Violence*, London: BAAF

Edwards BG (2019) 'Alarming effects of children's exposure to domestic violence', *Psychology Today*, available at: www.psychologytoday.com/progress-notes/201902

Eldridge H (2016) *Working with Children and Young People: Addressing disruptive behaviour*, in Bentovim A and Gray J (eds) *Hope for Children and Families: Building on strengths, overcoming difficulties*, York: Child and Family Training

Elliot P (1996) 'Shattering illusions: same-sex domestic violence', *Journal of Gay & Lesbian Social Services*, 4:1, pp. 1–8

Elliott GC, Avery R, Fishman E and Hoshiko BC (2002) 'The encounter with family violence and risky sexual activity among young adolescent females', *Violence and Victims*, 17:95, pp. 569–592

Elsley S (2013) *Developing a National Mentoring Scheme for Looked After Children and Young People*, available at: https://www.celcis.org./files/2714/4050/9227/LACSIG_Mentoring_Report-2014-09-02.pdf

Enlow MB, Egeland B, Blood E, Wright RO and Wright RJ (2013) 'Interpersonal trauma exposure and cognitive development in children to age 8 years: a longitudinal study', *Journal of Epidemiology and Community Health*, 66:11, pp. 1005–1010

Fahlberg V (1994) *A Child's Journey through Placement*, London: BAAF

Fahmy E, Williamson E and Pantazis C (2015) *Evidence and Policy Review: Domestic violence and poverty, A research report for the Joseph Rowntree Foundation*, Bristol: University of Bristol School for Policy Studies

Family Action (undated) *Looked After Children Support Services*, London: Family Action Head Office, www.family-action.org.uk

Family Action (2017) *Managing Birth Family Contact*, available at: https://www.specialguardiansupport.org.uk/content/uploads/2017/07/Managing-birth-family-contact-download.pdf

Family Futures (2009) *Planning Transitions for Children Moving to Permanent Placement: What do you do after you say "hello"?* available at: https://www.familyfutures.co.uk/wp-content/uploads/2015/06

Family Futures (2019) *Practice Paper: Assessing Sibling Placements*, available at: https://www.familyfutures.co.uk/we-content/uploads/2019/06/Practice-Paper-Siblings-June-2019.pdf

Farmer E (2009) 'How do placements in kinship care compare with those in non-kin foster care: placement patterns, progress and outcomes?', *Child & Family Social Work*, 14:3, pp. 331–342

Field T, Seligman S and Scafidi F (1996) 'Alleviating post-traumatic stress in children following hurricane Andrew', *Journal of Applied Developmental Psychology*, 17:1, pp. 37–50

Forrester D (2012) *Parenting a Child Affected by Parental Substance Misuse*, London: BAAF

Fox C, Corr M, Gadd D and Butler I (2013) *From Boys to Men: Phase one key findings*, available at: http://www.boystomenproject.com/wp-content/uploads/2012/12/Key-Findings-Phase-1.pdf

Foxon J with Argent H (2007) *Guidelines to the Text: Spark Learns to Fly*, London: BAAF

FRANK (undated) *Drugs and Young People in Foster Care: Information and resource guide for foster carers*, available at: https://www.caerphilly.gov.uk?CaerphillyDocs/Children-and-families/Foster_Carers_frank_drugs.aspx

Fursland E (2010) *Social Networking and Contact: How social workers can help adoptive families*, London: BAAF

Fursland E (2011) *Foster Care and Social Networking: A guide for social workers and foster carers*, London: BAAF

Galvani S (2004) 'Responsible disinhibition: alcohol, men and violence to women', *Addiction Research*, 12:4, pp. 357–374

Gass K, Jenkins J and Dunn J (2007) 'Are sibling relationships protective? A longitudinal study', *Journal of Child Psychology and Psychiatry*, 48:2, pp.167–75

Geddes H (2006) *Attachment in the Classroom*, London: Worth Publishing Ltd

Gerring C, Kemp S and Marcenko M (2008) 'The Connections Project: a relational approach to engaging birth parents in visitation', *Child Welfare*, 18: pp. 5-30

Gilbert L, El-Bassel N, Rajah V, Foleno A and Frye V (2001) 'Linking drug-related activities with experiences of partner violence: a focus group study of women in methadone treatment', *Violence Survivors*, 16:5, pp. 517–536

Gilchrist G, Dennis F, Radcliffe P, Henderson J, Howard LM and Gadd D (2019) 'The interplay between substance use and intimate partner violence perpetrations: a meta-ethnography', *International Journal of Drug Policy*, 65, pp. 8–23

Gilligan R (2001) *Life Story Work for Children and Young People in Care*, available at: https://Kentchildcare.proceduresonline.com/pdfs/life_story_work.pdf

Giovanardi G, Vitelli R, Vergano CM, Fortunato A, Chianura L, Lingiardi V and Speranza AM (2018) 'Attachment patterns and complex trauma in a sample of adults diagnosed with gender dysphoria', *Frontiers in Psychology*, 1; 9:60, available at: doi: 10.3389/fpsyg.2018.00060

Glaser D (2000) 'Child abuse and neglect and the brain: a review', *Journal of Child Psychology & Psychiatry*, 41:8, pp. 97–116

Gleeson C, Robinson M and Neal R (2002) 'A review of teenagers' perceived needs and access to primary healthcare: implications for school health services', *Primary Health Care Research and Development,* 3, pp. 184–193

Golding KS (2013) *Nurturing Attachments Training Resource*, London: Jessica Kingsley Publishers

Golding KS (2017) *Foundations for Attachment Training Resource*, London: Jessica Kingsley Publishers

Golding KS (2019) 'The development of DDP-informed parenting groups for parents and carers of children looked after or adopted from care', *Adoption & Fostering*, 43:4, pp. 400–412

Gordon A and Graham K (2016) *The National Independent Visitor Data Report*, London: Barnardo's, available at: www.basw.co.uk/system/files/resources/basw_50915-4_0.pdf

Gorin S (2004) *Understanding what Children Say: Children's experiences of domestic violence, parental substance misuse and parental health problems*, London: National Children's Bureau

Gov.Scot (2020) *Children's Social Work Statistics: 2019 to 2020*, available at: www.gov.scot/publications/childrens-social-work-statistics-2019-2020

Gov.UK (2019) *Adoption Support Fund (ASF)*, available at: www.gov.uk/.../Adoption

Gov.UK (2020) *Permanent and Fixed-Period Exclusions in England*, available at: www.gov.uk/Data collection and statistical returns

Gov.UK (2021a) *Pupil Absence in Schools in England: Autumn term*, available at: https://explore-education-statistics.service.gov.uk/pupil-absence-in-school-in-England:autumn-term-Autumn-Term-2020/21

Gov.UK (2021b) *£79 Million to Boost Mental Health Support for Children and Young People*, available at: www.gov.uk/government/news/79-million-to-boost

Graham-Bermann SA and Levendosky AA (1998) 'Traumatic stress symptoms in children of battered women', *Journal of Interpersonal Violence*, 13:1, pp.111–128

Gray S, Hahn R, Cater K, Watson D, Williams K, Metcalfe T and Meineck C (2020) 'Towards a design for life: redesigning for reminiscence with looked after children', *CHI '20: Proceedings of the 2020 CHI Conference on Human Factors in Computing Systems*, pp. 1–14

Green H, McGinnity A, Meltzer H, Ford T and Goodman R (2005) *Mental Health of Children and Young People in Great Britain, 2004*, London: ONS

Gribble K (2016) 'Promoting attachment in foster parents: what we can learn from the experiences of parents of premature infants', *Adoption & Fostering*, 40:2, pp. 113–127

Guy J with Feinstein L and Griffiths A (2014) *Early Intervention in Domestic Violence and Abuse,* Early Intervention Foundation, available at: www.eif.org.uk /pdf/early-intervention-in-domestic-violence-and-abuse

Hamburger ME, Leeb RT and Swahn MH (2008) 'Childhood maltreatment and early alcohol use among high-risk adolescents', *Journal of Studies on Alcohol and Drugs*, 69:2, pp. 291–295

Hammond SP and Cooper NJ (2013) *Digital Life Story Work*, London: BAAF

Healy C, Brannigan R, Dooley N, Coughlan H, Clarke M, Kelleher I and Cannon M (2019) 'Childhood and adolescent psychotic experiences and risk of mental disorder: a systematic review and meta-analysis', *Psychological Medicine*, 49:10, pp. 1589–1599

Heismann E and Day L (2010) *Non-Violent Resistance Programme*, available at: http://www.pavpub.com/children-and-families/non-violent-resistance-programme

Heismann E, Jude J and Day L (2019) *Non-Violent Resistance: Innovations in practice*, available at: http://www.pavpub.com/health-and-social-care/non-violent-resistance-innovations

Heismann E, Frimpong D, Target L and McClay S (2020) *Whose Tune Are We Dancing To Anyway?*, available at: https://www.pavpub.com/children-and-families/whose-tune-dancing

Herba MH and Glover V (2021) 'The developmental effects of prenatal maternal stress: evolutionary explanations', in Wazana A, Szekely E and Oberlander TF (eds) *Prenatal Stress and Child Development*, New York: Springer

Hester M and Radford L (1996) 'Safety matters! Domestic violence and child contact, towards an interdisciplinary response', *Representing Children*, 8:4, pp. 49–60

Hester M, Pearson C and Harwin N with Abrahams H (2007) *Making an Impact: Children and domestic violence, A reader* (2nd edn), London: Jessica Kingsley Publishers

Hestia (2016) *From Victim to Survivor: Domestic abuse in 21st Century London*, available at: https://hestia.org/Handlers/Download.ashx?IDMF=401af254-1e2f-495d-84f8-947c1e2fb5eb

Hestia (2019) *Impact On Adults Who Have Experienced Domestic Violence In Childhood*, available at: https://www.hestia.org/Handlers/Download.ashx?IDMF=b1b2a3aa-9a26-4306-8080-5e711bbda1f8

Hirst M (2005) *Loving and Living with Traumatised Children: Reflections by adoptive parents*, London: BAAF

HM Government (2010) *Safeguarding Children and Young People who may be Affected by Gang Activity*, available at: https://assets.publishing.service.gov.uk/government/uploads/system/uploads/attachment_data/file/189392/DCSF-00064-2010.pdf.pdf

HM Government (2018a) *Working Together to Safeguard Children: A guide to inter-agency working to safeguard and promote the welfare of children*, available at: https://assets.publishing.service.gov.uk/government/uploads/system/uploads/attachment_data/file/942454/Working_together_to_safeguard_children_inter_agency_guidance.pdf

HM Government (2018b) *Serious Violence Strategy*, available at: https://assets.publishing.service.gov.uk/government/uploads/system/uploads/attachment_data/file/698009/serious-violence-strategy.pdf

Hogan F and O'Reilly M (2007) *Listening to Children: Children's stories of domestic violence*, Dublin: Department of Health and Children, available at: https://www.womensaid.ie/assets/files/pdf/listening_to_childrens_stories_of_domestic_violence.pdf

Holt A and Birchall J (2021) 'Their mum messed up and Gran can't afford to: violence towards grandparent kinship carers and the implications for social work', *British Journal of Social Work*, 52:3, pp. 1-18, available at: https://doi.org/10.1093/bjsw/bcab156

Holt S, Buckley H and Welan S (2008) 'The impact of exposure to domestic violence on children and young people: a review of the literature', *Child Abuse & Neglect*, 32:8, pp. 797–810

Home Office (2013) *Information for Local Areas on the Change to the Definition of Domestic Violence and Abuse*, available at: https://assets.publishing.sevice.gov.uk/government/uploads/system/uploads/attachment_data/file/142701/guide-on-definition-of-dv.pdf

Home Office (2015) *Controlling or Coercive Behaviour in an Intimate or Family Relationship: Statutory guidance framework*, available at: https://assets.publishing.service.gov.uk/government/uploads/system/uploads/attachment_data/file/482528/Controlling_or_coercive_behaviour_-_statutory_guidance.pdf

Home Office (2020) *Criminal Exploitation of Children and Vulnerable Adults: County lines*, available at: www.gov.uk/government/publications/criminal-exploitation-of-children-and-vulnerable-adults

Homes A and Grandison G (2021) *Trauma-Informed Practice: A toolkit for Scotland*, Edinburgh: Scottish Government, available at: https://www.careknowledge.com/media/49988/trauma-informed-practice-toolkit-scotland.pdf

Howell KH, Barnes SH, Miller LE and Graham-Bermann SA (2016) 'Developmental variations in the impact of intimate partner violence exposure during childhood', *Journal of Injury & Violence*, 8:1, pp. 43–57

Humphreys C and Mullender A (1999) *Children and Domestic Violence*, Dartington: Research in Practice

Humphreys C and Stanley N (eds) (2006) *Domestic Violence and Child Protection: Directions for good practice,* London: Jessica Kingsley Publishers

Humphreys C and Houghton C (2008) 'The research evidence on children and young people experiencing domestic violence', in Humphreys C, Houghton C and Ellis J (eds) *Literature Review: Better outcomes for children and young people experiencing domestic abuse – directions for good practice*, Edinburgh: Scottish Government

Humphries T, Kushalnagar P, Mathur G, Napoli DJ, Padden C, Rathmann C and Smith SR (2012) 'Language acquisition for deaf children: reducing the harms of zero tolerance to the use of alternative approaches', *Harm Reduction Journal*, 9:16, pp. 2–9

Hunt J (2020) *Two Decades of UK Research on Kinship Care: An overview*, London: Family Rights Group, available at: https://www.frg.org.uk/images/e-publications/Overview-research-kinship-care.pdf

Institute of Alcohol Studies (2014) *Alcohol, Domestic Abuse and Sexual Assault,* available at: www.ias.org/uploads/pdf/IAS%20report%20Alcohol%20domestic%20abuse%20

Ironside J (2004) 'Living a provisional existence: thinking about foster carers and the emotional containment of children placed in their care', *Adoption & Fostering*, 28:4, pp. 39–49

Ivaldi G (2000) *Surveying Adoption: A comprehensive analysis of local authority adoptions 1998–1999, England*, London: BAAF

James E (2020) *Not Just Collateral Damage: The hidden impact of domestic abuse on children*, Essex: Barnardo's, available at: https://www.barnardos.org.uk/sites/default/files/uploads/%27Not%20just%20collateral%20damage%27%20Barnardo%27s%20Report_0.pdf

Jenkins JM, Smith MA and Graham PJ (1989) 'Coping with parental quarrels', *Journal of the American Academy of Child & Adolescent Psychiatry*, 28:1, pp. 182–189

Johnson JE (2011) *Children Who Are Cruel to Animals: When to worry*, available at: www.psychologytoday.com/blog/the-human-equation

Johnson JK, Haider F, Ellis K, Hay DM and Lindow SW (2003) 'The prevalence of domestic violence in pregnant women', *BJOG: An international journal of obstetrics and gynaecology*, 110, pp. 272–275

Johnson K and Barlow C (2018) *Researching Police Responses to Coercive Control*, Policing Research Partnership, available at: https://www.n8prp.org.uk/2018/04/05/researching

Johnson MK and Mollborn S (2009) 'Growing up faster, feeling older: hardship in childhood and adolescence', *Social Psychology Quarterly*, 72:1, pp. 39–60

Jones D (2001) 'Assessment of parenting', in Horwath J, *The Child's World* (2nd edn), London: Jessica Kingsley Publishers

Jones D (2003) *Communicating with Vulnerable Children: A Guide for Practitioners*, London: Royal College of Psychiatrists & Gaskell

Joseph S, Govender K and Bhagwanjee A (2006) '"I can't see him hit her again, I just want to run away…hide and block my ears"', *Journal of Emotional Abuse*, 6:4, pp. 23–45

Julien RM (1995) *A Primer of Drug Action: A concise, non-technical guide to the actions, uses, and side effects of psychoactive drugs* (7th edn), New York: WH Freeman & Co

Kaniuk J (2010) *Supporting Adopters*, London: BAAF

Karakurt G and Silver KE (2013) 'Emotional abuse in intimate relationships: the role of gender and age', *Violence and Victims*, 28:5, pp. 804–821

Karr M (1995) *The Liars' Club*, Harmondsworth: Penguin

Katz E (2016) 'Beyond the physical incident model: how children living with domestic violence are harmed by and resist regimes of coercive control', *Child Abuse Review*, 25: pp. 46–59

Kaufman TL and Baams L (2021) 'Disparities in perpetrators, location, and reports of victimization for sexual and gender minority adolescents', *Journal of Adolescent Health*, pp.1–9, available at: https://doi.org/10.1016/j.jadohealth.2021.06.024

Kaur M (2021) 'Calls to Sikh domestic abuse group more than double in pandemic', *BBC News, 12 March*, available at: https://www.bbc.co.uk-calls-to-sikh-domestic

Kaysen D, Dillworth T, Simpson T, Waldrop A and Larimer ME (2006) 'Domestic violence and alcohol use: trauma-related symptoms and motives for drinking', *Addictive Behaviour.* 32:6, pp. 1272–1283

Kenyon P and Forde E (2020) *Thousands of Siblings Split up in Care System*, available at https://bettercarenetwork.org/thousands-of-siblings-split-up-in-care-system

Khalifeh H, Hargreaves J, Howard LM and Birdthistle I (2013) 'Intimate partner violence and socioeconomic deprivation in England: findings from a national cross-sectional survey', *American Journal of Public Health*, 103:3, pp. 462–472

Kidger J, Heron J, Lewis G, Evans J and Gunnell D (2012) 'Adolescent self-harm and suicidal thoughts in the ALSPAC cohort: a self-report survey in England', *BMC Psychiatry*, 12:69

Koenen KC, Moffitt TE, Caspi A, Taylor A and Purcell S (2003) 'Domestic violence is associated with environmental suppression of IQ in young children', *Development and Psychopathology*, 15:2, pp. 297–311

Kroll B and Taylor A (2003) *Parental Substance Misuse and Child Welfare*, London: Jessica Kingsley Publishers

Lee-Kelland R and Finlay F (2018) 'Children who abuse animals: when should you be concerned about child abuse? A review of the literature', *Archives of Disease in Childhood*, 103:8, pp. 801–805

Leeds City Council (2014) *Kinship Care (Family and Friends) Policy*, available at: https://democracy.leeds.gov.uk/documents/s128961/2Leeds

Levendosky AA, Huth-Bocks AC, Semel MA and Shapiro DL (2002a) 'Trauma symptoms in preschool-age children exposed to domestic violence', *Journal of Interpersonal Violence*, 17, pp. 150–164

Levendosky AA, Huth-Bocks AC and Semel MA (2002b) 'Adolescent peer relationships and mental health functioning in families with domestic violence', *Journal of Clinical Child and Adolescent Psychology*, 31:2, pp. 206–218

Lloyd M (2018) 'Domestic violence and education: examining the impact of domestic violence on young children, children, and young people and the potential role of schools', *Frontiers in Psychology*, 9:13, article no. 2094

Local Government Association (2021 *Tackling Child Exploitation: Resources pack*, available at: https://www.local.gov.uk/publications/tackling-child-exploitation

Lord J and Borthwick S (2008) *Together or Apart: Assessing siblings for permanent placement* (2nd edn), London: BAAF

Luthra R, Abramovitz R, Greenberg R, Schoor A, Newcorn J, Schmeidler J, Levine P, Nomura Y and Chemtob CM (2009) 'Relationship between type of trauma exposure and post-traumatic stress disorder among urban children and adolescents', *Journal of Interpersonal Violence* 24:11, pp. 1919–1927

Lyons M and Brewer G (2021) 'Experiences of intimate partner violence during lockdown and the Covid-19 pandemic', *Journal of Family Violence*, 26 February, pp. 1–9

McCloskey LA and Lichter EL (2003) 'The contribution of marital violence to adolescent aggression across different relationships', *Journal of Interpersonal Violence*, 18:4, pp. 390–412

McDonald SE, Collins EA, Nicotera N, Hageman TO, Ascione FR, Williams JH and Graham-Bermann SA (2015) 'Children's experiences of companion animal maltreatment in households characterised by intimate partner violence', *Child Abuse & Neglect*, 50, pp. 11–127

McGaha-Garnett V (2013) *Effects of Violence on Academic Progress and Classroom Behavior: From a parent's perspective*, ACA Knowledge Center, available at: https://www.counselling.org/docs/default-source/vistas/the-effects-of-violence-on-academic-progress-and-classroom-behavior.pdf?sfvrsn=1828de3f_12

McGee C (2000) *Childhood Experiences of Domestic Violence*, London: Jessica Kingsley Publishers

McGill L, Coman W, McWhirter J and O'Sullivan C (2018) 'Social workers' experiences of using the narrative model to talk to children about why they are in care and other sensitive issues', *Adoption & Fostering*, 42:1, pp. 49–57

McMullan P (2008, updated 2016 by Dibben E) 'Life story work', *Community Care Inform*, available at: https://www.ccinform.co.uk/topic/adoption/life-story-work

McParlin P (2019) 'We have to get serious about child-on-adoptive-parent violence', *Community Care*, available at: www.communitycare.co.uk/2019/08/07/get-serious

Malone LP (2017) *Gender Identity and Childhood Experiences: An introductory qualitative study of the relationships between gender identity and adverse childhood experiences*, Smith ScholarWorks, available at: https://scholarworks.smith.edu/cgi/viewcontent.cgi?article=2979&context=theses

Marchetti D, Musso P, Verrocchio MC, Manna G, Kopala-Sibley DC, De Berardis D, De Santis S and Falgares F (2021) 'Childhood maltreatment, personality vulnerability profiles, and borderline personality disorder symptoms in adolescents', *Development and Psychopathology*, 26:1–14

Martinez-Torteya C, Bogat GA, Lonstein J, Granger DA and Levendosky AA (2017) 'Exposure to intimate partner violence in utero and infant internalising behaviors: moderation by salivary cortisol-alpha amylase asymmetry', *Early Human Development*, 113, pp. 40–48

Maye J (2011) *Me and My Family*, London: BAAF

Meakings S and Selwyn J (2016) '"She was a foster mother who said she didn't give cuddles": the adverse early foster care experiences of children who later struggle with adoptive family life', *Clinical Child Psychology and Psychiatry*, 21:4, pp. 509–519

Meltzer H, Gatward R, Corbin T, Goodman R and Ford T (2003) *The Mental Health of Young People Looked After in Local Authorities in England*, London: The Stationery Office

Mental Health Foundation (2002) *The Mental Health of Looked-After Children*, available at: https://www.mentalhealth.org.uk/sites/default/files/mental_health_looked_after_children.pdf

Mental Health Foundation (2006) *Truth Hurts: Report of the National Inquiry into Self-Harm among Young People*, available at: https://www.mentalhealth.org.uk/sites/default/files/truth_hurts.pdf

Mertin P and Mohr PB (2002) 'Incidence and correlates of post-trauma symptoms in children from backgrounds of domestic violence', *Violence and Victims*, 17:5, pp. 555–567

Metro (2020) *Growing up with a Violent Father has Affected Every Relationship I've Had*, available at:

https://metro.co.uk/2020/02/27/growing-violent-father-affected-every-relationship-ive-12312524/?ito=cbshare

Meuleners LB, Lee AH, Janssen PA, Fraser ML (2011) 'Maternal and foetal outcomes among pregnant women hospitalised due to interpersonal violence: a population based study in Western Australia, 2002–2008', *BMC Pregnancy Childbirth*, 11:70

Meyer S, Reeves E and Fitz-Gibbon K (2021) 'The intergenerational transmission of family violence: mothers' perceptions of children's experiences and use of violence in the home', *Child & Family Social Work*, 26:3, pp. 476-484

Mezey GC and Bewley S (1997) 'Domestic violence and pregnancy', *British Journal of Obstetric Gynaecology*, 104:55, pp. 528–531

Mind (2020) *What is Psychosis?*, available at: www.mind.org.uk/types-of-mental-health-problems/about/psychosis

Moffitt TE and Caspi A (1998) 'Implications of violence between intimate partners for child psychologists and psychiatrists', *Journal of Child Psychology and Psychiatry*, 39:2, pp. 137–144

Monk D and Macvarish J (2018) *Siblings, Contact and the Law: An overlooked relationship*, available at: http://www.nuffieldfoundation.org/siblings-contact-and-law-overlooked-relationship

Monckton Smith J (2021) *In Control: Dangerous relationships and how they end in murder*, London: Bloomsbury Publishing

Morrison M (2016) *Undertaking a Child Assessment (Scotland)*, London: CoramBAAF

Morrison M (2018) *Effective Adoption and Fostering Panels in Scotland*, London: CoramBAAF

Mullender A and Morely R (eds) (1994) *Children Living with Domestic Violence*, London: Whiting & Birch

Mullender A, Hague G, Imam U, Kelly L, Malos E and Regan L (2002) *Children's Perspectives of Family Violence*, London: Sage Publications

Mullender A (2006) 'What children tell us: "He's said he was going to kill our mum"', in Humphreys C and Stanley N, *Domestic Violence and Child Protection: Directions for good practice*, London: Jessica Kingsley Publishers

Murray L and Andrews L (2000) *The Social Baby*, Richmond, Surrey: CP Publishing

Narey M and Owers M (2018) *Foster Care in England: A review for the Department for Education*, available at: https://assets.publishing.service.gov.uk/government/uploads/system/uploads/attachment_data/file/679320/Foster_Care_in_England_Review.pdf

National Assembly for Wales' Health and Social Care Committee (2015) *Inquiry into Alcohol and Substance Misuse: Consultation responses*, available at: https://senedd.assembly.wales/documents/b8731/Inquiry%20into%alcohol%20and%20substance%20misuse%20consultation%20responses%20Wednesday%2004-Feb-2015%2009.15%20Hea.pdf?T=9

National Child Trauma Stress Network (2010) *Domestic Violence and Children: Questions and answers for domestic violence project advocates*, available at: https://www.doj.state.or.us/wp-content/uploads/2017/08/domestic_violence_and_children.pdf

National Institute for Health and Care Excellence (2017) *Child Abuse and Neglect [NG76] Guideline*, available at: www.nice.org.uk/guidance-child-abuse-and-neglect-guideline

National Scientific Council on the Developing Child (2007) *The Science of Early Childhood Development*, available at: https://46y5eh11fhgw3ve3ytpwxt9r-wpengine.netdna-ssl.com/wp-content/uploads/2015/05/Science

National Statistics (2018) *Health Survey for England 2017: Adult and child overweight and obesity*, NHS Digital, available at: https//www.health survey.hscic.gov.uk/media/78619/HSE17-Adult-Child-BMI-rep.pdf

NCH Action for Children (1994) *The Hidden Victims: Children and domestic violence,* London: NCH Action for Children

Neil E, Young J and Hartley L (2018) *The Joys and Challenges of Adoptive Family Life: A survey of adoptive parents in the Yorkshire and Humberside region*, Norwich: Centre for Research on Children and Families, University of East Anglia (UEA)

Neil E, Beek M and Schofield G (2020) *The UEA Moving to Adoption Model: A guide for adoption social workers, fostering social workers and children's social workers*, Norwich: Centre for Research on Children and Families, UEA, available at: https://www.movingtoadoption.co.uk/wp-content/2020/07/Moving-to-Adoption-Practice-Programme-2020-v6.pdf

New Economics Foundation (2014) *Relationships for Children in Care: The value of mentoring and befriending,* available at: https://b.3cdn.net/nefoundation/ff6e91d7f5a3ca8a7d_ccm6ba7cj.pdf

Newberry M (2017) 'Pets in danger: exploring the link between domestic violence and animal abuse', *Aggression and Violent Behavior*, 34, pp. 273–281

NHS (2018) *Mental Health of Children and Young People in England, 2017*, available at: https://files.digital.nhs.uk/A6/EA7D58/MHCYP%202017%20Summary.pdf

NHS Digital (2018) *Mental Health of Children and Young People in England, 2017: Summary of key findings*, available at: https://files.digital.nhs.uk/A6/EA7D58/MHCYP%202017%20Summary.pdf

NHS Digital (2019) *Smoking, Drinking and Drug Use among Young People in England 2018*, available at: www.digital.nhs.uk/publications/statistical/smoking-drinking-and-drug-use-among-young-people-in-England-2018

NHS England (2017) *Child Sexual Exploitation: Advice for healthcare staff*, available at: https://www.england.nhs.uk/wp-content/uploads/2017/02/cse-pocket-guide.pdf

NICE (2016) *Psychosis and Schizophrenia in Children and Young People: Recognition and management*, available at: https://www.nice.org.uk/guidance/cg155/resources/psychosis-and schizophrenia-in-children-and-young-people.pdf

NSPCC (2018) *Children Living in Families Facing Adversity: NSPCC Helplines report,* London: NSPCC

NSPCC (2020a) *Calls about Domestic Abuse Highest on Record Following Lockdown Increase*, available at: www.nspcc.org.uk/about-us/new-opinion/Calls-about-domestic-abuse-highest-on-record-following-lockdown-increase/

NSPCC (2020b) *Signs of Self-Harm in Children and Teenagers*, available at: www.nspcc.org.uk/childrens-mental-health/self-harm

NSPCC (2020c) *Grooming*, available at: www.nspcc.org.uk /what-is-child-abuse/types-of-abuse

NSPCC (2021a) *Life Story Work*, available at: https://learning.nspcc.org.uk/life-story-work

NSPCC (2021b) *Criminal Exploitation and Gangs*, available at: https://www.nspcc.org.uk/types-of-abuse/gangs-criminal

Nuffield Trust (2019) *Teenage Pregnancy*, available at: www.nuffieldtrust.org.uk/teenage-pregnancy

Nuffield Trust (2021) *Obesity*, available at: www.nuffieldtrust.org.uk/resource/obesity

Nuttall D, Rea D, Bennett CV, Hollen L, Mullen S, Maguire S, Emond A, Kemp A and Deave T (2020) 'Would shared health visitor and emergency department records improve recognition of child maltreatment within the emergency department? A multicentre study', *Child Abuse Review*, 29:6, pp. 518–528

Nwabunike C and Tenkorang EY (2015) 'Domestic and marital violence among three ethnic groups in Nigeria', *Journal of Interpersonal Violence*, 32:18, pp. 1–26

Oakley MW and Masson J (2000) 'Official friends and friendly officials', included in O'Quigley A, *Listening to Children's Views: The findings and recommendations of recent research*, York, Joseph Rowntree Foundation, available at: www.jrf.org.uk/default/files/jrf/migrated/files/1859353363.pdf

Office for National Statistics (2016) *Intimate Personal Violence and Partner Abuse*, available at: www.ons.gov.uk/Intimate-personal-violence-and-partner-abuse

Office for National Statistics (2018a) *Domestic Abuse in England and Wales: Findings from the Crime Survey for England and Wales: Year ending March 2018*, available at: www.ons.gov.uk/Domestic-abuse-in-England-Wales-year-ending-March2018

Office for National Statistics (2018b) *Partner Abuse in Detail, England and Wales: Year ending March 2018*, available at: www.ons.gov.uk /Partner-abuse-in-detail-year-ending-March2018

Office for National Statistics (2019) *Domestic Abuse Victim Characteristics England and Wales: Year ending March 2019*, available at: www.ons.gov.uk/Domestic-abuse-victim-characteristics-year-ending-March2019

Office for National Statistics (2020a) *Domestic Abuse in England and Wales Overview: November 2020*, available at: www.ons.gov.uk /Domestic-abuse-in-England-and-Wales-overview-November2020

Office for National Statistics (2020b) *Child Abuse Extent and Nature, England and Wales: Year ending March 2019*, available at: www.ons.gov.uk/Child-abuse-extent-and-nature-year-ending-March2019

Office for National Statistics (2020c) *Conceptions in England and Wales: 2018*, available at: www.ons.gov.uk/conceptionandfertilityrates/bulletins

Office on Women's Health (2018) *Domestic Intimate Partner Violence*, available at: www.women'shealth.gov

Ofsted (2020) *Fostering in England 2018 to 2019: Main findings*, available at: https://www.gov.uk/government/statistics/fostering-inengland-1-april-2018-to-31-march-2019

Onyskiw JE (2003) 'Domestic violence and children's adjustment', *Journal of Emotional Abuse*, 3:1–2, pp. 11–45

Overup CS, DiBello AM, Brunson JA, Acitelli LK and Neighbors C (2015) 'Drowning the pain: intimate partner violence and drinking to cope prospectively predict problem drinking', *Addictive Behaviour*, 41: pp. 152–161

Oxleas NHS (2007) *An Eye for an Eye will make the Whole World Blind*, available at: www.oxleas.nhs.uk/sitemedia/cmsdownloads/NVR_for_parents_web_mgRKEiw.pdf

PAC-UK (2012) *Specialist Therapy, Advice, Support, Counselling and Training for all Affected by Adoption and Permanency*, London: Family Action

PAC-UK and Department for Education (2017) *Meeting the Needs of Adopted and Permanently Placed Children: A guide for school staff*, available at: https://www.pac-uk.org/wp-content/uploads/2017/10/Meeting-the-needs-of-adopted-and-permanently-placed-children-A-guide-for-school-staff.pdf

Page S (2020) '"People get killed cause of there [their] skin. IT CANNOT BE STOPPED": a Midlands case study considering experiences of racism amongst pupils in UK secondary schools and the community', *British Journal of Community Justice*, 16:1, pp. 64–81

Parliamentary Taskforce (2020) *First Thought Not Afterthought: Report of the Parliamentary Taskforce on Kinship Care*, available at: https://www.frg.org.uk/family-and-friends-carers/cross-party-parliamentary-taskforce

Parrot A and Cummings N (2006) *Forsaken Females: The global brutilization of women*, New York: Rowman and Littlefield

Partnership Projects (2021) *Introduction to NVR*, available at: https://www.partnershipprojectsuk.co./introduction-to-NVR

Peake A (undated) *Life Story Work: A resource for foster carers, residential social workers, adoptive parents, and kinship carers, to support this work*, available at: https://www2.oxfordshire.gov.uk/cms/sites/default/files/folders/documents/childreneducationandfamilies/educationandlearning/schools/virtualschools/Life_Story_Work_Booklet.pdf

Peckover S (2001) 'Domestic violence and the protection of babies: the role of health care professionals', in Gordon R and Harran E (eds) *Fragile: Handle with Care: Protecting babies from harm: Reader*, Leicester: NSPCC

Perry BD, Pollard RA, Blakley TL, Baker WL and Vigilante D (1995) 'Childhood trauma, the neurobiology of adaptation and "use-dependent" development of the brain: how states become traits', *Infant Mental Health Journal*, 16:4, pp. 271–291

Petkova H, Simic M, Nicholls D, Ford T, Prina A, Stuart R, Livingstone N, Kelly G, Macdonald G, Eisler I, Gowers S, Barrett BM and Byford S (2019) 'Incidence of anorexia nervosa in young people in the UK and Ireland: a national surveillance study', *BMJ Open*, 2019:9, e027339

Phillips R (2004) *Children Exposed to Parental Substance Misuse*, London: BAAF

Pietrangelo A (2018) *How to Recognise the Signs of Mental and Emotional Abuse*, Healthline, available at: www.healthline.com/health/signs-of-mental-abuse

Pires de Almeida C, Sa E, Cunha F and Pires EP (2012) 'Violence during pregnancy and its effects on mother–baby relationship during pregnancy', *Journal of Reproductive and Infant Psychology*, 31:4, pp. 370–380

Pitcher D and Jaffar S (2018) '"To another's house": the experiences of Muslim young people in foster care', *Adoption & Fostering*, 42:3, pp. 219–233

Platt L (2007) *Poverty and Ethnicity in the UK*, Bristol: Joseph Rowntree Foundation

Powell A (2010) *Sex, Power and Consent: Youth culture and the unwritten rules*, Cambridge: Cambridge University Press

Public Law Working Group (2020) *Recommendations to Achieve Best Practice in the Child Protection and Family Justice Systems: Special guardianship orders*, available at: https://www.judiciary.uk/wp-content/uploads/2020/06/PLWG-SGO-Final-Report-1.pdf

Quilgars D, Johnsen S and Pleace N (2008) *Youth Homelessness in the UK: A decade of progress?*, York: Joseph Rowntree Foundation, available at: https://www.jrf.org.uk/sites/default/files/jrf/migrated/files/2220-homelessness-young-people.pdf

Radcliffe P, d'Oliveira AFPL, Lea S, dos Santos Figueiredo W and Gilchirist G (2017) 'Accounting for intimate partner violence perpetration. A cross-cultural comparison of English and Brazilian male substance users' explanations', *Drug Alcohol Review*, 36:1, pp. 64–71

Radford L, Corral S, Bradley C, Fisher H, Bassett C, Howat N and Collishaw S (2011) *Child Abuse and Neglect in the UK Today*, London: NSPCC

Rainer, Prince's Trust and Mentoring and Befriending Foundation (2008) *Mentoring for Looked After Children*, Kent: Rainer

Ramsey S, Randour ML, Blaney N and Gupta M (2010) 'Protecting domestic violence victims by protecting their pets', *Juvenile & Family Justice Today*, Spring 2010

Ran Kim J (2009) *Ambiguous Loss Haunts Foster and Adopted Children*, North American Council on Adoptable Children, available at: fosteringperspectives.org/ambiguous

Reed J with Parish N (2021) *Working for Babies: Lockdown lessons from local systems*, London: Parent Infant Foundation, available at: https://parentinfantfoundation.org.uk/wp-content/uploads/2021/01/210115-F1001D-Working-for-Babies-Report-FINAL-v1.0-compressed.pdf

Rees G and Lee J (2005) *Still Running 2: Findings from the second national survey of young runaways*, London: The Children's Society

Rees G (2011) *Still Running 3: Early findings from our third national survey of young runaways, 2011*, London: The Children's Society, available at: https://www.childrenssociety.org.uk/sits/default/files/tcs/still_running_3_full_report_final.pdf

Reimer D (2010) '"Everything was strange and different": young adults' recollections of the transition into foster care', *Adoption & Fostering*, 34:2, pp. 14–22

Reynolds M with Reynolds L (2021) *The Wild Track: Adopting, mothering, belonging*, London: Doubleday

Rice F, Frederickson N, Shelton K, McManus C, Riglin L and Ng-Knight T (2019) *Identifying Factors that Predict Successful and Difficult Transitions to Secondary School*, available at: https://nuffieldfoundation.org/wp-content/uploads/2019/11/STARS_report.pdf

Rigopoulo M (2015) 'Inviting in the storm' in Cleaver H, *Parenting a Child Affected by Domestic Violence*, London: BAAF

Robinson C and Fielding M (2007) *Children and their Primary Schools: Pupils' voices*, Primary Review Research Survey 5/3, available at: https://cprtrust.org.uk/wp-content/uploads/2014/06/Research_Survey_5_3.pdf

Rolle L, Giardina G, Caldarera AM, Geriono E and Brustia P (2018) 'When intimate partner violence meets same sex couples: a review of same sex intimate partner violence', *Frontline Psychology*, 21:9, 1506, available at doi:10.3389/psyg.2018.01506

Rose R and Philpot T (2004) *The Child's Own Story: Life story work with traumatised children*, London: Jessica Kingsley Publishers

Rose W (2006) 'The developing world of the child: children's perspectives', in Aldgate J, Rose W and Jeffery C (eds), *The Developing World of the Child*, London: Jessica Kingsley Publishers

Ross N, Cocks J, Johnston L and Stoker (2017) *'No voice, no opinion, nothing': Parent experiences when children are removed and placed in care*, available at: https://www.lwb.org.au/assets/Parental-perspectives-OOHC-Final-Report-Feb-2017.pdf

Rushton A (2004) 'A scoping and scanning review of research on the adoption of children placed from public care', *Clinical Child Psychology and Psychiatry*, 9:1, pp. 89–106

Rutgers AH, Bakermans-Kranenburg MJ, van Ijzendoorn MH and van Berckelaer-Onnes IA (2004) 'Autism and attachment: a meta-analytic review', *Journal of Child Psychology and Psychiatry*, 45:6, pp. 1123–1134

Rutter M (1981) *Maternal Deprivation Reassessed*, London: Penguin

Rutter M (2007) 'Resilience, competence, and coping', *Child Abuse & Neglect*, 31:2, pp. 205–210

Rutter M, Graham P, Chadwick O and Yule W (1976) 'Adolescent turmoil? Fact or fiction', *Journal of Child Psychology and Psychiatry*, 7, pp. 35–56

Ryan T and Walker R (2016) *Life Story Work: Why, what, how and when*, London: CoramBAAF

SafeLives (2014) *In Plain Sight: Effective help for children exposed to domestic abuse*, available at: https://safelives.org.uk/sites/default/files/resources/Final%20policy%20report%20In%20plain%20sight%20-%20effective%20help%20for%20children%20exposed%20to%20domestic%20abuse.pdf

SafeLives (2015) *Insights Idva National Dataset 2013–14*, Bristol: SafeLives

SafeLives (2016) *A Cry for Health: Why we must invest in domestic abuse services in hospitals*, available at: https://safelives.org.uk/sites/default/files/resources/SAFJ4993_Themis_report_WEBcorrect.pdf

REFERENCES

St Giles (2021) *Child Criminal Exploitation: Advice and support for parents and caregivers*, available at: www.stgilestrust.org.uk/help-for-parents-and-children

Saleem Khan I (2020) 'Consent in marriage: a radical feminist analysis of Pakistani law', *William & Mary Journal of Women and the Law*, 26:3

SAMHSA (2014) *SAMHSA's Concept of Trauma and Guidance for a Trauma-Informed Approach*, available at: www.samhsa.gov

Sayers A and Roach R (2011) *Child Appreciation Days*, London: BAAF

Schofield G (2006) 'Middle childhood: five to eleven years', in Aldgate J, Jones D, Rose W and Jeffery C (eds) *The Developing World of the Child*, London: Jessica Kingsley Publishers

Schofield G (2009) 'Permanence in foster care', in Schofield G and Simmonds J (eds) *The Child Placement Handbook: Policy, research and practice*, London: BAAF

Schofield G and Beek M (2014) *The Secure Base Model*, London: BAAF

Schofield G and Beek M (2018) *Attachment Handbook For Foster Care and Adoption* (2nd edn), London: CoramBAAF

Schofield G, Beek M and Ward E (2012) 'Part of the family: planning for permanence in long-term family foster care', *Children and Youth Services Review*, 34, pp. 244–253

Scott S, McNeish D, Bovarnick S and Pearce J (2019) *What Works in Responding to Child Sexual Exploitation*, London: Barnardo's, available at: www.dmss.co.uk/pdfs/what-works-incse.pdf

Scottish Government (2010) *Guidance on Looked After Children (Scotland) Regulations 2009 and the Children Adoption and Children (Scotland) Act 2007*, available at http://www.scotland.gov.uk/Publications/2010/06/01094202/1

Scottish Government (2018) *Improving Attainment for Looked After Children*, available at: https://www.gov.scot/improving-attainment-for-looked-after-children

Scottish Government (2021) *Care Experienced Children and Young People Fund: National operational guidance*, available at: https://www.gov.scot/care-experienced-children-and-young-people-national-operational-guidance

Selwyn J, Quinton D, Harris P, Wijedasa D, Nawaz S and Wood M (2010) *Pathways to Permanence for Black, Asian and Mixed Ethnicity Children*, London: BAAF

Selwyn J, Wijedasa D and Meakings S (2014) *Beyond the Adoption Order: Challenges, interventions and adoption disruption*, DfE, available at: https://assets.publishing.service.gov.uk/government/uploads/system/uploads/attachment_data/file/301889/Final_Report_-_3rd_April_2014v2.pdf

Shah S (ed) (2014) *Preparing to Adopt in England: Applicant's workbook*, London: BAAF

Shah S (ed) (2019) *Preparing to Adopt in Scotland: Applicant's workbook*, London: CoramBAAF

Silverstein M, Augustyn M, Cabral H and Zuckerman B (2006) 'Maternal depression and violence exposure: double jeopardy for child school functioning', *Pediatrics*, 118:3 e792-e800

Simmonds J, Harwin J, Brown R and Broadhurst K (2019) *Special Guardianship: A review of the evidence: Summary report*, London: Nuffield Family Justice Observatory, available at: https://www.nuffieldfjo.org.uk/files/documents/NuffieldFJO-Special-Guardianship-190731-WEBfinal.pdf

Simpson JE and Clapton G (2020) 'A brief history of contact in fostering and adoption: practice and power, and the coming of the mobile phone', *Adoption & Fostering*, 44:3, pp. 272–284

Sinclair I (2005) *Fostering Now: Messages from research*, London: Jessica Kingsley Publishers

Sinclair I, Baker C, Lee J and Gibbs I (2007) *The Pursuit of Permanence: A study of the English child care system*, London: Jessica Kingsley Publishers

Singer E (2016) *Children and Adoption: The school age years (6-11)*, Center for Adoption Support and Education, available at: https://adoptionsupport.org/wp-content/uploads/2015/12/02-The-School-Age-Years.pdf

Skafida V, Morrison F and Devaney J (2021) *Mothers Living with Domestic Abuse in Scotland – A tale of poverty and social inequality*, available at: https://www.crfr.ac.uk/wp-content/uploads/2021/03/Mothers-living-with-domestic-abuse-in-Scotland-CRFR-94.pdf

Smith PK and Cowie H (1993) *Understanding Children's Development*, Oxford: Blackwell

Social Care Institute for Excellence (2004) *Fostering: Placement stability*, available at: www.scie.org.uk/publications/guides/guide07/

Solmi F, Sharpe H, Gage SH, Maddock J and Lewis G (2020) 'Changes in the prevalence and correlates of weight-control behaviors and weight perception in adolescents in the UK, 1986-2015', *JAMA Pediatrics*, available at: doi: 10.1001/jamapediatrics.2020.4746

Stafford A, Stead J and Grimes M (2007) *The Support Needs of Children and Young People Who Have to Move Home Because of Domestic Abuse*, Edinburgh: Scottish Women's Aid

Stanley N, Miller P, Richardson Foster H and Thomson G (2010) *Children and Families Experiencing Domestic Violence: Police and children's social services responses*, available at: www.nspcc.org.uk/inform

Stein M, Rees G, Hicks L and Gorin S (2009) *Neglected Adolescents: Literature review*, London: DCSF

Stonewall (2017) *School Report: The experiences of lesbian, gay, bi and trans young people in Britain's schools in 2017*, available at: www.stonewall.org.uk/get-involved/education

Stoye DQ, Blesa M, Sullivan G, Galdi P, Lamb GJ, Black GS, Quigley AJ, Thrippleton MJ, Bastin ME, Reynolds RM and Boardman JP (2020) 'Maternal cortisol is associated with neonatal amygdala microstructure and connectivity in sexual dimorphic manner', *eLife*, e60729

Stuewig J and McCloskey LA (2005) 'The relation of child maltreatment to shame and guilt among adolescents: psychological routes to depression and delinquency', *Child Maltreatment*, 10: pp. 324–336

Sullivan CM, Juras J, Bybee D, Nguyen H and Allen N (2000) 'How children's adjustment is affected by their relationships to their mothers' abusers', *Journal of Interpersonal Violence,* 15:6, pp. 587–602

Summers R and Hoffman AM (2002) *Domestic Violence: A global view*, Westport, CT: Greenwood Press

Swain V (2016) *Keeping Connected: Maintaining relationships when moving on*, The Fostering Network, available at: https://www.thefosteringnetwork.org.uk/sites/default/files/2021-03/keep_connected_4_feb_v2_...

Swan C, Gambone LJ, Caldwell JE, Sullivan TP and Snow DL (2008) 'A review of research on women's use of violence with male intimate partners', *Violence and Victims*, 23:3, pp. 301–314

Swift R (2020) *Adopting a Child in Scotland* (2nd edn), London: CoramBAAF

Taub A (2020) 'As domestic abuse rises, UK failings leave victims in peril', *New York Times*, 2 July 2020, available at: https://www.nytimes.com/interactive/2020/07/02/world/europe/uk-coronavirus-domestic-abuse.html

Teicher HM and Vigtaliano GD (2011) 'Witnessing violence toward siblings: an understudied but potent form of early adversity', *Plus One*, 6:12

The Care Inquiry (2013) *Making not Breaking: Building relationships for our most vulnerable children*, available at: https://www.becomecharity.org.uk/media/1129/care_inquiry_-_full_report_april_2013.pdf

The Child Psychology Service CIC (2015) *Therapeutic Parenting for Looked After and Adopted Children*, available at: www.thechildpsychologicalservice.co.uk

The Children's Society (2011) *Make Runaways Safe*, available at: www.childrenssociety.org.uk/sites/default/files/tcs/make-runaways-safe-report.pdf

The Conversation UK (2014) *How Taking Drugs While Pregnant Harms Unborn Babies*, available at: www.theconversation.com

The Fostering Network (2016) *Delegated Authority*, available at: https://www.thefosteringnetwork.org.uk/delegated-authority

The Fostering Network (2019) *Not Forgotten: The importance of keeping in touch with former foster carers*, available at: https://www.thefosteringnetwork.org.uk/sites/default/files/2001-03/Not%20forgotten%20report

The Fostering Network (2021) *State of the Nation's Foster Care*, available at: www.thefosteringnetwork.org.uk/sotn

The Guardian (2021) 'I've seen women who have been abused for more than 20 years', *The Guardian G2*, 2021, 17 February, pp. 4–7

The Institute of Public Care at Oxford Brookes University (2020) *Evaluation of the Adoption Support Fund: Local authority and provider experiences*, available at: https://assets.publishing.service.gov.uk/government/uploads/system/uploads/attachment_data/file/869762?Eval_of_ASF_draft_LA_provider_report_March-2020.pdf

The Law Commission (LAW COM. No 205) (1992) *Criminal Law Rape within Marriage*, London: HMSO

The Mental Health Foundation (2002) *The Mental Health of Looked After Children, Bright Futures: Working with vulnerable young people*, London: Mental Health Foundation, available at: https://www.mentalhealth.org.uk/sites/default/default/files/mental_health_looked_after_children.pdf

The Observer (2020) *Revealed: Surge in domestic violence during Covid-19 crisis*, available at: www.theguardian.com

Thomas C and Beckford V with Lowe N and Murch M (1999) *Adopted Children Speaking*, London: BAAF

Townsend H (2019) *What Survival Looks Like at Home*, available at: https://beaconhouse.org.uk/wp-content/uploads/2019/09/What-Survival-Looks-Like-At-Home.pdf

Tsavoussis A, Stawoclo SPA, Stoicea N and Papadimos TJ (2014) 'Child-witnessed domestic violence and its adverse effects on brain development: a call for societal self-examination and awareness', *Frontiers in Public Health*, 2:178

Umana-Taylor AJ, Lee RM, Rivas-Drake D, Syed M, Seaton E, Quintana SM, Cross WE, Schwartz SJ, Yip T, and Ethnic and Racial Identity in the 21st Century Study Group (2014) 'Ethnic and racial identity during adolescence and into young adulthood: an integrated conceptualisation', *Child Development*, 85:1, pp. 21–39

UNICEF (2006) *Behind Closed Doors: The impact of domestic violence on children*, London: UNICEF and Body Shop International, available at: www.unicef.org/media/files/BehindClosedDoors

United Nations Convention on the Rights of the Child (1990) *Convention on the Rights of the Child*, London: UNICEF, available at: www.unicef.org.uk

University of Oxford, Centre for Suicide Research (2015) *Coping with Self-Harm: A guide for parents and carers*, available at: www.psych.ox.ac.uk/files/news/copy_of_coping-with-self-harm-brochure_final_copyright.pdf

Varese F, Smeets F, Drukker M, Lieverse R, Lataster T, Viechtbauer W, Read J, van Os J and Bentall RP (2012) 'Childhood adversities increase the risk of psychosis: a meta-analysis of patient-control, prospective and cross-sectional cohort studies', *Schizophrenia Bulletin*, 38:4, pp. 661–671

Victims' Commissioner (2020) *Recognition of Children as Victims of Domestic Abuse, and Improved Protections for Victims in Family Courts Announced*, available at: www.victimscommissioner.org.uk/news/recognition-of-children

Victims' Commissioner (2021) *Commissioners Endorse Non-Fatal Strangulation Amendment to the Domestic Abuse Bill*, available at: www.victimscommissioner.org.uk/news/commissioners-endorse-non-fatal-strangulation-amendment

Walby S (2004) *The Cost of Domestic Violence*, available at: https://eprints.lancs.ac.uk/id/eprint/55255/1/cost_of_dv_report_sept04.pdf

Walby S and Allen J (2004) *Domestic Violence, Sexual Assault and Stalking: Findings from the British Crime Survey*, available at: www.nomsintranet.org.uk/roh/official-documents/HomeOfficeResearchStudy276

Ward H (2019) *Permanent Exclusions of Looked-After Children at Five-Year Low*, available at: https://www.tes.com/news/permanent-exclusions-looked-after-children-five-year-low

Ward H and Skuse T (2001) 'Performance targets and stability of placements for children long looked after away from home', *Children and Society*, 15, pp. 333–346

Ward H, Munro ER and Dearden C (2006) *Babies and Young Children in Care*, London: Jessica Kingsley Publishers

Ward H, Brown R and Westlake D (2012) *Safeguarding Babies and Very Young Children from Abuse and Neglect*, London: Jessica Kingsley Publishers

Warman A (2016) 'Eating well and nurturing others: the role of food in good fostering practice', *Adoption & Fostering*, 40:2, pp. 140–152

Watson D, Lancaster B and Meineck C (2018) 'Adopted children's co-production and use of "trove" (a digitally enhanced memory box) to better understand their care histories through precious objects', *Clinical Child Psychology and Psychiatry*, 23:4, pp. 614–628

Wellings K, Nanchahal K, Macdowall W, McManus S, Mercer CH, Johnson AM, Copas AJ, Korovessis C, Fenton KA and Field J (2001) 'Sexual behaviour in Britain: early heterosexual experience', *The Lancet*, 358:9296, pp. 1843–1850

Welsh Government and Barnardo's Wales (2013) *Sexual Exploitation: Sex, secrets and lies*, available at: https://www.dorset.police.uk/media/1425/cse_booklet_sex_secrets_lies_engver.pdf

Whitaker DJ, Haileyesus T, Swahn M and Saltzman LS (2007) 'Differences in frequency of violence and reported injury between relationships with reciprocal and nonreciprocal intimate partner violence', *American Journal of Public Health*, 97:5, pp. 941–947

White T (2022) *I was a Child Victim of Domestic Abuse – I Know how Badly Kids like me Need Support*, available at: https://www.theguardian.com/commentisfree/2022/feb/03/child-victim-domestic-abuse-support-bill-services

Wijedasa D (2015) *The Prevalence and Characteristics of Children Growing up with Relatives in the UK*, Bristol: Hadley Centre for Adoption and Foster Care Studies, University of Bristol, available at: https://www.bristol.ac.uk/media-library/sites/sps/documents/kinship/Kinstat_%20Briefing%20Paper%20001_v2.pdf

Williams JR, Ghandour RM and Kub JE (2008) 'Female perpetration of violence in heterosexual intimate relationships: adolescence through adulthood', *Trauma Violence Abuse*, 9:4, pp. 227–249

Williamson E, Lombard N and Brooks-Hay O (2020) 'Domestic violence and abuse, coronavirus, and the media narrative', *Journal of Gender-Based Violence*, 4:2, pp. 289–294

Wojtczak H (2009) *British Women's Emancipation since the Renaissance*, available at: www.historyofwomen.org

Women's Aid and TUC (2015) *Unequal, Trapped and Controlled: Women's experiences of financial abuse and the potential implications for Universal Credit*, available at: www.womensaid.org.uk/financial-abuse-report

Women's Aid (2019) *The Domestic Abuse Report 2019: The Economics of Abuse,* Bristol: Women's Aid

Women's Aid (2020) *A Perfect Storm: The impact of the Covid-19 pandemic on domestic abuse survivors and the services supporting them*, Bristol: Women's Aid

Young Lives Foundation (undated) *Care Leaver Mentoring*, available at: https://ylf.org.uk/how-we-help/care-leaver-mentoring

YoungMinds (undated) *Parents' Guide to Support A-Z*, available at: www.youngminds.org.uk/parents-guide-to-support-a-z/pa

Youth Justice Board/Ministry of Justice (2020) *Youth Justice Statistics 2018/19*, available at: https://assets.publishing.service.gov.uk/government/uploads/system/uploads/attachment_data/file/862078/youth-justice-statistics-bulletin-march-2019.pdf

Youth Justice Board/Ministry of Justice (2021) *Youth Justice Statistics 2019/20*, available at: https://assets.publishing.service.gov.uk/government/uploads/system/uploads/attachment_data/file/956621/youth-justice-statistics-2019-2020.pdf

YMCA (2020) *Young and Black: The young black experience of institutional racism in the UK*, London: YMCA, available at: https://www.ymca.org.uk/wp-content/uploads/2020/ymca-young-and-black.pdf

Zeitlin D, Dhanjal T and Colmsee M (1999) 'Maternal-foetal bonding: the impact of domestic violence on the bonding process between a mother and child', *Archive of Women's Mental Health*, 2, pp. 183–189